GW00361251

The Sunday Papers

THE SUNDAY PAPERS

A history of Ireland's weekly press

Joe Breen & Mark O'Brien

EDITORS

FOUR COURTS PRESS

Set in 11.5 pt on 13.5 pt Centaur for
FOUR COURTS PRESS LTD
7 Malpas Street, Dublin 8, Ireland
www.fourcourtspress.ie
and in North America for
FOUR COURTS PRESS
c/o IPG, 814 N Franklin St, Chicago, IL 60622

A catalogue record for this title is available
from the British Library.

ISBN 978-1-84682-727-3

Printed in England,
by CPI (Group) UK Ltd, Croydon.

If you want to know 'bout the bishop and the actress
If you want to know how to be a star
If you want to know 'bout the stains on the mattress
You can read it in the Sunday papers

—'Sunday papers', written and performed
by Joe Jackson, 1979

Contents

Abbreviations

ABC	Audit Bureau of Circulations
BBC	British Broadcasting Corporation
DÉD	Dáil Éireann Debates
EEC	European Economic Community
EH	*Evening Herald*
EP	*Evening Press*
EU	European Union
FJ	*Freeman's Journal*
GAA	Gaelic Athletic Association
HP	*Hot Press*
IFA	Irish Farmers' Association
IFJ	*Irish Farmers Journal*
II	*Irish Independent*
INLA	Irish National Liberation Army
INM	Independent News and Media
IP	*Irish Press*
IRA	Irish Republican Army
IT	*Irish Times*
IWI	*Irish Weekly Independent*
NAI	National Archives of Ireland
NLI	National Library of Ireland
NNI	National Newspapers of Ireland
NUJ	National Union of Journalists
RTÉ	Raidió Teilifís Éireann
SBP	*Sunday Business Post*
SDLP	Social Democratic and Labour Party
SÉD	Seanad Éireann Debates
SF	*Sunday Freeman*

SI	*Sunday Independent*
SJ	*Sunday Journal*
SP	*Sunday Press*
SR	*Sunday Review*
ST	*Sunday Tribune*
SW	*Sunday World*
UVF	Ulster Volunteer Force
VAT	value added tax
WFJ	*Weekly Freeman's Journal*
WIT	*Weekly Irish Times*

Contributors

JOE BREEN is a former managing editor at the *Irish Times*. Previously he held a number of senior positions including chief sub-editor, op-ed editor, online editor and production and design editor. Since leaving the newspaper he has completed a master's degree in media and international conflict at University College Dublin and has lectured there and at Dublin City University. He contributed to *Periodicals and journalism in twentieth-century Ireland: writing against the grain* (2014) and to *Independent Newspapers: a history* (2012).

PAT BRENNAN is a former news editor and deputy editor of the *Sunday Tribune* (1985–91), and previously worked as a reporter and feature writer for the *Irish Press* and *Magill*. She was a producer and television programme editor for RTÉ news from 1991–2016. She is co-author, with Gene Kerrigan, of *This great little nation: the A–Z of Irish scandals and controversies* (1999).

RAY BURKE worked for the Irish Press Group from 1983 to 1995. He was news editor of the *Irish Press* from 1991 to 1995 and he is the author of *Press delete: the decline and fall of the* Irish Press (2005). He has written on Irish Press newspapers for the National Library of Ireland and *Irish Communications Review*. He is a member of the executive committee of the Newspaper and Periodical History Forum of Ireland and contributed to *The Irish regional press, 1892–2018: revival, revolution and republic* (2018). He was a news editor at RTÉ news from 1996 to 2007 and chief news editor there from 2007 to 2018.

MICHAEL FOLEY is professor emeritus at the School of Media, Dublin Institute of Technology. He is a former lecturer in journalism and media correspondent with the *Irish Times*. He is the author of *Death in every paragraph: journalism and the Great Irish Famine* (2015) and has written and broadcast extensively on media issues and press history. He is a consultant on media development, has worked for the BBC's development wing, Media Action, the International Federation of Journalists, UNICEF and UNESCO and is a member of the NUJ's Ethics Council.

FELIX M. LARKIN, a retired public servant, has written extensively about the history of the press in late nineteenth- and early twentieth-century Ireland.

He is a co-founder and former chairman of the Newspaper and Periodical History Forum of Ireland, and the author of *Terror and discord: the Shemus cartoons in the* Freeman's Journal, *1920–1924* (2009). With Mark O'Brien, he co-edited *Periodicals and journalism in twentieth-century Ireland: writing against the grain* (2014). He is a former academic director of the Parnell Summer School, and currently serves as chairman of An Post's Philatelic Advisory Committee.

MARY MULDOWNEY is a labour historian and the author of books and many journal articles in which she uses oral history interviews as a primary source. She is historian in residence for Dublin Central and is also an adult-education consultant, designing and delivering training courses for community and trade union activists. As a founding member and organizer of the Stoneybatter & Smithfield People's Project she has edited and contributed to their publications, which focus on the working-class history of Dublin.

ED MULHALL is an editorial advisor and media consultant with forty years' experience in broadcast and news media. He was previously managing director of RTÉ news and current affairs (2002–12) and director of news (1997–2002). Since retiring from RTÉ in 2012 he has worked as an editorial advisor for the European Broadcasting Union's news department, Century Ireland and a number of national and international media projects. He has written on broadcasting and the Irish financial crisis as well as on history and literature. He is currently a research associate at Trinity College and on advisory boards for the Mary Raftery Journalism Fund, Brainstorm, Benefacts and the Museum of Literature, Ireland.

SIÚN NÍ DHUINN is the digital coordinator for Irish at RTÉ. She produces and co-hosts RTÉ's first Irish-language podcast, *Beo ar Éigean*. She is the co-editor of *Solas ar na Dumhchannaí* (2016) and editor of *An Ghaeilge i gCéin* (2011). She is also the editor of bilingual online publication *As an Nua* and is a board member of Raidió na Life and IMRAM (the Irish Language Literature Festival). A regular contributor on RTÉ and TG4, her research interests include Flann O'Brien's *Irish Times* columns and fashion in Ireland.

MARK O'BRIEN is associate professor at the School of Communications, Dublin City University, where he teaches media and journalism history and chairs the university's Media History Collection Advisory Board. He is the author of *The fourth estate: journalism in twentieth-century Ireland* (2017), *The* Irish Times*: a history* (2008) and *De Valera, Fianna Fáil and the* Irish Press*: the truth in the news?* (2001). He is co-editor, with Felix M. Larkin, of *Periodicals and journalism in* *twentieth-century Ireland* (2014), with Donnacha Ó Beacháin of *Political communication in the Republic of Ireland* (2014) and, with Kevin Rafter, of *Independent Newspapers: a history* (2012).

KEVIN RAFTER is professor of political communication and head of the School of Communications at Dublin City University. He is the author/editor of over a dozen books and has published numerous book chapters and academic journal articles with a specific focus on Irish media and politics. He is chair of the expert advisory committee of Culture Ireland and also chairs the compliance committee of the Broadcasting Authority of Ireland. Prior to 2008, he worked as a senior political journalist and held senior editorial positions with the *Irish Times*, the *Sunday Times*, *Sunday Tribune*, *Magill* and RTÉ.

BRIAN TRENCH is a researcher and trainer in science communication, co-editor with Massimiano Bucchi of *Routledge handbook of public communication of science and technology* (2008, 2014) and of *Public communication of science*, a four-volume anthology (2016), and, with Padraig Murphy and Declan Fahy, of *Little country, big talk: science communication in Ireland* (2017). He was president of the international Public Communication of Science and Technology Network, 2014–18. He was formerly senior lecturer and head of the School of Communications, Dublin City University, and, before that, a full-time journalist for twenty years, serving in various positions with the *Sunday Tribune*, 1981–6, and as editor of *Magill*, 1987.

REGINA UÍ CHOLLATÁIN is a professor at (and the head of) the School of Irish, Celtic Studies and Folklore and the head of Irish Studies at University College Dublin. Her research interests include Irish-language revival, media and print culture, and she has published nationally and internationally on these areas. Her most recent publications are *Saothrú na Gaeilge scríofa i suímh uirbeacha na hÉireann, 1700–1850* (co-editor, 2017), which examines urban Irish-language writing in Ireland, and *Litríocht na Gaeilge ar fud an Domhain* (co-editor, 2015), which is the first comprehensive study of Irish-language literature in a global context. She was awarded the Ireland Canada University Foundation senior visiting professorship (2011–12) and is a former board member of TG4.

Preface

In an interview published in the then nascent *Sunday Business Post* in 1991 the former long-time editor of the *Sunday Independent*, Hector Legge, declared that, morally, Ireland was 'on a downward path that leads to the bonfire'.[1] Whatever about morality, Ireland, and its Sunday newspaper market, had changed utterly since Legge had retired in 1970 after thirty years at the helm of the *Independent*. When Legge had assumed the editorship in 1945, the state was still a member of the British Commonwealth, nine out of ten children left school after primary level, emigration was rife and there existed only one indigenous Sunday newspaper – which he edited.[2] By the time Legge retired, the state had become a republic, abandoned economic protectionism in favour of free trade and launched a national television service. Also, free second-level education had been introduced and the state was well on its way to joining the European Economic Community, later the EU.

By that time too, the indigenous Sunday newspaper market had expanded. The *Sunday Press* appeared in 1949 and very quickly became the dominant title. The *Press* was followed by Ireland's first tabloid, the relatively short-lived *Sunday Review*, in 1957. In many ways, the irreverent *Review* was ahead of its time and it would not be until 1973 that another tabloid, the *Sunday World*, took up where the *Review* left off – with more success. The *World* somehow caught the zeitgeist of a changing Ireland that was beyond the third tabloid to appear: the short-lived *Sunday Journal*. Other titles, such as the *Sunday Tribune* (1980) and the *Sunday Business Post* (1989), had greater success, as did a radically reinvented *Sunday Independent* from the mid-1980s onward. All this activity took place against strong competition from the imported British Sunday titles: one estimate put sales of such titles at over 20 million copies in 1949.[3] By the 1990s this competition had intensified, with several British titles, such as the *Sunday Times*, establishing offices in Ireland and producing Irish editions.

It is this nexus – the changing nature of the state and its Sunday newspaper market – that forms the core of this volume. The past twenty years has witnessed intense research into the daily press, the provincial press, periodicals and journalism generally. But Sunday newspapers have remained unexplored and it

1 *SBP*, 8 Sept. 1991.   2 School attendance figures from DÉD, vol. 80, col. 1581. (6 June 1940).   3 DÉD, vol. 121, col. 993 (31 May 1950).

is this gap that the volume addresses. By no means is it the final word on the Sunday newspaper market or on its individual titles; the histories of the press and journalism and the biographies of editors and journalists are too multifaceted and too rich an area of study for such a definitive claim. We do, however, hope that it prompts more research into the unique role and character of the Sunday papers and their role in Irish social, cultural and political life.

The editors gratefully acknowledge support for this publication from the Humanities and Social Sciences Book Publication Fund at Dublin City University and from the Newspaper and Periodical History Forum of Ireland. They also record their gratitude to the volume's contributors, to all at Four Courts Press and to Derek Speirs, Martyn Turner, John Burns and the National Library of Ireland for their permission to reproduce images.

This volume is dedicated to the memory of Joe Breen (1915–1993), a fervent Irish republican who, nonetheless, read the *Sunday Independent* and the *Sunday Express* each week, and to Dominick O'Brien, pioneer of the rural electrification scheme and weekly purchaser of the *Sunday Independent* and the *Sunday World*.

Joe Breen & Mark O'Brien

1 / The Irish Sunday newspaper: its role, character and history

JOE BREEN & MARK O'BRIEN

In his foreword to his 1967 edited volume, *Your Sunday paper*, British culture critic Richard Hoggart noted that 'though a great deal has been written on the press in general, there is relatively little on the Sunday press in itself'.[1] Many more words and volumes have addressed the general topic of newspapers since 1967, but, peculiarly, there remains something of a lacuna regarding study of the history of the Sunday press in Britain or in Ireland. Kevin Williams echoes that sentiment when he notes that the 'role of Sunday is often neglected in standard histories of the British press, where they appear in a secondary role to the exploits of the daily newspaper', while Brake, Kaul and Turner argue that the history of press scholarship privileges 'daily press above all else'.[2] This lack of critical scrutiny is all the more surprising when the Sundays have long lorded over their daily competitors in circulation and, some might argue, in influence.

Williams notes that the earliest Sunday newspapers were serious publications, and that it was 'the format of sex, gossip and crime developed by papers such as the *News of the World*, *Reynolds News* and *Lloyd's Weekly News* which enabled the Sundays to become Britain's best-selling newspapers from the mid-nineteenth century'.[3] He also records that the *News of the World* reached its sales peak in 1950 when it was calculated that 8.44 million people bought the paper; the highest daily sale recorded was 5.27 million for the *Daily Mirror* in 1967.[4] The oldest Sunday newspaper in these islands, and possibly in the world, is the *Observer*, which was first published in London in December 1791 and was, 'in varying degrees a scurrilous gossip sheet, government propaganda rag and provocative thorn-in-the-side of the establishment. Throughout the nineteenth

1 Richard Hoggart (ed.), *Your Sunday paper* (London, 1967), p. 9. 2 Kevin Williams, *Read all about it: a history of the British newspaper* (London, 2010), p. 8; Laurel Brake, Chandrika Kaul & Mark W. Turner (eds), *The News of the World and the British press, 1843–2011: journalism for the rich, journalism for the poor* (London, 2016), p. 7. Other works include Cyril Bainbridge & Roy Stockdill, *The News of the World: 150 years of the world's bestselling newspaper* (London, 1993) & Harold Hobson et al., *The pearl of days: an intimate memoir of the Sunday Times, 1822–1972* (London, 1972). 3 Williams, *Read all about it*, p. 8. 4 Ibid.

century, however, the paper's character changed and came to reflect the more sober morality of the age.'[5] It was founded by W.S. Bourne on the simple premise that 'the establishment of a Sunday newspaper would obtain him a rapid fortune'. However, within three years Bourne found himself £1,600 in debt; he would not be the last person to find out the hard way that investing in Sunday newspapers was a dice with debt.

SUNDAYS AND WEEKLIES

The history of Sunday newspapers in Ireland is, as subsequent chapters illustrate, more recent though no less colourful. This collection covers effectively three eras of Sundays in Ireland. The first, from 1905 (the launch of the *Sunday Independent*) to 1949 (the launch of the *Sunday Press*), is a quiet period in which the *Independent* essentially had the market to itself, apart from British imports and the short-lived *Sunday Freeman*. The second period, from 1949 to the launch of Teilifís Éireann in 1961, was a more competitive environment in which the *Press* emerged as the biggest-selling newspaper on the island. The final period ran from 1961 through to the end of the Aengus Fanning era at the *Sunday Independent* in 2010.[6]

The *Sunday Independent* was founded in 1905 and is the oldest surviving Sunday title in Ireland. But there were other Sunday publications before it, such as *The Oracle*, which enjoyed a short life between 1796 and 1797, and the first iteration of the *Sunday Freeman*, which was published from January to August in 1817.[7] (It would be ninety-six years before the next *Sunday Freeman* would be published, as Felix Larkin recounts in his chapter on the newspaper.) The picture is clouded by the number of weekly newspapers which were published on the island in the nineteenth and twentieth centuries. As Marie-Louise Legg has pointed out 'an important feature of the 1880s was not just the increase in numbers of [weekly] provincial newspapers, but the increase in the number of newspapers which claimed to have nationalist politics. Their readers were an increasingly literate populace who had moved away from rural labouring and into serving in shops and clerking in offices.'[8]

5 theguardian.com/gnm-archive/2002/jun/06/2.   6 Aengus Fanning was editor of the *Sunday Independent* from 1984 to 2012.   7 *The Oracle* was published between Sept. 1796 and Apr. 1797 and underwent numerous iterations as *The Oracle /Sunday Gazette*, during which it published intermittently on Sundays and Wednesdays. Averaging four pages per issue, it cost three pence and covered sittings of the Irish parliament and of the British House of Commons as well as providing an 'Essence of domestic news from all the other papers of the week'. Copies of the newspaper are available to view on microfilm at Dublin City Library and Archive.   8 Marie-Louise Legg, *Newspapers and nationalism: the Irish provincial press, 1850–1892* (Dublin, 1999), p. 120

Other weeklies were extensions of existing daily newspapers. For instance, the *Weekly Irish Times* was published from June 1875 to November 1941, when it was replaced by the *Times Pictorial*. Similarly, the *Irish Weekly Independent* appeared between April 1893 and August 1960 and the *Weekly Freeman's Journal* was published between January 1818 and December 1924. Typically, such weeklies repurposed the best of the respective daily's content from the previous week. They were a cheap and cheerful way to, in modern parlance, sweat your asset; the writing and setting of the texts had been done for the daily so the content just had to be repackaged. The weeklies were published mid-week (Wednesday in the case of the *Weekly Irish Times*, and Thursday in the case of both the *Irish Weekly Independent* and the *Weekly Freeman's Journal*) and were aimed at those, particularly in rural areas, who visited the market or attended Mass at urban centres once a week. In addition, Dublin had three weekly sports papers, *Sport*, *Sports Mail* and the *Irish Field*, all of which published multiple editions throughout Saturday so as to carry cross-Channel racing and football results.[9]

Sunday newspapers were (and are) different from their weekly competitors. In Britain, in the mid-nineteenth century, they were standalone operations and not offshoots of daily titles – that would come later. They were also publishing in a hostile religious environment. The sabbath was widely observed, particularly among non-conformist denominations, and newspapers, especially those that traded in sensationalism and stories arousing prurient interest, were considered unsuitable material. Williams notes that several attempts were made to close down such publications in the 1830s.[10] But, having survived the 1830s, the Sunday press in Britain expanded rapidly in the next decade as it mixed politics and sensationalism – 'a combination that was highly successful in attracting readers, particularly from a working class background'.[11] As time moved on their circulations increased and the content grew more and more racy – the newspapers had learned that entertainment in all its forms, from lurid court cases to sensationalist exclusives, was a magnet for readers. Williams argues that it was the Sundays that 'laid the foundations for the formula that would drive the rise of the popular press, with their emphasis on murders, executions, elopements and a miscellany of small features'.[12]

In Ireland, however, there is little evidence of the newspaper industry expanding into Sunday titles in the second half of the nineteenth century. Indeed, until William Martin Murphy decided to launch the *Sunday Independent* in 1905, there was a conspicuous absence of local titles. And even this title

9 *Sport* (1880–1931) was published by the *Freeman's Journal* and, from 1924, Independent Newspapers, which acquired the *Freeman* titles that year. *Sports Mail* (1921–39) was a reinvention of the *Irish Weekly Mail* which was published by the (Dublin) *Daily Express* (1851–1921). The *Irish Field* was sold by the *Irish Times* to the Agricultural Trust (publisher of the *Irish Farmers Journal*) in 2003 and today concentrates on the bloodstock industry. 10 Williams, *Read all about it*, p. 118. 11 Ibid., pp 118–19. 12 Ibid., p. 119.

was essentially 'a grand Sunday edition' of the weekly, containing, as the paper promised, 'the very latest and fullest news', with special attention 'devoted to sport in all its forms'.[13] The delay in Ireland spawning an indigenous Sunday newspaper market can, arguably, be attributed to a number of factors. Unlike Britain, with its booming industrialized economy, Ireland in the second half of the nineteenth century was a predominantly agrarian society recovering from the devastation of the Great Famine (1846–9). In the space of sixty years, the population on the island had fallen by almost half, from 8,175,124 in 1841 to 4,456,546 in 1901.[14] And, although literacy levels rose from 47 per cent to 75 per cent between 1841 and 1881, the strength of the local weekly press most likely obviated the need for a national Sunday press and the relatively primitive transport infrastructure inhibited circulation of newspapers from a Dublin base, or made it so costly as to make it uncompetitive.[15]

Certainly, there seems to have been no rush to create a native Irish Sunday press, but as British Sundays, fuelled by the popular energy of the new journalism at the close of the nineteenth century, began to circulate in Ireland it must have dawned on Irish publishers that a Sunday publication might prove a valuable investment. However, as has been noted elsewhere, the idea of newspapers reporting gossip, scandal and crime, and conducting investigations, was one far removed from Irish journalism at the turn of the century, as such topics 'were taboo and the publication of such stories in imported British titles was viewed by the Catholic Church as contributing to moral degeneration of the local population'.[16] Judging by their sales though, many Irish readers did not agree (or did not care). By 1910, the popular British Sunday newspapers were reportedly selling between 80,000 and 120,000 copies a week.[17] It was clearly a feverish atmosphere that would lead to actions such as the burning of newspapers, calls for import bans and actual bans. William Martin Murphy saw that there was a gap in the market for an Irish Sunday; in time, the Irish Sunday newspaper would become distinctly Irish in character and, in some cases, very profitable – not least Murphy's own creation.

WHAT IS IT ABOUT SUNDAY?

To understand the importance of Sunday newspapers it is essential to grasp the nature of Sunday life and the centrality of Sunday in the weekly calendar,

13 *EH*, 18 Nov. 1905.   14 Diarmaid Ferriter, *The transformation of Ireland, 1900–2000* (London, 2004), p. 20.   15 L.M. Cullen, *Eason & Son: a history* (Dublin, 1989), p. 5.   16 Mark O'Brien, *The fourth estate: journalism in twentieth-century Ireland* (Manchester, 2017), pp 6–7.   17 Kevin Rafter, 'The Irish edition: from "filthy scandal sheet" to "old friend" of the taoiseach' in Brake et al., *The* News of the World, pp 179–94 at p. 180.

particularly in Ireland. The day has been long observed by Christians worldwide as a day of rest and worship. Within that wide geographical and time-delineated arc there are extremes. While sabbatarianism – the belief that Sunday should constitute a day of strict religious observance and abstinence from work – carries little weight in the twenty-first century, pockets of it still exist. It was only in November 2007 that the Irish Football Association voted to allow matches in Northern Ireland to take place on the sabbath, ending a sixty-year ban and 'bringing the Irish league in line with the rest of the world'.[18]

Sabbatarianism was weak in Catholic countries as, according to one scholar, Catholics preferred what was known as the 'Continental sabbath', which was considered both a holy day and a holiday. However, fears about the growing secularization of Sunday worried the Catholic Church. As recently as 1998, Pope John Paul II, in an apostolic letter, *In Dies Domini*, stated that many Christians no longer understood the significance of Sunday, and he 'exhorted the "disciples of Christ" ... to avoid any confusion between the celebration of Sunday, which should truly be a way of keeping the Lord's Day holy, and the "weekend", understood as a simple time of rest and relaxation'.[19]

In the one hundred-plus years of Sunday newspapers in Ireland much has changed in society. In 1905, Ireland would have observed the day with religious fervour. Hearing weekly mass was an obligation for Catholics, who comprised the overwhelming majority in the twenty-six counties and, as the decades passed, became as much a social and cultural habit as it was religious. It represented an opportunity for the community to gather together and, in many ways, represented a form of political communication – and not just from the clergy delivering the sermon or the latest Lenten pastoral. Every major political party held an annual 'church-gate collection' outside churches, and at election time candidates would address congregations, often from the back of a lorry, as they dispersed after mass. And the array of newspapers outside the church – caught so well by Derek Speirs in the photograph on the cover of this book – is a reminder of the ties between the spiritual and secular in a previous time. Indeed, in the latter half of the twentieth century most Irish Sunday titles had priests as columnists – Fr Robert Nash in the *Sunday Press*, Fr Michael Cleary in the *Sunday Independent*, Fr Colm Kilcoyne in the *Sunday Journal* and Fr Brian D'Arcy in the *Sunday World*. Though religious observance has declined dramatically in recent years – with weekly mass attendance falling from 90 per cent to 34 per cent between 1973 and 2012 – Sunday retains cultural significance as a day of reflection on the six days preceding it.[20] Although that pulpit of reflection is

18 Theguardian.com/uk/2007/nov/30/northernireland.ireland.   19 Stephen Miller, *The peculiar life of Sundays* (London, 2008), pp 12 & 18.   20 Research & Development Commission, *Survey of religious*

now shared with television and radio programmes, the Sunday papers continue
to generate debate and controversy, whether through loudly proclaimed exclusives or striking commentary. 'The Marion Finucane Show' on RTÉ radio, for
instance, uses the content of the various newspapers to generate and frame discussion on the topics of the week. The newspapers, and their commentary and
stories, are positioned as integral to our understanding of the week, reinforcing
their status as respected arbiters of cultural and political norms. It helps that
most people do not work on Sunday, leaving them plenty of time to read their
favourite titles – and frequently, though perhaps not as frequently as in the past,
they purchase multiple newspapers.

Sunday's role as a day of reflection on what has passed and what was to
come has been helped by the growth of the weekend concept. While a week
is defined in the *Concise Oxford dictionary* as 'a period of seven days', there
is a second definition: 'the five days from Monday to Friday, or the time
spent working during this period'. The five-day week was a US gift to the
twentieth century. According to one account, it took decades for Saturday
to change from a half-day to a full day's rest.[21] In Ireland it was only in the
second half of the twentieth century that a five-day week became the norm.
Thus the weekend took root. This was an important development for newspapers published on Saturday and Sunday, with the latter becoming more
conscious of leisure-based features such as travel, gardening, wine and books.
The demise of the national weeklies – the *Irish Times* ended its title in 1941
and the *Independent* in 1960 – allowed the dailies to publish more reflective and
analytical content on Saturdays, as well as more features. This was recognition that readership was increasingly more concerned with leisure, sport and
entertainment. The Sundays also upped their game. In the dying days of
the *Sunday Review* in late 1963, the newspaper published a separate 'Women's
Review' supplement. It did not save the newspaper, but in time supplements
covering sport, business, property and culture would become part of the
Sunday offering. The same would apply to Saturday titles, where multiple
section newspapers would become the norm.

---

practice, attitudes and beliefs in the Republic of Ireland, 1973–74 (Dublin, 1975), and *IT*, 5 June 2012.   **21** theat-
lantic.com/business/archive/2014/08/where-the-five-day-workweek-came-from/378870. In 1908, a
New England mill became the first American factory to institute the five-day week. It did so to
accommodate Jewish workers, whose observance of a Saturday sabbath forced them to make up their
work on Sundays, offending some in the Christian majority. The mill granted these Jewish workers
a two-day weekend, and other factories followed this example. The Great Depression cemented the
two-day weekend into the economy, as shorter hours were considered a remedy to underemployment.

BRITISH IMPORTS AND IRISH SENSITIVITIES

The Sunday market in Ireland is particularly vulnerable, by dint of language and culture, to British imports, much to the chagrin of the native industry, which has long accused British competitors of 'dumping' and 'predatory pricing'. Earlier objections centred on the perceived 'gilded filth' of the papers' content. The history of antipathy to imported British newspapers is as old if not older than the indigenous Irish market. In 1899 the hierarchy called for action against the 'printing presses in Great Britain [that] daily pour out a flood of infidel and immoral publications some of which overflows into this country'. There followed the establishment of the Catholic Truth Society of Ireland, the aim of which was to distribute 'cheap publications of sound Catholic literature in popular form [to] remove the temptation of having recourse to filthy garbage'.[22] By 1902, the society had 120 branches nationwide and had sold over 800,000 penny books.[23]

It was an issue that inspired heated passions. In Limerick in October 1911 twenty-two newsagents, under pressure from the Holy Family sodality, signed a pledge not to sell copies of 'undesirable publications' and newsboys undertook not to sell the 'objectionable prints'.[24] After this tactic failed, other methods were used, as when a large crowd gathered at Limerick train station and intercepted the delivery of Sunday newspapers. According to one account 'the papers were solemnly burned, amidst a scene of great enthusiasm, the band playing hymns while the obnoxious journals burned, and then the Dead March (Saul) over their ashy remains'.[25] In February 1926 the minister for justice, Kevin O'Higgins, set up a Committee on Evil Literature to consider the possibility of the state taking action to prohibit the sale of certain publications. Various professional bodies, youth associations and other organizations were asked to submit evidence. These included the Catholic Truth Society, the Irish Vigilance Association, the Irish Christian Brothers, the Catholic Headmasters' Association and the Irish National Teachers' Organisation. Limerick-born Jesuit and social activist Rev. Richard S. Devane also gave evidence.[26] The Christian Brothers, represented by its superior general, Brother J.L. Craven, made a particularly strong submission by noting that, in terms of indecent literature, the Free State had:

> the vulgar and the course, the suggestive, the unsavoury, the offensive,
> the smutty, the ill-smelling; we have gilded filth, unvarnished filth, gross

22 *IT*, 4 Dec. 1899.   23 *IT*, 28 June 1902.   24 *IT*, 26 Oct. 1911.   25 *FJ*, 31 Oct. 1911.   26 Michael Adams, *Censorship: the Irish experience* (Tuscaloosa, AL, 1968), pp 24–5. Aidan Beatty provides a good summary of Fr Devane's career at aidanbeatty.com/2017/03/29/the-strange-career-of-r-s-devane.

animalism, sex-knowledge series, sexual science … Is it any wonder that
we should have so many houses of infamy – the resorts of night birds
and wild cats? … At present the spiritualised Irishman is quickly passing
away and all of the brute that is in him is being fed almost to the point of
moral leprosy, to be followed by a tempest of fire from heaven.[27]

While the Irish Vigilance Association told the committee that it objected to
the publication of 'revolting details of sexual crimes and of divorce cases'
the Catholic Truth Society listed the weekly circulation figures of the British
Sunday newspapers to which it objected:

News of the World	132,444
Empire News	76,698
Sunday Chronicle	46,188
Sunday People	30,660
Reynold's News	28,772
Sunday News	22,198
Sunday Herald	15,842
Total	352,802[28]

In relation to the *News of the World*, the society noted that it was 'devoted almost
entirely to reports of murders, suicides, divorces, bigamy cases, indecent assault,
incest, affiliation cases and crime in general, but particularly sexual crime'.
There was no great surprise when, in spring 1927, the committee recommended
that a censorship board be established. In addition, it wanted a clampdown on
the availability of information relating to contraception.[29] The government's
decision to draft a censorship bill was welcomed by the archbishop of Dublin,
Edward Byrne, who noted 'with most lively satisfaction that the state has initiated measures to provide a remedy against the traffic in vile literature'. He was
not alone. Referring to the 'abundance of error and filth served up under cheap
and attractive covers', the archbishop of Tuam, Thomas Gilmartin, declared it
the government's duty 'to pass with all haste such legislation that will deliver
our country from a dire evil'.[30] Lay groups also kept up the pressure. In May

27 Adams, *Censorship*, pp 26–7.   28 Ibid., pp 27–8.   29 Section 16 of the 1929 Censorship Act
made it unlawful for anyone to print, publish, sell or distribute any book or periodical that advocated 'the unnatural prevention of conception or the procurement of abortion or miscarriage or any
method, treatment, or appliance to be used for the purpose of such prevention or such procurement'.   30 *WIT*, 5 Mar. 1927.

1927 the *Irish Times* reported that masked men armed with revolvers had taken over Dundalk railway station, unloaded several thousand copies of British Sunday newspapers from a train, stacked them on the station platform, sprinkled them with petrol and set them alight.[31] In the south, the Cork Angelic Warfare Association led the charge by seizing copies of the *News of the World*. When proceedings were taken against one of those involved, a priest called as a character witness declared that there was nothing wrong with seizing objectionable newspapers. He had even done it himself; while walking on the quays he had stopped a newsboy, seized his copies of the *News of the World* and thrown them into the river Lee – 'the only congenial place for such filth'.[32]

To resolve the problem of imported newspapers that carried too much crime coverage Section 7 of the Censorship of Publications Act allowed the minister for justice to ban for three months any publication that 'devoted an unduly large proportion of space to the publication of matter relating to crime'. In November 1930 the minister indicated that he had in June that year used the section to ban six imported newspapers.[33] At this time the *News of the World* – the main target of the law, which allowed the paper's ban – was selling 130,000 copies in Ireland each Sunday. The ban was not accepted meekly – such healthy sales would have provided healthy revenues. The *News of the World* sent a delegation to meet the censorship board and the minister for justice, but without reward. It would be 1961 before a variation of the ministerial order that had banned the title in Ireland allowed a special Irish edition to be sold.[34]

With the circulation of the *Sunday Independent*, the sole Irish Sunday newspaper, standing at a mere 83,399 copies per week in March 1930 it is fair to say that British imports had a firm grip on the Sunday market.[35] Interestingly, the opposite was the case in the daily market, where British imports were about 170,000 per day but sales of Irish papers totalled 280,000 per day.[36] At a time of huge change in Ireland, the dominant news source on Sundays originated in the recently departed colonial power, with attempts to regulate the importation of papers via the imposition of duties adding to the confusion. While the 1932 Finance Act imposed a duty on imported newspapers and periodicals it exempted daily papers and papers 'of which the superficial area of page or front cover does not exceed three hundred and twenty square inches'.[37] This resulted

31 *IT*, 2 May 1927.   32 Cullen, *Eason*, p. 267.   33 DÉD, vol. 36, col. 719–20 (28 Nov. 1930). Initial bans lasted for three months, and a second offence resulted in a perpetual ban. The periodicals banned were *World's Pictorial News and Competitor's Guide*, *News of the World*, *Empire News*, the *Sunday People*, *Thomson's Weekly News* and *Weekly Record*. The *News of the World* was banned in Ireland in perpetuity after it fell afoul of the provision a second time in Nov. 1930.   34 Rafter, 'The Irish edition', pp 195 & 181–3.   35 *II*, 30 Apr. 1930.   36 Horgan and Flynn, *Irish media: a critical history* (Dublin, 2017), p. 50.   37 Finance Act 1932, second schedule.

in British Sunday titles ensuring they complied with the page measurements to avoid the duty. However, the following year's Finance Act imposed a duty on *all* imported daily newspapers – but left the size exemption in place, to the benefit of British Sundays.[38] As one commentator noted, the value of imported daily papers declined from £216,000 in 1932 to £99,000 in 1934.[39] By the early 1940s wartime newsprint shortages and transport difficulties resulted in British newspapers temporarily pulling back from the Irish market. Post-war, British titles returned, the revenue commissioners reporting that the annual total number of imported Sunday newspapers had increased from 15,704,988 in 1947 to 20,268,360 in 1949.[40] In 1950 one Clann na Poblachta TD, Seán Ó Tiománuidhe, questioned whether the anomaly in duty arrangements that favoured British Sundays resulted from the fact that the only Irish Sunday was the Fine Gael-supporting *Sunday Independent*. If, he asserted, the Fianna Fáil government had 'put a tariff on British Sunday newspapers it would have the immediate effect of increasing the sales of the *Sunday Independent*'.[41]

In 1949, now in opposition, the attention of Fianna Fáil turned towards establishing a Sunday title to accompany its daily title, the *Irish Press*. The *Sunday Press* exuded confidence from the beginning; its first editorial announced the newspaper as 'an event of national importance, whether considered socially, culturally or politically'. It wore its nationalist politics on its sleeve – so much so that in 1954 the Northern Ireland nationalist MP, Cahir Healy, wrote to the department of external affairs to suggest that it reproduce one of the paper's articles on partition as 'an excellent leaflet for distribution at meetings outside Ireland'. The civil servant who replied, one Conor Cruise O'Brien, noted that he had been directed by the minister (future Taoiseach Liam Cosgrave) to state that Healy's suggestion would 'be borne in mind', though in a note to his superior O'Brien stated that he did not think Healy's suggestion was practical and his reply was 'merely an acknowledgment for the sake of courtesy'.[42]

The *Press* and the *Independent* seemed set to battle it out throughout the 1950s to be the leading Sunday title. By the middle of 1955 the *Press* had become the first Irish newspaper to sell over 400,000 copies, and the *Sunday Independent* was not far behind. In 1957, a 'popular' tabloid, the *Sunday Review*, attempted to break into this challenging and fiercely competitive market. Published by the *Irish Times* with the aim of broadening the financially strapped company's revenue base, the *Review* lasted six years before the money ran out. When it closed, the paper was selling 190,000 copies per week. Among its legacies was

38 Finance Act 1933, part II, section 8.   39 Donat O'Donnell [Conor Cruise O'Brien], 'The *Irish Independent*: a business idea', *The Bell*, 9:5 (1945), 386–94 at 392–3.   40 DÉD, vol. 121, col. 993 (31 May 1950).   41 Ibid., col. 994.   42 NAI, DFA/5/305/14/273 (memo dated 8 Nov. 1954).

'Inside Politics by Backbencher', editor John Healy's pseudo-anonymous column, which would gain a second life in the *Irish Times* and help to change the nature of political journalism.

Meanwhile, the British Sundays had not gone away, though their main circulation engine, the *News of the World*, remained banned.[43] Indeed, by the mid-1950s there was again growing anxiety about the presence of British Sundays in the Irish market. At a meeting of the Prices Advisory Body in November 1955, John J. Dunne, director and general manager of Independent Newspapers, stated that 'a matter of grave anxiety to the two Dublin offices publishing a Sunday newspaper was the vigorous drive by English Sunday newspapers'. He told the committee that some 435,000 of these Sunday newspapers arrived in Dublin every weekend and it looked as if some British newspaper companies were seeking to print a portion of their Sunday output in Dublin each Saturday night. The drive for Irish circulation was, Dunne concluded, 'an intense one' and Irish publishers could not compete in the matter of expenditure 'because of the vast disparity in profits' involved.[44] The figure presented by Dunne seems accurate: a government memorandum from around that time estimated the sales of British Sunday newspapers in Ireland in 1958 as being 430,000 per week.[45]

There was occasional disruption to the distribution of British titles. In 1953 a newspaper distributor's van was held up by masked men as it left Dublin. Telling the driver that they 'objected to the circulation of filthy newspapers and in particular to the *People*', the men took bundles of the *Sunday People* and, having failed to set fire to them, 'scattered all the papers on the roadway tearing up a number of them'. While the Garda commissioner's office proffered the view that the holdup arose from the formation of a new group called Cosc ar Foillseacháin Gallda (Ban on Foreign Publications), which 'contained members from Sinn Féin and Connradh na Gaedhilge [*sic*]', the secretary of the department of justice, Peter Berry, believed that there was 'no particular reason to believe that this seizure of English newspapers was political – it is more likely "Catholic Action" at work'.[46] In 1956 the *Observer* published a series on sex and society, the third instalment of which was headed 'Family Planning'. Since section 16 of the Censorship of Publications Act 1929 made it an offence to print, publish, sell or distribute any publication that advocated the 'unnatural prevention of conception', the theme of the forthcoming instalment caught the eye of Brian MacMahon, secretary of the censorship of publications board.

43 The ban clearly irked the London paper's executives. In 1958, they leveraged their power to stop the *Sunday Review* being made available in Britain on the day of publication. Their action was noted in an official complaint to the Irish government; see NAI, DFA/5/379/127 (*Sunday Review*, 1958).   44 *IT*, 19 Nov. 1955.   45 NAI, DFA/5/379/127 (*Sunday Review*, 1958).   46 NAI, JUS/8/1013, memos dated 28 Sept. & 2 Oct. 1953.

Unbeknownst to the department of justice, the censorship board had an agreement with the Irish Retail Newsagents, Booksellers and Stationers Association
whereby the board would warn the association 'in cases where purely informal
complaints indicated that periodicals (especially those with no previous case
histories) were inclined to go off the rails'. MacMahon telephoned the chair
of the association, who in turn contacted the *Observer*'s Irish distributor, a Mr
Kirwan who, on contacting MacMahon, declared that 'he had no intention of
getting into trouble over "birth control stuff" for the *Observer* people and that
he would telephone them not to send the copies'.[47] According to the revenue
commissioners' account of the incident, Kirwan then telephoned the *Observer*'s
editor 'requesting the omission of the offending article. The editor told him
that this was impossible as they had only one edition and indicated, apparently, that what was good enough for English circulation was good enough
for this country.' Having travelled to Dublin Airport on 1 April 1956 to collect
the consignment of newspapers, Kirwan and the customs officer on duty read
the article in question and 'both formed the conclusion that it was objectionable' with Kirwan expressing the opinion that it was 'particularly inappropriate
that such an article should appear in a newspaper circulating on Easter Sunday
morning'. Since the customs service could not seize the consignment as the
paper had not been banned by the censorship board, Kirwan simply abandoned
the goods to the state.[48] These interruptions aside, British Sunday newspapers
circulated without hindrance.

GREATER COMPETITION

The 1960s was a time of great change in Ireland. Teilifís Éireann broadcast
for the first time on New Year's Eve, 1961. The print media was also undergoing major change. The *Irish Times*, having flirted with bankruptcy due to its
failed attempts to be a major player with the *Sunday Review* and the *Evening Mail*,
now suddenly prospered under the editorship of Douglas Gageby, catching
the liberal breeze blowing through Irish society. This breeze was resisted in
some quarters, with the two Irish Sunday titles often utilized by members of
the hierarchy to denounce what they viewed as politicians interfering in the
church's sphere of influence, and the pernicious influence of television. This
relationship reached its zenith in February 1966 when hierarchical thundering
dominated the front pages of the *Sunday Independent* and the *Sunday Press* for
two weeks running. In the first instance, Bishop Michael Browne addressed a

47 NAI, 90/102/139, memo from MacMahon to Thomas Coyne, department of justice, 6 Apr.
1956. 48 NAI, 90/102/139, memo dated 6 Apr. 1956.

Saturday-night public meeting in Galway at which, in the presence of the minister for education, Fianna Fáil's Jim Ryan, he lambasted the government's plan to close a number of one- and two-teacher schools. Browne then announced that, owing to the 'lateness of the hour', he needed to leave and could not remain to hear the minister's response. To ensure press coverage of his speech, Browne had sent it in advance to the religiously sympathetic *Sunday Independent* – but not to the Fianna Fáil-supporting *Sunday Press*. The *Sunday Independent* duly ran the story under the attention-grabbing page-one banner headline 'Bishop Attacks Minister'.[49] The following week, both the *Sunday Independent* and the *Sunday Press* carried Bishop Thomas Ryan's denunciation of the previous evening's *Late Late Show*, in which its host, Gay Byrne, had, in the midst of a competition, asked an audience member about the nightie she had worn on her honeymoon and received the answer that no nightie had been worn. Such entertainment was, Ryan declared, 'immorally suggestive'. And to get his message across, Ryan circulated the thundering sermon that he intended to deliver at 8.00 a.m. mass the following morning to the *Sunday Independent* and the *Sunday Press* – both of which carried the story on page one.[50]

The arrival of Teilifís Éireann in 1961 presented far-reaching challenges for Irish Sunday papers. While the instantaneous news cycle was still a long way off and the station's news and current-affairs programming impacted more on daily than Sunday titles, the new arrival presented competition for the public's attention and for advertising revenue. The Irish took to television with gusto. As of December 1967, 59 per cent of all private households had a television set, with programmes being watched by 67 per cent of all individuals and by 72 per cent of all those aged 15 to 34. And while Irish Sunday newspapers were estimated to be read by 81 per cent of all adults, television proved a strong competitor for advertising revenue.[51] Total advertising expenditure through Irish advertising agencies rose from £2.9 million in 1961 to £8.5 million in 1968 (an increase of 192 per cent), press advertising rose only from £2.4 million to £4.3 million (a rise of 80 per cent). In 1961 Irish television had only 2 per cent of all advertising spend; by 1968 this had risen to 32 per cent. In the same period the share of total advertising spend acquired by newspapers fell from 82 per cent to 51 per cent.[52]

The two Irish Sundays continued their head-to-head competition through the 1960s. In his chapter on the *Sunday Press*, Ray Burke recalls that circulation peaked at over 500,000 at the end of 1963, when the paper included a four-page, full-colour souvenir supplement on John Fitzgerald Kennedy. At the *Independent*, Hector Legge's religiosity was beginning to look out of place. But

49 *SI*, 6 Feb. 1966.   50 *SI & SP*, 13 Feb. 1966.   51 *IT*, 6 Feb. 1968.   52 *IT*, 13 Mar. 1971.

shortly before he departed as editor in 1970 he declined to publish what would
have been probably the biggest scoop of his career – the untold story of what
became known as the Arms Crisis. Within a year he was succeeded by Conor
O'Brien, but the circulation gap between both Irish Sunday newspapers had
widened: in 1969, sales for the *Sunday Press* hit 420,000 per week compared to
331,000 for the *Sunday Independent*.[53]

In the 1970s, the sense of change in the republic continued, but this was
also the decade when the Troubles in the North – and the spin-off impact in
the South – dominated the front pages. Ten years after the demise of the first
Irish tabloid, the *Sunday Review* in 1963, the *Sunday World* was launched. It would
prove a remarkable success, colourful, brash, controversial and popular. It tested
as many cultural boundaries as possible, including taboos such as the mention
of sex – as typified by its provocative slogan 'Are you getting it every Sunday?'[54]
As noted by Siún Ní Dhuinn and Regina Uí Chollatáin, the paper's content
indicates clearly that it viewed itself as part of 'a backlash against the cultural
force-feeding' that Ireland had experienced in previous decades. Within its first
six months of publication, it achieved weekly sales of 206,442.[55] One of those
involved in establishing the title, Gerry McGuinness, took exception to the way
'British papers were being dumped on to the Irish market at a lower price purely
to boost circulation figures for ABC audit purposes, which, in turn, would
help them sell more advertising'. At this stage, all British newspapers circulated
tariff-free, as a result of the Anglo-Irish Free Trade Agreement of 1965, which
allowed for the removal of the duty on imported newspapers. McGuinness also
took issue with governmental concern about how British television channels
were being picked up in the republic and the declared intention to establish a
second Irish television channel to counter this trend. It was odd, McGuinness
concluded, 'that the government considers it would not be in the national interest to have the influence of British television available nationwide on the one
hand, yet appears to have no feelings at all about the effect freely available and
cheaper UK newspapers have in the Irish market'.[56]

Leaving aside the continuing presence of British titles, it is important to
note that the success of the *Sunday World* broke the Irish duopoly. During the
first half of 1975 sales of the *Sunday Press* fell below 400,000 copies for the first
time in a dozen years. And by 1977 the respective sales stood at 381,611 (*Press*),
272,359 (*Independent*) and 293,000 (*World*) copies per week.[57] The figures imply a
weak performance by the *Independent*, but Conor O'Brien's short period as editor
before he was replaced in 1976 by Michael Hand resulted in much outstanding

53 Ibid.   54 This notable slogan was coined by newspaper executive John Thompson. See *IT*, 21 Oct.
2006.   55 *IT*, 10 Jan. 1978.   56 *IT*, 9 Nov. 1976.   57 *IT*, 25 May 1974 & 31 Aug. 1977.

journalism, not least by investigative reporter Joe MacAnthony. The most celebrated story was MacAnthony's three-page investigation (plus banner-headline treatment on page one) that exposed the Irish Hospital Sweepstakes as a grubby money-making exercise that benefitted, among others, Sweepstakes chief executive Joe McGrath. Although originally planned as a two-part series, O'Brien famously decided to run it all in one edition because he feared that he would be forced to drop the content planned for the second week. Michael Hand's term was also relatively short but eventful. In 1982 he refused to publish an investigation by *Independent* news editor Kevin O'Connor that detailed a range of suspect activities involving then minister for justice Sean Doherty. Many years later, O'Connor established that Taoiseach Charles Haughey had asked a government minister to request that Hand spike the story.[58] There were other, lighter, moments but by November 1983 Hand's race was run. He was moved upstairs and later enjoyed a journalistic Indian summer when he penned features, some award-winning, for the *Sunday Tribune*.

The *Tribune* had earlier entered the Sunday market in October 1980. An unlikely partnership of Hugh McLaughlin – one of the figures behind the *Sunday World* – and former *Hibernia* magazine editor John Mulcahy identified a gap in the market for a quality Sunday. It was, note Pat Brennan and Brian Trench in their chapter on the newspaper, 'an attempt to continue by other means that magazine's dissenting journalism'. McLaughlin recruited rising *Irish Times* journalist Conor Brady as editor after a disillusioned Mulcahy left, selling his shares to the Smurfit Group and, state Brennan and Trench, in the process becoming the 'only man to make a capital gain from the *Sunday Tribune*'. Within a short time its audited circulation was 110,000, propelled by a stream of political exclusives written by political editor Geraldine Kennedy, another young former *Irish Times* journalist. Both would return to the *Irish Times* and both would record firsts there: Brady as the first Catholic editor; Kennedy as the first woman editor.

Having been acquired by Vincent Browne (with the backing of Tony Ryan, who had built a fortune through aircraft leasing) the *Tribune* declared its position clearly on several current and controversial issues such as the bans on divorce and contraception. Brennan and Trench wonder whether the paper's 'attention to these issues' led to an informant calling with news of a teenage girl, Ann Lovett, and her baby dying after childbirth at a grotto in Granard, Co. Longford. The resulting story, note Brennan and Trench, 'had ripple effects far greater than the size of the report might have suggested … as Ann Lovett became an instantly recognised symbol of something much greater than a single girl's experience'.[59] They also argue that the *Tribune*'s openness to 'points of view beyond the

58 Kevin O'Connor, *Sweetie: how Haughey spent the money* (Dublin, 2009), pp 28–9.   59 *ST*, 5 Feb. 1984.

spectrum generally covered in media was seen most clearly but also most controversially in relation to Northern Ireland and republicanism'. Indeed, an interview
with INLA leader and fugitive Dominic McGlinchey prompted Tony Ryan to
summon Browne and managing director John Kelleher to his home, where the
confrontation was physical as well as verbal. Within a year, Ryan wanted out.
Browne found friends to buy his shares. But the company's future remained on a
knife edge, as it would until its final edition on 30 January 2011.

The *Sunday Tribune* was not alone in making its debut in 1980. Earlier that
year the first edition of the *Sunday Journal* rolled off the presses. While the
Tribune spoke to a largely urban audience, the *Journal* was aimed at a rural readership in its first iteration. But, as Mary Muldowney recounts in her chapter,
the paper was in trouble almost from the start, despite a claimed circulation of
50,000 copies. By July 1980 the original investors had pulled out and Joe Moore,
of the insurance company PMPA, had agreed to step in. It was not the happi-
est of arrangements: Moore did not want the *Journal* to continue as a 'farming
paper'; his intention, states Muldowney, was to change the paper's focus to general features, 'with some news but with a strong motoring emphasis'. It did not
fare well. Sales and advertising revenue continued to fall and the *Journal*'s final
edition was published in June 1982. A year later, an administrator was appointed
to PMPA, Joe Moore was sacked and the government was forced to bail out the
company at the taxpayers' expense.

In the late 1970s and early 1980s the landscape changed again. A second television channel (RTÉ2) began broadcasting in November 1978, an economic
recession hindered people's purchasing power and a change to canon law in 1983
removed the obligation for Catholics to attend Sunday mass, if they attended
a Saturday evening mass instead. The church's rationale for the change was that
Sunday had lost its 'traditional rhythm and society had created difficulties in cel-
ebrating the Lord's Day'.[60] This change resulted in the transfer of nearly 20 per
cent of church congregations from Sunday morning to Saturday evening mass,
with knock-on effects on Sunday-newspaper deadlines and circulations. Sales of
the *Sunday Press* dropped from 369,156 in 1981 to 281,992 in 1984; over the same
period, sales of the *Sunday Independent* fell from 267,109 to 227,003.[61] In a similar
vein, the move towards Sunday trading resulted in a slow and then rapid altera-
tion of Sunday from a day on which only newsagents and small shops opened for
a few hours to allow for the purchase of 'Sunday goods', to a day when almost
every shop and restaurant was open from noon to 6.00 p.m. By early 1985 trade
unions were acknowledging that Sunday trading was 'a fact of life' in large urban
areas. And, despite regular appeals from members of the Catholic hierarchy for

60 *IT*, 14 Nov. 1983.   61 *Business & Finance*, 13 Sept. 1984.

people to 'make Sunday a day of joy and freedom from work' and to beware the dangers of turning their minds 'from God to mammon', by the early 1990s Sunday trading was endemic across all commercial sectors nationwide.[62]

With an emphasis on the previously neglected Mammon, the *Sunday Business Post* was launched in 1989. It was, as Ed Mulhall states in his chapter, 'a venture that would come close to collapse on several occasions, make millionaires of some of its journalist founders, have several significant changes in its owner-ship structure with the different foreign and domestic entities, yet still operate in 2018 under the banner of "Independent journalism on Sunday"'. Mulhall recounts the dramatic last-minute manoeuvres as the first publishing deadline approached, the newspaper's early difficulties as it struggled to find its feet and how Stephen Ryan's outstanding design 'gave it a distinctive look'. The four founders divided the responsibilities, with Damien Kiberd, a former business editor of the *Irish Press*, taking the role of editor; Frank Fitzgibbon, formerly editor of *Irish Business* magazine, as managing director; Aileen O'Toole, formerly editor of *Business and Finance* magazine, as news editor; and James Morrissey, for-merly deputy business editor of the *Irish Independent*, as senior reporter. Mulhall's chapter focuses on the Kiberd era, which ended in November 2001. Four years earlier, the *Post* was in its prime, in profit and circulation had climbed to near 42,000 copies per week. In August 1997 British regional press group Trinity International Holdings bought the paper for £5.55 million.

As the new kids on the block made their presence felt, matters at the *Sunday Press* went from bad to disastrous with numbing speed. In 1984 circulation of the *Press* was put at 281,992, down about 100,000 copies since 1981. This compared unfavourably with 227,003 for the *Sunday Independent* and 93,175 for the rising star, the *Tribune*. Michael Keane succeeded Vincent Jennings as editor in 1986, but the sales continued southward. In 1989 the circulation of the *Independent* passed that of the *Press*. In his chapter, Ray Burke details the end: 'the decline was terminal, hastened by haemorrhaging sales, worsening management-staff relations and a disastrous partnership with a US newspaper publisher, Ralph Ingersoll III'. The last edition of the *Sunday Press* was published on 21 May 1995.

In contrast, the *Sunday Independent* was going from strength to strength under the editorship of Aengus Fanning, who, in one interview, stated his determina-tion 'to do something slightly different. What's needed is a chemistry which makes a newspaper compulsive, that you can't ignore it, you've got to buy the bloody thing.'[63] As Kevin Rafter outlines in his chapter, the reinvented title, as

62 *IT*, 9 Apr. 1985, 25 Dec. 1987, 12 Dec. 1988 & 11 July 1991.   63 Ivor Kenny, 'Aengus Fanning – the *Sunday Independent*' in *Talking to ourselves: conversations with editors of the Irish news media* (Galway, 1994), pp 208–24 at p. 214.

well as delivering headline-grabbing exclusives and the views of controversial columnists, very often itself became the news.

The demise of the Press Group disturbed the Irish market, with British and Irish Sundays seeking to mop up *Press* readers. There was also room for entrepreneurs. On 28 July 1996 a novel new Sunday was launched. Building on reader interest in sport, the *Title* restricted its coverage to games of all hues, though mostly soccer, GAA and rugby. It was edited by well-known sports journalist Cathal Dervan and the managing director was former Meath GAA footballer and *Sunday Press* journalist Liam Hayes. Described as a 'brave and colourful effort, but a gamble that did not quite come off', within a year it had morphed into *Ireland on Sunday*, a more general-interest newspaper which, by the end of 1999, was selling more than 65,000 copies. Horgan and Flynn describe the editorial content as a 'mixture designed to appeal at least in part to the slightly more conservative, more nationalist readers who had been left high and dry by the collapse of the *Sunday Press*'.[64] In June 2000 it was taken over by the rapidly expanding Scottish Radio Holdings, which, six years later, sold the paper to DMG, publishers of the *Daily Mail*. It was then rebranded for a second time, becoming the *Irish Mail on Sunday*.

As already noted, imports of British newspapers, particularly Sunday titles, have been a feature of the Irish market since the turn of the twentieth century. Our focus in this volume is on the Sunday press in the Irish republic. But given the long-held determination of British publishers to tap into the Irish market – and equally the desire of Irish readers to read British publications – there is a history of hybridity between core British Sunday newspapers and their Irish offspring. In the past this may have amounted to little more than inserting Irish sports reports and the occasional news story written by a 'stringer', an industry term for freelance or moonlighting journalists who regularly contribute to a title. These 'stringers' would augment staff journalists based in Ireland such as Chris Ryder at the *Sunday Times*, with editorial control residing in London. However, in recent years the Irish editions of the *Sunday Times* and the *News of the World* (which published a distinct Irish edition from 1996 until that title's demise in 2011) have represented a more significant investment in Irish content and staff, while still adhering to the model of customizing the core product for the local market. The same can be said in varying degrees of the other hybrid titles: the *Irish Mail on Sunday*, the *Irish Sun on Sunday* and the *Irish Sunday Mirror*. Together these three titles and the *Sunday Times* sold 225,712 copies per week in Ireland between July and December 2017.[65]

---

64 Horgan and Flynn, *Irish media*, p. 177.   65 newsbrandsireland.ie/data-centre/circulation.

This issue of hybridity, with its complex balancing of British and Irish interests and opinions, is explored in Michael Foley's chapter, with particular focus on the experience of the *Sunday Times* in Ireland. Foley argues that the development of the modern hybrid press was 'made possible by a number of factors: the historic presence in Ireland of the British press, new technology that allowed a high degree of editorial change between Irish and UK editions, and the health of the Irish economy as it entered what would be called the Celtic Tiger era'. Cultural fluidity is another important factor; the popular culture stars in Britain are stars in Ireland too; football supporters share the same passions and the same teams; and radio and television know no borders. But there are important differences. While the launch slogan for the Irish edition of the *Sunday Times* was 'The English just don't get it', the paper has always been, and remains, a British-managed and -controlled newspaper.[66]

While many of the titles examined in this volume produced Northern editions, for the most part readers in Northern Ireland gravitated towards British Sunday titles, with indigenous Sunday titles only emerging from the 1960s onwards. This may have been influenced by the widespread observance of the sabbath in the North. However, in 1965 the *Belfast News Letter* entered the Sunday market with the *Sunday News* – an attempt by the unionist-oriented *News Letter* to engage with those not of that political persuasion. Its first editor, Pat Carville, was recruited from the nationalist leaning *Irish News*. As the only Sunday title published in Northern Ireland, with a 2.00 a.m. deadline on Sunday mornings, the paper was well placed to build on the demand for news that accompanied the outbreak of the Troubles. Among those who worked on the paper in its early days was chief sub-editor Andy Barclay, who later went on to work with, respectively, the *Sunday Tribune* and the *Irish Times*. There was also Jim Campbell (later of the *Sunday World*) who, as news editor, was responsible for assigning a young reporter, Colin McClelland (later editor of the *Sunday World*), to Belfast's hot spots. Ironically, it was the huge success of the Northern edition of the *Sunday World* (with Campbell as its Northern editor) that helped bring about the demise of the *Sunday News*. The death-knell for the title came, however, when, in 1988, the *Belfast Telegraph* launched the tabloid *Sunday Life*, to huge success. From

---

66 Just as British titles 'editionized' for the Irish market, Irish Sunday titles also 'editionized' with specific editions printed in the order of how far these needed to travel to reach readers. Generally, the production schedule took the order of British, Northern, country, Dublin and (Dublin) city editions. The infrastructure needed to distribute these newspapers was substantial. In 1979 a government report noted that every Saturday night/Sunday morning over 1 million newspapers were printed in Dublin city before being dispatched by trucks and vans to focal points around the county, after which local distribution contractors took over. Report of enquiry into the supply and distribution of daily and Sunday newspapers published in Ireland, and of newspapers, periodicals and magazines distributed by wholesalers (Dublin, 1979), pp 12–14.

Figure 1: *Irish Times* cartoonist Martyn Turner's view in May 1995 on the domination of
the Irish newspaper industry by Independent Newspapers (now INM).

sales of over 100,000 a week in the 1970s, the *Sunday News* dropped to less than
25,000 copies a week in 1993, the year it ceased publication.[67] *Sunday Life* was
recorded as selling 32,892 copies per week for the six months between July and
December 2017.[68]

It is important to note that some short-lived recent Sunday titles – *Stars
on Sunday* (March–May 2003) and the *Irish Daily Star Sunday* (2003–11) – are not
examined in this volume for reasons of space. For the same reason, we were
unable to explore the recent history and impact of the *Irish Mail on Sunday*.

HOW SUNDAY NEWSPAPERS WORK

Sunday newspapers are different to their daily counterparts in appearance,
content, attitude and pace. Some titles, such as the *Sunday Independent*, are part
of an established stable of newspapers, while others, like the *Sunday Business
Post*, are stand-alone publications. And while the current dramatic decline in
the fortunes of print newspapers has resulted in many changes in journalistic
work practices, with smaller staffs and greater flexibility across company titles,
Sundays remain distinctly separate publications. This is different to the US,
for example, where newspapers often operate a seven-day production cycle; the
Sunday *New York Times* is still the *New York Times*. In Ireland, the *Sunday Independent*
would never be viewed as the *Irish Independent* on Sunday, nor would the staff of
either title wish it so, though in recent years rationalization has resulted in some
overlap of personnel and function.

67 Hugh Oram, *Paper tigers: stories of Irish newspapers by the people who make them* (Belfast, 1983), p. 74. See
also *IT*, 25 Mar. 1993. **68** Information courtesy of Audit Bureau of Circulations.

The conscious creation of a separate visual identity is not new. British culture critic Raymond Williams recalled that 'by the 1840s, when the Sunday papers had become even more successful, there was a distinctive "Sunday-paper look", which we can still often recognise'.[69] While the tone varies according to the title – from the ominously serious to the entertainingly flippant – the Sunday papers call out to readers in a loud voice, staking their claim to define the day, the week.

But, asks Paul Barker, 'in what sense are the Sundays *news*papers?' How often do Sunday newspapers share a lead story? Really hard news, he states, 'sometimes demands its own priorities'.[70] Of course, Sundays will share a lead story when something happens of such import that they cannot avoid it, but generally a Sunday newspaper is seeking not to cover common ground but to be seen to be different, to stand out. In sport, however, it is different. Most games are still played over the weekend, so a Sunday has the advantage of news reports on games or previews of same. Sunday titles also labour under the difficulty of rarely having a set news agenda to follow. While the daily diary of news events such as the courts, the Dáil, the stock exchange, financial announcements, political announcements and press conferences dictate, to a large degree, news coverage in the dailies, the Sundays generally have to generate their own stories. They can, for instance, produce a wrap-up on a running celebrity court case, but even here they have to find an angle that has not been exhausted in daily coverage.

As such, reporters have to unearth new stories or new angles on old stories. The former results in Sundays generating a high number of exclusives, often through investigative journalism, while the latter is achieved by accentuating one or more of the five 'Ws' and 'H' often mentioned in journalism studies as the essential ingredients of a story: who, what, where, when, why and how. In theory they have a week to do this, but Sunday newspapers present significant production headaches. They demand discipline from journalists, both reporters and production staff, to pull together the disparate parts into a cohesive package, with deadlines running through the week so that page output can be managed efficiently. This is also why soft news, such as gossip (social diaries), celebrity profiles, general features and opinion/comment are so prominent. Generally they are not time-critical. Social diaries, defined by Stuart Hall as 'often inconsequential stories about consequential people' can sometimes be much sharper – as with socialite and journalist Terry Keane's 'The Keane Edge', which ran in the *Sunday Independent* throughout the 1990s.[71]

69 Raymond Williams, 'General profile' in Hoggart, *Your Sunday paper*, pp 13–29 at p. 14.   70 Paul Barker, 'No news is good news', ibid., pp 30–42 at p. 30.   71 Stuart Hall, 'The world of the gossip

Over the years Sunday newspapers have grown beyond the news-and-features paradigm to include magazines, sports supplements, property supplements and any and every idea that might attract the all-important advertising. As a once-a-week publication, it must generate enough cash in a single edition to keep full-time and part-time staff employed and shareholders happy. And there are clear threats to the Sunday business model. In a declining market, as print increasingly gives way to digital, the distinctive look of the Sunday press is increasingly lost in generic home pages. However, one leading international editorial figure believes that the future for weekend print titles is brighter compared to that facing their daily counterparts. Former *Guardian* editor Alan Rusbridger has stated that he did not believe there would be many daily print newspapers in ten years' time: 'I would have thought that many newspapers would produce a weekly edition and the weekend papers would be probably more long-lasting.'[72]

It should be noted that a history of Sunday newspapers is also a history of Sunday newspaper readers, of power, culture, taste and morality, and of difference, as competition entered the indigenous Irish market in the shape of the *Sunday Press, Sunday Tribune* and the *Sunday Business Post.* The *Sunday Independent* of the 1990s was, it could be argued, a creature of the Celtic Tiger era, of expressions of wealth and loud annunciations of power, opinion, entitlement and privilege. But it could also be viewed as a newspaper that shook up a complacent establishment and challenged the political power and cultural control of 'official Ireland'. Equally, the earlier *Sunday Independent* of the Hector Legge era mirrored an Irish society under the yoke of a strict Catholic sensibility. However, generalizations about the role enjoyed by the Sunday press can and should be challenged by particular examples. For instance, the *Independent* in the 1970s under editor Conor O'Brien was also responsible for Joe MacAnthony's truly groundbreaking journalism about the Irish Hospital Sweepstakes.

Sunday newspapers were, up to recent times, by and large gendered publications, written by men for men, with some minor roles for women. While this changed in the modern era when first Geraldine Kennedy and later Emily O'Reilly were appointed to frontline political positions – the former in the *Sunday Press* and the *Sunday Tribune*, the latter in the *Tribune* and the *Business Post* – it is still worth noting that there have been only three female editors of Sunday newspapers in Ireland: Fiona McHugh at the *Sunday Times* (2000–5); Nóirín Hegarty at the *Sunday Tribune* from 2005 until its closure in 2011; and Anne Harris at the *Sunday Independent* (2012–14).

While this collection is a study of newspapers, not a socio-cultural analysis of Ireland in the twentieth century, understanding the socio-cultural backdrop and the social forces at play at any given time helps to better appreciate the work of journalism, and particularly Sunday newspaper journalism. It also illustrates that, beyond simply using newspapers as sources, understanding the nature of newspapers — as shaped by their ownership structures, production routines, financing, journalistic ethos, editors and journalists — helps us construct a far deeper understanding of the processes of political and social change and the role that print media played, and continues to play, in such processes.

2 / 'The Sham Squire's youngest child': the *Sunday Freeman*, 1913–16

FELIX M. LARKIN

The *Sunday Freeman*, launched on 22 June 1913, was the first Sunday newspaper in Ireland that was distinct, in content as well as in branding, from its weekly stablemate. The *Freeman's Journal* newspaper – founded in 1763 – had since 1818 published a weekly newspaper, the *Weekly Freeman's Journal*, which was essentially a compendium of news items and editorials published in the daily *Freeman* during the previous week.[1] It was targeted at country readers to whom it was not possible, even in the early years of the twentieth century, to distribute a daily newspaper published and printed in Dublin in a timely fashion – and the rural character of the *Weekly Freeman* was reinforced from 1871 by the incorporation of the *Irish Agriculturist* within the title. This model of a weekly compendium was copied by the *Irish Daily Independent* in the 1890s and early 1900s – and by its successor from 1905 onwards, the *Irish Independent*. When the *Independent* began publishing a Sunday edition, it was essentially a version of the *Weekly Independent* – albeit with its own branding and sold on Sunday instead of on Thursday, the publication day for both the *Weekly Freeman* and the *Weekly Independent*. The *Sunday Freeman*, however, was different from the *Weekly Freeman*, aimed not at country but at urban – and specifically Dublin – readers, and its target market was essentially those who had begun taking English Sunday newspapers.

The entry of English Sunday newspapers into the Irish market was a very recent phenomenon, but these newspapers had been enjoying considerable success in Ireland. An editorial in the *Freeman's Journal* on 6 November 1911 commented that 'a few years ago these journals had only a limited circulation in this country. Now they flood every Irish city on Sunday morning.'[2] Their success was widely regretted, both by the Irish nationalist establishment and by the Catholic Church; they lacked any Irish identity and were regarded as sensationalist and even salacious. The *Sunday Freeman* aimed to offer an Irish alternative to these English newspapers. In its first editorial, it apologized for daring 'to

1 The *Freeman's Journal* would celebrate its third jubilee with an elaborate supplement published on 10 Aug. 1913 – just one month after the launch of the *Sunday Freeman*. 2 L.M. Cullen, *Eason & Son: a history* (Dublin, 1989), p. 252.

further overcrowd the ranks of journalism' with another title, but it justified its existence in unequivocal terms:

> The fact that there is a growing demand for a readable, interesting, newsy paper for Sunday reading has, so far, received little recognition from Irish journalists. Newspaper owners on the other side of the Channel have been quicker to recognise the demand, but their anxiety to profit by it seems to have left them little opportunity of discriminating between news that a self-respecting man or woman would care to read and that which, for decency's sake, should be suppressed.

The new paper would be 'fit for free circulation in an Irish home', and the editorial concluded with the hope 'that the new paper will merit and receive the support of all who believe that the spirit and the life of Ireland can best be rendered by an Irish press'.[3] Its Dublin focus was evident in the statement in the editorial that the new paper was making 'our first timid bow to the discerning inhabitants of the Irish Metropolis' – and also in the device above the editorial, which incorporated the coat of arms of the city.[4] The device also included the legend 'All the news that's *fit* to print'.[5]

The sentiments of the first editorial were repeated by the chairman of the *Freeman's Journal* company, Sir Walter Nugent MP, at the annual general meeting of the company in March 1914. Referring to the *Sunday Freeman*, he said that:

> it was a venture they had started during the past year and of which they were very proud. It had met with a hearty welcome and ... it filled a long-felt want in Dublin. It was a clean paper. They endeavoured to make it a paper that every man could have in his house without anxiety or shame, at the same time as they endeavoured to give the latest news.[6]

Nugent had become chairman of the *Freeman* company in 1912, after a period of serious decline in the fortunes of the company. The new venture represented by the *Sunday Freeman* was part of an attempt – ultimately unsuccessful – to save the company and its titles. The *Freeman's Journal* was the semi-official organ of the Irish Parliamentary Party, and its survival was regarded by the party as essential to their continued political success. Thus, in 1907, John Dillon had written to his party leader, John Redmond, that:

3 *SF*, 22 June 1913.   4 In the 'Aeolus' episode of *Ulysses* (1922), set in the offices of the *Freeman's Journal*, James Joyce locates the newspaper 'in the heart of the Hibernian metropolis' – the opening words of the 'Aeolus' episode.   5 Author's emphasis. The *New York Times* had been using this slogan since 1896.   6 *FJ*, 23 Mar. 1914.

the chief weakness of the party lies in the management of the *Freeman* …
I do not believe it is possible to maintain the Irish party without some
newspaper in Dublin which can be counted on to give it loyal, active and
intelligent support.[7]

In 1912, the party leaders had intervened in the affairs of the *Freeman* so as to
avert its collapse – and had installed a new board, under Nugent as chairman,
with the promise of subsidies from party sources in order to keep the company
afloat.[8] The new management identified the launch of a Sunday newspaper to
compete with English imports as a possible means of increasing revenue.

It is impossible now to say whether or not the *Sunday Freeman* was a commercial success – but the evidence would suggest that any success it may have
enjoyed was fleeting. The *Freeman* company claimed that it was successful in its
early days: at its 1914 annual general meeting, Nugent stated that 'the circulation
of the *Sunday Freeman* was very large and increasing week by week and, with its
increased sales, its attraction as an advertising medium must become apparent
to advertisers'.[9] Its first issue comprised twenty-four pages and, along with news
on the home rule bill, on suffragette 'outrages' in London and on proposals for
a motorised bus service in Dublin, it carried a parliamentary news page written by Irish Party stalwart T.P. O'Connor MP. Alongside sports and financial
news, its other features included a news miscellany page ('Talk of the Town'), a
social diary column ('In Hibernian Circles'), a short story and numerous book
extracts and reviews. Its pagination was increased to thirty-two pages for the
second and subsequent issues in 1913 – to meet the demand for advertising,
according to the paper itself.[10] The pages were initially smaller in size than those
of the daily *Freeman*, and it had more advertisements than the latter – and these
were more prominently displayed. There were also more illustrations – mostly
well-executed cartoon drawings complementing feature articles, but some photographs too. More generally, the layout of the pages was less rigid than in the
daily *Freeman*, a staid newspaper in appearance even by the standards of 1913. The
new style of newspaper that the *Sunday Freeman* aspired to be is symbolized by
the jaunty, angled presentation of its title in the masthead. The paper, however,
soon lost its impetus. It reverted to twenty-four pages in January 1914. This

---

7 NLI, John Redmond Papers, MS 15,182/15, John Dillon to John Redmond, 31 July 1907.
Confirmation of the *Freeman*'s role in the decline and fall of the Irish Party is to be found in an
anonymous memorandum, also in the Redmond Papers, which concluded *c*.1916 that 'the press was the
weakest side of the constitutional movement' (MS 15,262/1).   8 Felix M. Larkin, 'Two gentlemen
of the *Freeman*: Thomas Sexton, W.H. Brayden and the *Freeman's Journal*, 1892–1916' in Ciara Breathnach
& Catherine Lawless (eds), *Visual, material and print culture in nineteenth-century Ireland* (Dublin, 2010), pp
210–22 at pp 219–220.   9 *FJ*, 23 Mar. 1914.   10 *SF*, 29 June 1913.

Figure 2: The *Sunday Freeman* front page from 2 August 1914.

was reduced further to a mere twelve pages in June 1914 – and at that time it changed to a broadsheet format, thereby assuming more of the character of a traditional newspaper. So, even before the First World War broke out in August 1914 and newsprint shortages forced the *Freeman* company to scale back the production of all its titles, it would seem that the hopes that had been entertained for the *Sunday Freeman* were not being realized – and that the title, born with such flourish, was only adding to the difficulties of the company.

'A READABLE, INTERESTING, NEWSY PAPER'

The root of these difficulties lay in the Parnell Split of 1890–1. Prior to that, the *Freeman's Journal* had been the leading daily organ in Dublin – at least since 1841, when it was purchased by Sir John Gray. Gray and his son, Edmund Dwyer Gray, made the *Freeman* an important newspaper. The repeal in the 1850s of oppressive duties on advertisements and on the newspapers themselves opened the way for great expansion in the newspaper market, and Sir John Gray exploited this opportunity – growing the circulation of the *Freeman* from between 2,000 and 3,000 copies per day to approximately 10,000 at the time of his death in 1875. Under his son, the *Freeman's* production capacity was further increased, its circulation grew threefold – to 30,000 copies per day – and it became extremely profitable.[11] So successful was it that in 1887 Edmund converted it into a public company, while retaining control for himself and his family.

Edmund Dwyer Gray died at the early age of 42 in 1888, and his widow, Caroline, effectively controlled the *Freeman* for the next four years. The Parnell Split occurred during that period, ushering in a time of unprecedented volatility in Irish politics that had huge implications for the newspaper market in Dublin. Caroline Gray and the *Freeman* initially supported Parnell in the Split. However, once the anti-Parnellites launched their own daily newspaper, the *National Press*, in March 1891, and the *Freeman* began as a result to lose circulation and revenue, she wavered. Under the influence of her son, also named Edmund Dwyer Gray, and just turned 21, Mrs Gray resolved that the paper should switch sides. This it did in late September 1891, a fortnight before Parnell's unexpected death. The Parnellites then launched the *Irish Daily Independent* to fill the vacuum

---

11 See Cullen, *Eason*, pp 45, 76–7. I have assumed that the pattern of newspaper sales in Ireland through W.H. Smith – the antecedent of Eason's – was representative of the market generally at this time. I have also assumed that W.H. Smith's share accounted for one-third of total sales of newspapers in Ireland (Cullen, *Eason*, p. 355). All estimates of newspaper circulation in Ireland in the nineteenth and early twentieth centuries should be regarded as extremely tentative; figures were generally neither published nor independently verified. No circulation figures are available for the *Sunday Freeman*.

caused by the *Freeman*'s defection. This only compounded the *Freeman*'s difficulties: it now had two competitors instead of one. The *Freeman* and the *National Press* later merged in March 1892, with Mrs Gray selling her shareholding as part of the deal. In simultaneous transactions, the *Freeman* company bought the *National Press* newspaper for £36,000 and the *National Press* company bought Mrs Gray's shares for exactly the same sum. The *National Press* then ceased publication, and Mrs Gray's shares were distributed to the shareholders of the defunct *National Press* company.[12]

The Parnell Split had a devastating effect on the *Freeman's Journal*. First, the damage inflicted by the *National Press* was huge: the *Freeman*'s circulation fell by a quarter in 1891, and the cost of purchasing the *National Press* – £36,000, equivalent to over £2.5 million sterling today – was crippling.[13] Secondly, it had to contend with the ongoing competition from the pro-Parnell *Irish Daily Independent*, which survived as the organ of the Parnellite wing of the Irish Party until the party's reunification under John Redmond in 1900, when it was purchased by William Martin Murphy. In 1905, Murphy transformed the paper into the modern *Irish Independent*, at half the price of the *Freeman* – a halfpenny, instead of a penny – and with a more popular format and a less partisan editorial policy. He copied what Lord Northcliffe had done in London in 1896 when Northcliffe launched the *Daily Mail*, the first mass-circulation newspaper in these islands.[14] When the *Sunday Freeman* was launched in 1913, it too cost one penny – though the *Weekly Freeman* cost 1½ pence (expressed in its masthead as 'three-halfpence').

After its merger with the *National Press*, the *Freeman's Journal* operated first as the organ of the anti-Parnell faction of the Irish Party and then, after the party came together again in 1900, as the organ of the re-united party. Thomas Sexton MP, the Irish Party's foremost financial expert, became chairman of the company in 1893. This proved an unhappy arrangement – at least from the Irish Party's perspective – because in 1896 Sexton, disillusioned with the continuing divisions within the party, unexpectedly retired from parliament. Afterwards he seemed to regret his loss of influence and compensated for it by using the

12 For further information about the Gray family's association with the *Freeman's Journal*, see Felix M. Larkin, 'Mrs Jellyby's daughter: Caroline Agnes Gray (1848–1927) and the *Freeman's Journal*' in Felix M. Larkin (ed.), *Librarians, poets and scholars: a festschrift for Dónall Ó Luanaigh* (Dublin, 2007), pp 121–39. 13 Trinity College, Dublin, John Dillon Papers, MS 6804/126–8. 14 Patrick Maume, 'Commerce, politics and the *Irish Independent*, 1891–1919', unpublished paper read before the 24th Irish Conference of Historians held at University College Cork, 20–2 May 1999; my thanks to Dr Maume for making a copy of this paper available to me. See also Donal McCartney, 'William Martin Murphy: an Irish press baron and the rise of the popular press' in Brian Farrell (ed.), *Communications and community in Ireland* (Dublin & Cork, 1984), pp 30–8.

Freeman to try to impose his will on his erstwhile colleagues. He was increasingly out of sympathy with them, and this was reflected in the *Freeman*.

Moreover, Sexton proved incapable of meeting the commercial challenge to the *Freeman* represented by Murphy's revamped *Irish Independent* after 1905. Because of its tribulations in the 1890s, the *Freeman* lacked funds for investment – and Sexton, afraid of losing control, would not raise new capital. The paper was not, therefore, in a position to take advantage of the growing demand for newspapers in Ireland, as elsewhere, at this time. Total sales of daily newspapers in Ireland grew by a factor of seven between the early 1880s and the 1920s – from 75,000 copies per day in the 1880s to over half a million in the 1920s.[15] However, the *Freeman*'s circulation – at between 30,000 and 35,000 copies per day – remained much the same as it had been under Edmund Dwyer Gray in the 1880s, and was quickly exceeded by the *Independent*.[16] With the consequent loss of advertising, the paper began to incur heavy trading losses and no dividends were paid to its shareholders after 1908.[17]

It was against this background that the Irish Party leaders moved to save the *Freeman* in 1912, replacing the board and installing Sir Walter Nugent – a prominent businessman, and a safer pair of hands politically than Sexton – as chairman. It was too little, too late. The *Irish Independent* had by then an unassailable market advantage. The launch of the new title within the *Freeman* stable of newspapers, even if it had been a resounding success, could not have stopped the decline and fall of the venerable *Freeman's Journal*. Nevertheless, the *Sunday Freeman* was a significant new development in the Irish newspaper market and is noteworthy for being the first distinctively Sunday newspaper in Ireland – not just a newspaper, and not a compendium of the previous week's news, but a combination of 'a readable, interesting, newsy paper' and 'a magazine of fresh and current literature' suitable for Sunday reading in an Irish family household.[18]

Much of the content of the *Sunday Freeman* was feature articles, at least in its first phase up to June 1914 – its lighter content being modelled on the so-called new journalism that W.T. Stead and others had pioneered in Britain in the late nineteenth century. These articles regularly addressed some aspect of Irish history, especially recent history during the 'long' nineteenth century – and the *Sunday Freeman*'s approach to Irish history is well illustrated by a striking full-page cartoon published on 28 December 1913, the last Sunday of that year.[19]

15 Cullen, *Eason*, pp 77, 307 – but see also footnote 11 above. Raymond Williams likewise calculates a sevenfold increase in aggregate daily newspaper circulation in Britain between 1880 and 1920; see Williams, *The long revolution* (paperback ed., London, 1965), p. 198.   16 The circulation figures given here for the *FJ* refer to 1915 (NLI, John Redmond Papers, MS 15,262/7). By 1915, the *II* claimed to have a circulation of 110,000 (*Newspaper Press Directory*, 1915).   17 *FJ*, 29 Apr. 1912.   18 *SF*, 22 & 29 June 1913.   19 *SF*, 28 Dec. 1913.

Figure 3: Cartoon from the *Sunday Freeman* of 28 December 1913.

It shows the iconic female figure of Erin – with the obligatory harp, the long-established symbol of Ireland – and she anticipates the passage of the third home rule bill into law in the following year; 1914 is thus added to a list of iconic dates in Ireland's 'long' nineteenth century. Three of these dates mark other great parliamentary achievements by Irish representatives at Westminster: Catholic emancipation in 1829; Gladstone's home rule bill of 1886; and his second home rule bill of 1893.

These achievements are, however, put on an equal footing with three Irish rebellions: the United Irishmen's rebellion of 1798 – which was, in fairness, a very serious uprising – and the rather pathetic revolts of the Young Ireland movement in 1848 and of the Fenians in 1867. These manifestations of the physical-force tradition in Irish politics are claimed by the *Sunday Freeman* as milestones on the road to home rule. Here was a clear message for those attracted by the idea of armed insurrection – namely, that the constitutional nationalists of 1913 felt that such action, at least in the past, was legitimate. This tended to undermine the ideological underpinnings of the home rule movement, and the Irish Party would reap the whirlwind in 1918 – when, in the general election of that year, they were wiped out by Sinn Féin, which had taken on the mantle of the 1916 rebels. By identifying with – and glorifying – the physical-force tradition and thereby accustoming Irish men and women 'to the thought of arms, to the sight of arms, to the use of arms' (a quotation from Patrick Pearse),[20] the Irish Party and its organ, the *Sunday Freeman*, may have inadvertently helped to sow the seeds of its own destruction post-1916. To adapt a phrase from John F. Kennedy's presidential inaugural address in 1961, by riding on the back of the tiger the party ended up inside its belly.

The rebels in 1916 claimed to be acting 'in the name of God and of the dead generations', and they went on to state in their Proclamation of the Irish Republic that 'in every generation the Irish people have asserted their right to national freedom and sovereignty; six times during the past three hundred years they have asserted it in arms'. Three of those six rebellions are celebrated in that cartoon in the *Sunday Freeman*. The rebels were not alone in remembering them with approbation. The attitude of the Irish Party towards this militant heritage is well summed up in a recent study of the Redmond family in their political stronghold of Waterford city as follows: 'When he thought it expedient, Redmond could "wrap the green flag round me, boys" and link himself to a revolutionary past while pointing to a constitutional future.'[21]

---

20 From Pearse's article 'The coming revolution', *An Claidheamh Soluis*, Nov. 1913 – quoted in Vivian Mercier, 'Literature in English, 1891–1921' in W.E. Vaughan (ed.), *A new history of Ireland*, vi: *Ireland under the Union, II, 1870–1921* (Oxford, 1996), pp 357–84 at p. 377.   21 Pat McCarthy, *The Redmonds and Waterford: a political dynasty* (Dublin, 2018), p. 41.

The acceptance by the party and by the wider home rule movement of a tradition antipathetical to its values was, at least in part, an attempt to forge the widest possible political base for the movement and obviate the danger of being outflanked by more extreme nationalists. It also reflected a complacency on the part of the parliamentarians that republican violence was a thing of the past – and, in fact, the so-called 'New Departure' negotiated by Parnell, Davitt and Devoy in 1878–9 had effectively removed guns from Irish politics for the thirty-five years before the Ulster Volunteers landed their arms at Larne. As Conor Mulvagh has remarked, 'for Fenians, the New Departure represented a renewed experiment in constitutionalism' – and the Irish Party leaders felt confident that they had appropriated the Fenian tradition and irrevocably absorbed it within the home rule movement, and so could celebrate it without risking a revival.[22]

Moreover, many home rulers had murky backgrounds in more radical politics, even physical-force republicanism – and still harboured feelings of nostalgia for their youthful indiscretions and the romance of it all, much more glamorous than the long, hard slog of constitutional politics and parliamentary endeavour. As Vincent Comerford has written, 'there has scarcely been between 1872 and 1918 a Westminster parliament, or since then a Dáil Éireann, that did not include members who, at some stage, had dabbled in Irish rebellion'.[23] Such nostalgia for the revolutionary past is evident in the many articles about Irish history that appeared in the *Sunday Freeman*, as it is evident also in, for example, the memoirs of William O'Brien – one of Parnell's principal lieutenants and a member of parliament almost continuously from 1883 to 1918.[24]

Robert Emmet's rebellion of 1803 is – quite surprisingly – not included in that cartoon of 28 December 1913, though it would be one of the six from which the 1916 rebels drew inspiration. It was no less insignificant than the 1848 and 1867 episodes – it has been characterized as little more than a 'drunken street riot' – but Emmet was an attractive figure who was executed for his pains and he secured his status as an Irish republican hero with an eloquent speech from the dock after he had been condemned to death.[25] He may have been absent from the cartoon, but the *Sunday Freeman* did not forget him: it celebrated the 110th anniversary of his arrest with a full-page feature in August 1913.[26] During 1913, the paper also ran a series of laudatory pieces on the 1798 rebels, including one on a notable leader of the Wexford rebels, Fr John Murphy – described as

22 Conor Mulvagh, 'Home rulers at Westminster, 1880–1914' in Thomas Bartlett (ed.), *The Cambridge history of Ireland, iv: 1880 to the present* (Cambridge, 2018), pp 62–88 at p. 62.   23 R.V. Comerford, 'Stephens, Devoy and Clarke' in Eugenio Biagini & Daniel Mulhall (eds), *The shaping of modern Ireland: a centenary assessment* (Dublin, 2016), pp 13–25 at p. 24.   24 William O'Brien, *Recollections* (New York, 1905), pp 115–28.   25 Patrick M. Geoghegan, 'Emmet, Robert' in *Dictionary of Irish biography* (dib.cambridge.org).   26 *SF*, 24 Aug. 1913.

'a sainted hero' – and, in November 1913, they gave two pages to a feature on the three Fenians known as the 'Manchester Martyrs', who had been hanged in 1867 for killing a policeman in a successful bid to free two fellow Fenians from a prison van in Manchester.[27] The subheading on this article tells the readers that it is a 'thrilling story' – and the thrilling story is accompanied on the next page by a highly emotive image of the execution of the three.[28]

Similarly, the *Sunday Freeman* in 1914 published sympathetic pieces on various Fenian leaders, including John O'Leary and Jeremiah O'Donovan Rossa – though, significantly, the paper did not refer to the latter's later avocation as the mastermind behind dynamite campaigns in British cities.[29] And in 1915, the *Sunday Freeman* hailed John Mitchel, the most militant of the Young Irelanders of 1848, as a 'great revolutionist' with 'a heroic heart'.[30] Mitchel was one of Patrick Pearse's 'four great nationalist evangelists',[31] his *Jail journal* being an immensely important text for Irish republicans. By focusing the attention of its readers on such people, rather than on the heroes of the Irish constitutional tradition such as Grattan, O'Connell and Parnell, the *Sunday Freeman* was certainly riding on the back of a tiger.

'HISTRIONIC PLAYBOYS'

A legitimacy derived from history was important for the 1916 rebels, as it was for the Young Ireland movement in 1848 and for the Fenians in the 1860s. Whereas the United Irishmen in 1798 and Emmet in 1803 had formulated a political agenda derived from the American and French revolutions, which reflected the progressive ideals of the Enlightenment, Young Ireland, the Fenians and the 1916 rebels tended to look backwards to an idealized, even mythological, past. Their sense of freedom was not 'republican' in the French understanding of the concept, but was rather simply separation from England – in other words, a narrow nationalism based on the supposition that the Irish were a distinct people who could trace their origins back into pre-history and had struggled gallantly in arms since time immemorial to maintain their nationhood against waves of invaders – to quote one of the leaders of the Young Ireland movement, Thomas Davis, 'against Dane and Saxon and Norman'.[32] This thinking is of dubious historicity, but it closely parallels that of other romantic nationalist movements in Europe in the mid- to late nineteenth century. These movements made skilful use of newspapers, pamphlets and cheap books to propagate their

27 *SF*, 12 Oct. 1913. 28 *SF*, 23 Nov. 1913. 29 *SF*, 11 Jan. 1914 (O'Leary); 18 Jan. 1914 (O'Donovan Rossa). 30 *SF*, 7 Nov. 1915. 31 From Pearse's pamphlet *Ghosts* (1915); quoted in James Quinn, *Young Ireland and the writing of Irish history* (Dublin, 2015), p. 139. 32 Quinn, *Young Ireland*, p. 11.

ideas and to create a mass solidarity that Benedict Anderson termed an 'imagined community' – in other words, a nation.[33] The *Sunday Freeman* can be seen to have played an analogous role in its feature articles on Irish history – and thereby to have contributed to the intellectual ferment that produced the 1916 Rising and all that flowed from it, including the destruction of the home rule movement that the *Freeman* otherwise supported faithfully.

The balance between features and news items in the *Sunday Freeman* favoured the former over the latter until its issue of 21 June 1914. That issue – exactly one year after the launch of the newspaper – introduced the new broadsheet format for the newspaper, reduced its size to twelve pages and altered the balance of its contents in favour of news. News for the first time appeared on its front page instead of a feature article – and that would henceforth be the practice each week. Its front page on 2 August 1914, for instance, carried the headlines: 'WAR DECLARED: Germany draws the sword. Britain, France, Russia and Austria involved'. Thereafter, the *Sunday Freeman* became essentially an organ of war news – with several later issues carrying prominently on the front page the legend 'War Special' – and, whether because of shortage of newsprint or otherwise, it was limited to eight pages per issue from August 1914.[34] This reduced the scope for features, though articles on Irish history and other topics did not completely disappear: for example, the article on John Mitchel mentioned above was published on 7 November 1915 to mark the centenary of his birth, and on 1 August 1915 there was a lengthy feature anticipating the funeral of O'Donovan Rossa, which took place that day, under the headline 'The nation's last tribute to a great Irish patriot'. That feature on the impending O'Donovan Rossa funeral quotes with approval a passage from the *New York Tribune* that is indicative of the attitude of the *Sunday Freeman* – and, by extension, the home rule movement generally – towards the physical-force tradition of Irish nationalism:

> The *New York Tribune* in an editorial in its issue of July 1st makes a telling differentiation between genuine physical force men of the type of O'Donovan Rossa and the histrionic playboys whose antics today, both in Ireland and in the States, are a travesty of the men who took part in a genuine movement at a time when no other way of winning Irish freedom seemed even remotely possible. 'Ireland today,' says the *Tribune*, 'has no rebels who can properly be likened to O'Donovan Rossa. He was of

33 Anderson proposed 'the following definition of the nation: it is an imagined community – and imagined as both inherently limited and sovereign'. See Benedict Anderson, *Imagined communities: reflections on the origin and spread of nationalism* (revised ed. London, 2006), pp 5–6. **34** The first time that legend appeared in the *SF* was on 18 Oct. 1914. See also, for example, the *SF*, 26 Dec. 1915.

another generation, living and fighting under the conditions of his own time … It is true that a few parasitic creatures of those days survive in the country, but it would be an affront to the memory of the valiant and desperate old revolutionist to associate his name with the blatant, noisy, but essentially mean-spirited little group of quasi-Irishmen who still endeavour to work up the symptoms of a dangerous patriotism.'[35]

It is, therefore, somewhat ironic that the *Sunday Freeman*'s short life was brought to an end by the Easter Rising of 1916 – led by those who, a few months earlier, the newspaper had dismissed as 'histrionic playboys'. The offices and plant of the *Freeman's Journal* – located alongside the General Post Office in Dublin, the headquarters of the rebels – were completely destroyed in the Rising, and publication of the *Sunday Freeman* was suspended as a result. Stopgap measures were put in place immediately to ensure that the daily *Freeman* continued to appear so that the Irish Party would still have a voice in the uncertain political landscape after the Rising – but the same priority did not attach to restoring the *Sunday Freeman*. It was never revived. The *Freeman's Journal* – in new premises in Townsend Street, Dublin, from early 1917 onwards – staggered on for another few years as the organ of the Irish Party. It was sold off to new owners in 1919 in the aftermath of the Irish Party's defeat in the general election of the previous year, and it ceased publication finally on 19 December 1924.[36]

The demise of the *Sunday Freeman* was celebrated prematurely by Arthur Griffith on the front page of his weekly newspaper *Nationality* on 12 February 1916 in a characteristically sardonic article entitled 'Death of the Sham Squire's youngest child'. What gave rise to this article was the fact that the *Sunday Freeman* had not been published on the previous weekend, but that was a false alarm – as the chairman of the *Freeman* company, Sir Walter Nugent, was able to report to the annual general meeting held on 10 March 1916:

> As to the *Sunday Freeman*, the Board were pleased to find it possible to continue the paper. The reason for its discontinuance for one or two Sundays was due altogether to the paper restrictions. When these were first proposed, it was thought that they would be much more drastic than had actually been the case and when the situation improved they were enabled to issue the Sunday paper again.[37]

35 *SF*, 1 Aug. 1915. 36 For an account of the *Freeman*'s last years, see Felix M. Larkin, '"A great daily organ": the *Freeman's Journal*, 1763–1924', *History Ireland*, 14:3 (May/June 2006), pp 44–9. 37 *FJ*, 11 Mar. 1916.

Griffith had a history of antagonism towards the *Freeman's Journal* on account of the fact that it was the organ of the Irish party and hostile to current advanced nationalist movements – and between June 1915 and April 1918, he published a series of articles that amounted to a sustained campaign of vilification of the *Freeman*.[38] He accused it bluntly of keeping 'Ireland quiet for the English politicians'.[39] His article about the *Sunday Freeman* was but one in that series.

Unfortunately for the *Freeman*, it had a skeleton in its cupboard that could be – and was – exploited by Griffith in making his case against the newspaper. This was Francis Higgins, a thoroughly disreputable figure known as the 'Sham Squire', who was editor and later proprietor of the *Freeman* at the end of the eighteenth century.[40] The *Freeman* had been founded to support the 'patriot' opposition in the Irish parliament in College Green. From the early 1780s, however, its independence was undermined by Higgins. He was a paid agent of the Dublin Castle authorities. Griffith characterized Higgins as 'originally a pot-boy in a public house in Fishamble Street, Dublin [who] became successively a forger, a convict, a brothel-keeper, a gambling house owner, a blackmailer, and editor and proprietor of the *Freeman's Journal*'.[41] Higgins was eventually awarded a secret-service pension of £300 per annum plus a bounty of £1,000 for information he provided to Dublin Castle on Lord Edward Fitzgerald and for facilitating his capture in 1798. The Sham Squire provided the leitmotif of Griffith's treatment of the *Freeman* – as in this extract from another of Griffith's papers, *Sinn Féin*, in October 1914:

> The body of Francis Higgins is turned to clay in bleak Kilbarrack's church-yard [in north Dublin], but the evil spirit of Francis Higgins still haunts the office where the blood of Lord Edward Fitzgerald was bought and sold, and guides the hand that writes the *Freeman's Journal* leading articles.[42]

That is the context for his designation of the *Sunday Freeman* as the 'Sham Squire's youngest child'.

Griffith's article on the supposed death of the *Sunday Freeman* in February 1916 begins with the statement that 'great commotion was caused in pro-English circles in Ireland by the death of the *Sunday Freeman* last week', and it then goes on to imagine its funeral:

---

38 See Felix M. Larkin, 'Arthur Griffith and the *Freeman's Journal*' in Kevin Rafter (ed.), *Irish journalism before independence: more a disease than a profession* (Manchester, 2011), pp 174–85.   39 *Nationality*, 30 June 1917.   40 Thomas Bartlett (ed.), *Revolutionary Dublin, 1795–1801: the letters of Francis Higgins to Dublin Castle* (Dublin, 2004), especially pp 23–30.   41 *Nationality*, 26 May 1917.   42 *Sinn Féin*, 31 Oct. 1914.

The remains of the *Sunday Freeman* were interred at midnight on Sunday in Kilbarrack churchyard beside the grave of Francis Higgins, the Sham Squire. Dear Mr Brayden [editor of the daily *Freeman* and a director of the *Freeman* company], who was very much affected, delivered a brief and eloquent address above the newly-made grave. He reminded his hearers that this world was transient, and as for the other one, no loyal member of the [*Freeman*] staff could afford to let his mind dwell upon it.[43]

This is Arthur Griffith at his savage best, and the article cleverly evokes an actual mock funeral that had taken place on 27 September 1891 after the *Freeman* defected to the anti-Parnell side in the split. On that occasion, a group of Parnellites arranged a solemn procession from Sir John Gray's statue in Dublin city centre to Kilbarrack churchyard, and copies of the *Freeman* were burnt and interred in the grave of the Sham Squire.[44] As a young man, Griffith was a committed Parnellite – and he may well have had a personal memory of that mock funeral on which he could draw for his article on the death of the *Sunday Freeman*. Though he was overhasty in February 1916 in recording its death, the 'youngest child of the Sham Squire' had then only a few more weeks of life left before it succumbed to the conflagrations that destroyed the General Post Office and its environs in Easter Week 1916.

The *Sunday Freeman* was published for a mere thirty-four months, an insignificant span as compared with the 161 years of continuous publication of the *Freeman's Journal*. It had, however, lasted for somewhat longer than an earlier Sunday newspaper launched in 1817 by the Sham Squire's successor as editor and proprietor of the *Freeman*, Philip Whitfield Harvey. Titled the *Sunday Freeman's Journal*, it survived for just a few months. A note in the *Freeman's Journal* in January 1817 observed of the new paper that it would give 'a complete epitome of the diurnal press ... the essence of six publications of the daily *Freeman's Journal*' and that it would be distributed 'to the interior [and] accessible to country readers'.[45] It seems, therefore, to have prefigured the *Weekly Freeman*, the first issue of which was dated 17 January 1818. In contrast, the *Sunday Freeman* of 1913–16 was clearly an autonomous paper – not a regurgitation of what had previously appeared in the daily *Freeman*. It was the first of its kind in Ireland.[46]

---

43 *Nationality*, 12 Feb. 1916. For further information on Brayden, see Larkin, 'Two gentlemen of the *Freeman*', pp 213–15, 220–1.   44 Stephen J. Brown, *The press in Ireland: a survey and a guide* (Dublin, 1939), p. 39.   45 *The Waterloo directory of Irish newspapers and periodicals, 1800–1900*, at irish.victorianperiodicals. com.   46 A section of this essay was given as a paper, 'Riding the back of the tiger: Irish rebellions of the nineteenth century as portrayed in the *Sunday Freeman* newspaper', in Northumbria University on 4 Nov. 2016 at a conference on 'Revolutionary pasts: representing the long nineteenth century's radical heritage'.

3 / 'A weekly newspaper unequalled in the annals of Irish journalism': the *Sunday Independent*, 1905–84

MARK O'BRIEN

The *Sunday Independent*, Ireland's oldest continuously published Sunday news-paper, began its life as the Sunday edition of the long-running *Irish Weekly Independent*. Launched in 1893 and aimed at those, particularly in rural areas, who did not purchase a daily paper, the *Irish Weekly Independent* was published every Thursday. The new Sunday title would, adverts announced, be 'the Grand Sunday edition' of the paper. Priced at one penny, it would 'contain the very latest and fullest news' with special attention 'devoted to sport in all its forms'.[1] While the *Irish Daily Independent* had been founded by Charles Stewart Parnell in the midst of the newspaper war that followed the Parnell-O'Shea divorce saga and the split in the Irish Parliamentary Party, it had been acquired by former Irish Party MP and successful entrepreneur William Martin Murphy in 1900. It was Murphy who, having seen the success that Alfred Harmsworth had made of the *Daily Mail* in London, reinvented the title by following Harmsworth's formula of a low price, condensed news, serials, interviews, features and compe-titions. Relaunched in January 1905, the halfpenny *Irish Independent* was an instant success. Prompted to enter the Sunday market by the huge popularity of British Sunday titles and the fact that he had invested heavily in printing machinery, Murphy's branding of the new Sunday title as an extension of the existing weekly paper allowed him to offer advertisers the opportunity to advertise in both versions of the weekly paper for the one price. Though a commercial rather than a political venture, the *Irish Independent* reflected Murphy's worldview – 'intensely Catholic, nationalist and conservative'.[2] And it was this worldview that also permeated the pages of the *Sunday Independent* – from its first edition in November 1905 right up to the early 1980s.[3] This chapter examines the paper

---

1 *EH*, 18 Nov. 1905. *IWI* continued to be published until 1960. 2 Padraig Yeates, 'The life and career of William Martin Murphy' in Mark O'Brien & Kevin Rafter (eds), *Independent Newspapers: a history* (Dublin, 2012), pp 14–25 at p. 14. 3 The first month of publication (10, 17, 24, 31 Dec. 1905) is missing from the National Library of Ireland and the Gilbert Library newspaper collection. It is also missing from the Irish Newspaper Archives database. These editions are, however, available at the British Library.

during these decades – a time of intense political change as the state secured its independence from Britain, engaged in a process of nation-building and slowly adjusted to modernity in the post-1960s period.

'A REALLY GOOD WEEKLY PAPER'

The launch of the *Sunday Independent* was preceded by an intense advertising and marketing campaign. Editorial content in Murphy's *Irish Independent* declared that the announcement of the new Sunday title had 'excited great interest all over Ireland'. Many letters, it was reported, 'lay stress on the flood of filthy literature with which certain of the imported papers teem week after week, and the necessity for counteracting this evil in the most effective form possible'. Responding to such sentiments, the *Irish Independent* declared that its new sister title would seek to be 'a really good weekly paper – bright, readable and newsy from beginning to end'. Other letters expressed surprise that Irish weekly newspapers had always been published 'mid-week, leaving the events of Thursday, Friday, and Saturday [to] pass unrecorded'. Again, it was stressed that the forthcoming *Sunday Independent* – as an extension to the revamped *Irish Weekly Independent* – would change this situation; in combination, they would be 'weekly papers in the best, brightest, and completest sense of the term'.[4] Adverts announcing the new paper were placed in all the provincial press, though at least one title, the *Cork Weekly Examiner*, declined to advertise the new venture. Accusing the *Examiner* of being 'afraid of what is to come', the *Irish Independent* observed that the same tactic had been employed, unsuccessfully, at the time of that title's relaunch. The *Sunday Independent* would, it declared, be 'found far superior to any weekly paper published in this country'.[5]

As a pre-launch publicity stunt, Murphy's company repeated a marketing tactic that had well served the relaunch of the *Irish Independent* earlier that year – the 'missing man' competition. This entailed the first edition of the *Sunday Independent* publishing a photograph of a man along with hints as to his changing daily geographical location. A reward of £20 awaited the first member of the public to identify and catch 'Mr Baffler'.[6] When 'Mr Baffler' was apprehended at Donegal railway station after a fortnight on the run, the *Sunday Independent* began a 'spot your face in the crowd' competition with a prize of half a guinea for those who identified themselves as being the person captioned.[7] On the Thursday of the relaunch of the *Irish Weekly Independent* it was described as 'a weekly newspaper unequalled in the annals of Irish journalism'.[8] The first edition of the *Sunday Independent* (10 December 1905) followed that

4 *II*, 20 Nov. 1905.   5 *II*, 25 Nov. 1905.   6 *II*, 4 Dec. 1905.   7 *II*, 29 Dec. 1905.   8 *II*, 7 Dec. 1905.

weekend and 'edition after edition was sold out with amazing rapidity'. The following day's *Irish Independent* noted that, of the two titles, the public was more enthusiastic towards the Sunday version of the weekly paper.[9] After the second edition of the *Sunday Independent*, the *Irish Independent* noted that while the title was the only Irish Sunday newspaper, it had to meet 'serious competitors across Channel'. Any comparison with the British titles, it declared, would show the *Sunday Independent* as 'far and away more up-to-date and infinitely more Irish than even the most advanced of its rivals'.[10]

Costing one penny, the *Sunday Independent*, unlike all the national daily titles, carried news on its front page, accompanied by a topical cartoon above the fold. Inside the paper were a humorous column, a short story, a serial story, editorial columns, a 'Letters from London' column and a roundup of provincial news. A second section carried news, sports coverage, market news, a women's page ('For Wife and Maid'), a children's section and an advice column. Among the frequent advertisers were Watkins Stout, Cadbury's Cocoa, Erasmic Soap – 'the dainty soap for dainty folk' – Player Cigarettes and Sunlight Soap.[11] Later in 1906 it began an extensive theatre column ('Flashes from the Footlights') and from 1909 it included photographs for display adverts and its theatre column. By the beginning of 1916 it had expanded its photographic coverage – with half-pages and full pages devoted to war photographs – and in 1922 it dropped its front-page cartoon in favour of the inclusion of photographs. Its 'Pictorial News of the Week' page, which began in May 1922, added a new dimension, but beyond that the paper's design and content remained remarkably consistent over the years.

The *Sunday Independent*'s first editor was the incumbent editor of the *Irish Weekly Independent*, P.J. Lynch. A Corkman, Lynch had begun his career with the *Cork Herald* and had joined the *Irish Daily Independent* as its first art editor. A life-long republican, his obituary noted that he 'took a prominent part in the fight for Irish freedom'. During the war of independence he was arrested at his office at Independent House and interned for ten months at the Curragh Camp. His arrest arose from a letter, intercepted by crown forces, that he had sent to Michael Collins offering to supply him with photographs of British personnel. On his release in December 1921 he resumed his position at the *Sunday Independent*, but he was plagued by ill-health and retired shortly afterwards.[12] Lynch was succeeded as editor by John Rice, who had worked for several Cork titles before joining the *Irish Independent*.[13] In turn, Rice was succeeded by Thomas O'Donnell, who would edit the *Sunday Independent* throughout the 1930s.

9 *II*, 11 Dec. 1905. 10 *II*, 18 Dec. 1905. 11 *SI*, 7 Jan. 1906. 12 *II*, 4 May 1934. 13 *II*, 13 Aug. 1941. Patrick Maume, 'Rice, John' in *Dictionary of Irish biography* (dib.cambridge.org).

A Mayoman, O'Donnell had begun his career at the *Western People* before joining the *Irish Independent* as a sub-editor in 1919. He later became assistant editor and then editor of the *Sunday Independent*.[14]

As with all the national newspaper titles, the *Sunday Independent* was highly critical of James Larkin and his attempts to unionize Dublin workers – an endeavour that brought him into direct conflict with the paper's owner, William Martin Murphy, proprietor of the Dublin Tramways Company and leader of the Dublin Employers' Federation. While Murphy took to the pages of his *Irish Independent* to denounce Larkin, it was coverage of the 1913 Lockout in British Sunday newspapers that most concerned the *Sunday Independent*.[15] It noted that the 'incurable sentimentality which makes the Englishman glory in elaborating the dramatic nature of any struggle ... is his practical sense which tells him that strikes and scenes in Ireland are exceedingly good copy when one is trying to capture a big Irish circulation'. This resulted, as the *Sunday Independent* saw it, in 'the glorification of the romantic personality of the strike-monger in prosy pictures and highly pictorial prose; and the exaggarating of the affair from the casting out of an unwanted group of agitators to the dimensions of a full-blown labour crisis'.[16] While distribution of all the Independent titles was impacted on by the Lockout, the *Sunday Independent* put the best gloss it could on such disruption by noting that 'the net sales of the *Weekly Independent* and the *Sunday Independent* exceeded the sales of any other weekly newspaper in Ireland'.[17] In its early years the circulation of the *Sunday Independent* was combined with that of the *Irish Weekly Independent*. In 1907 the combined circulation grew from 21,391 copies in January 1907 to 41,593 in October 1909; by 1911 the combined circulation stood at 47,038; and in 1913 it was 52,081.[18]

'SCENES OF HORROR'

As circulation increased so too did the political temperature. As a new newspaper, the *Sunday Independent* sought to find its voice in an Ireland that was undergoing immense political upheaval. When home rule was granted in 1912, it noted that the issue had been dealt with 'as a pure business matter as between country and country [and had] received the blessing of every party, except, of course, that of the eternal opponents of self-government for Ireland'.[19] When these 'eternal opponents' organized the signing of the Ulster Covenant – which pledged its signatories to use 'all means which may be found necessary to defeat

14 *IT*, 25 Dec. 1962. 15 For more on the *II* and the Lockout see Yeates, 'The life and career of William Martin Murphy'. 16 *SI*, 7 Sept. 1913. 17 *SI*, 5 Oct. 1913. 18 *SI*, 28 Nov. 1909, 29 Oct. 1911 & 5 Oct. 1913. 19 *SI*, 14 Apr. 1912.

the present conspiracy to set up a Home Rule Parliament in Ireland' – the paper expressed surprise at how militant resistance to parliamentary democracy was conducted in public and how 'modern revolutionaries simply use the efficient machinery placed at their disposal by a benevolent Government and an enthusiastic Press'. Who, it pondered, 'under such circumstances, would not be a rebel?'[20] When Ulster unionists later landed arms and ammunition at Larne to resist home rule, the newspaper condemned the 'gentlemen who are endeavouring to promote bloodshed and civil war in Ulster', and noted that the government had shown unionists 'a special leniency in this matter which has never been and – one is inclined to think – would never be shown to the Southern Nationalist'.[21] When, three months later, British army personnel interfered with the landing of arms at Howth by Irish Volunteers, interference that resulted in the deaths of three people, the paper described the action of the army as 'an unparalleled outrage'.[22] The outbreak of the First World War – which saw the paper observe 'rebel Ireland rallying to the defence of the Empire and people hob-nobbing with those whom they affected to believe a few weeks ago were preparing to murder them in their beds!' – resulted in the *Sunday Independent* dropping from twelve to eight pages per edition in August 1914.[23] Later newsprint shortages saw it drop to six pages per edition in 1916 and to four pages per edition in 1917.

During the Easter Rising of 1916, the rebels occupied Independent House on Abbey Street, just around the corner from the GPO, and while the building was not too badly damaged in the subsequent shelling of the city centre by the British gunboat *Helga*, the paper missed an edition. It returned the following week with a page-one headline – 'Dublin A City of Dead and Ruins' – that told its own story. It put the blame for the Rising on the ineffectual administration of Ireland and, in particular, the leniency shown to the Ulster unionists. 'If Ulster had not led the way', it declared, 'and if there had been no Larne gunrunning, there would have been no gun-running at Howth, no armed and drilled Sinn Féiners, and consequently, no scenes of horror such as were witnessed in Dublin last week'. While, in relation to the Rising's leaders, it believed that 'any feeling of sympathy with them in Ireland will be checked by the thought of what their mad venture has cost Dublin and Ireland in blood and suffering', it restrained itself, unlike its sister daily title, from calling for more executions.[24] Indeed, the following week it noted that 'all those responsible for this wildest

20 *SI*, 29 Sept. 1912. **21** *SI*, 3 May 1914. **22** *SI*, 2 Aug. 1914. **23** *SI*, 9 Aug. 1914. **24** *SI*, 20 Apr.–7 May 1916. For more on the daily title's reaction to the Rising, see Felix M. Larkin, 'No longer a political sideshow: T.R. Harrington and the "new" *Irish Independent*, 1905–31' in O'Brien & Rafter (eds), *Independent Newspapers*, pp 26–38.

of revolutionary outbursts have now paid the extreme penalty – and, one must add, paid it bravely and without complaint'.[25] In the aftermath of the 1918 general election, which saw Sinn Féin displace the Irish Parliamentary Party, the paper declared that 'the Irish people have very definitely and decidedly scrapped the old Party, which held power for so long, and which eventually presumed on its power to compromise the national demand'. The result meant that 'the nation has taken a new line, has handed over its trust to a new set of men, and has thereby created an entirely fresh political situation, which not only affects Ireland, but, must also have a considerable moral influence on the position of England at the Peace Conference'.[26]

The war of independence that followed saw the paper criticize Hamar Greenwood, the newly installed chief secretary of Ireland, for establishing a government-sponsored publication, the *Weekly Summary*, which he declared was needed 'to supply the police in Ireland with the truths they can obtain from no other source'. The *Sunday Independent* declared that the publication's 'special brand of truth is unique', and also criticized the 'similar propaganda in the matter of photographs, cinema films, and "plots" which is also being inspired and organized from official sources'. As an example of such propaganda, the paper printed two photographs of the same location: one showed an empty bridge in Dalkey, Co. Dublin and the other showed several bodies on the bridge. The propaganda element resided in the fact that the second photograph had been staged and circulated to British newspapers as the aftermath of an ambush in Tralee Co. Kerry. As the *Sunday Independent* noted, many British newspapers had published the staged photograph in good faith: there was, it concluded, an element in the British administration determined to 'stir up anti-Irish prejudice in England and abroad'.[27] Sales of the paper increased during the conflict – from 76,884 in January 1920 to 93,368 in February 1921 – as the demand for non-British reportage increased.[28] After the conflict it was resolutely pro-treaty: the agreement reached, it declared, 'secured the substance of all those demands for which generation after generation of Irishmen made such immense sacrifices'.[29] In January 1922 it published the result of the treaty vote under the banner headline 'Peace Treaty Ratified – Majority Seven' over a display list of how deputies had voted. While it acknowledged that the treaty did 'not fulfil the nation's ideals', it was a means 'to finally attaining them'.[30]

Given its function as a weekly read with a heavy emphasis on features, the *Sunday Independent* did not editorialize on current affairs as often or to the same extent as its sister daily title. As a result, it did not comment to any great extent

25 *SI*, 14 May 1916.   26 *SI*, 5 Jan. 1919.   27 *SI*, 28 Nov. 1920.   28 *II*, 22 Mar. 1921.   29 *SI*, 1 Jan. 1922.   30 *SI*, 8 Jan. 1922.

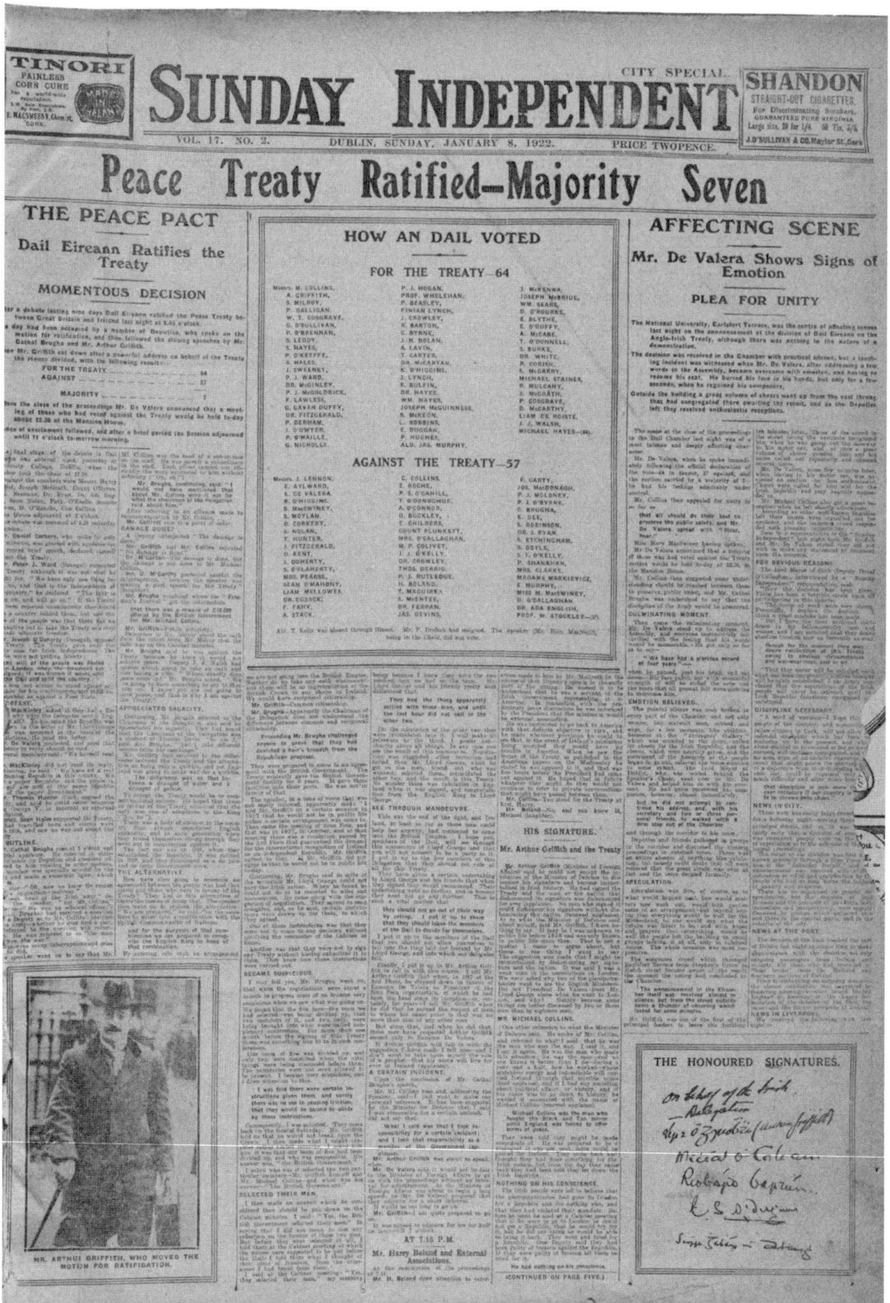

CITY SPECIAL

SUNDAY INDEPENDENT

VOL. 17. NO. 2. DUBLIN, SUNDAY, JANUARY 8, 1922. PRICE TWOPENCE.

Peace Treaty Ratified—Majority Seven

THE PEACE PACT

Dail Eireann Ratifies the Treaty

MOMENTOUS DECISION

After a debate lasting nine days Dail Eireann ratified the Peace Treaty between Great Britain and Ireland last night at 8.45 o'clock.

The day had been occupied by a number of Deputies, who spoke on the motion for ratification, and then followed the closing speeches by Mr. Cathal Brugha and Mr. Arthur Griffith.

When Mr. Griffith sat down after a powerful address on behalf of the Treaty the House divided, with the following result:—

FOR THE TREATY	64
AGAINST	57
MAJORITY	7

Before the close of the proceedings Mr. De Valera announced that a meeting of those who had voted against the Treaty would be held to-day about 12.30 at the Mansion House.

Scenes of excitement followed, and after a brief period the Session adjourned until 11 o'clock to-morrow morning.

HOW AN DAIL VOTED

FOR THE TREATY—64

Messrs. M. COLLINS,	P. J. HOGAN,	J. McKENNA,
A. GRIFFITH,	PROF. WHELEHAN,	JOSEPH McBRIDE,
S. MILROY,	P. BEASLEY,	WM. SEARS,
P. GALLIGAN,	FINIAN LYNCH,	D. O'ROURKE,
W. T. COSGRAVE,	J. CROWLEY,	E. BLYTHE,
G. O'SULLIVAN,	R. BARTON,	E. O'DUFFY,
P. O'BRENNAN,	C. BYRNE,	A. McCABE,
S. LEDDY,	J. N. DOLAN,	T. O'DONNELL,
S. HAYES,	A. LAVIN,	S. BURKE,
P. O'KEEFFE,	T. CARTER,	DR. WHITE,
S. HALES,	DR. McCARTAN,	R. CORISH,
J. SWEENEY,	K. O'HIGGINS,	S. McGARRY,
P. J. WARD,	J. LYNCH,	MICHAEL STAINES,
DR. McGINLEY,	E. BULFIN,	R. MULCAHY,
P. J. McGOLDRICK,	DR. HAYES,	J. McGRATH,
F. LAWLESS,	WM. HAYES,	P. COSGRAVE,
G. GAVAN DUFFY,	JOSEPH McGUINNESS,	D. McCARTHY,
DR. FITZGERALD,	S. McKEON,	LIAM DE ROISTE,
P. DERHAM,	L. ROBBINS,	J. J. WALSH,
J. O'DWYER,	E. DUGGAN,	MICHAEL HAYES—(64).
P. O'MAILLE,	P. HUGHES,	
G. NICHOLLS.	ALD. JAS. MURPHY,	

AGAINST THE TREATY—57

Messrs. J. LENNON,	C. COLLINS,	F. CARTY,
E. AYLWARD,	E. ROCHE,	JOS. MacDONAGH,
E. DE VALERA,	P. S. O'CAHILL,	P. J. MOLONEY,
B. O'HIGGINS,	T. O'DONOGHUE,	P. J. O'BYRNE,
S. MacSWINEY,	A. O'CONNOR,	C. BRUGHA,
S. MOYLAN,	D. BUCKLEY,	S. DEE,
D. CORKERY,	E. CHILDERS,	S. ROBINSON,
S. NOLAN,	COUNT PLUNKETT,	DR. J. RYAN,
T. HUNTER,	MRS. O'CALLAGHAN,	S. ETCHINGHAM,
J. FITZGERALD,	M. P. COLIVET,	S. DOYLE,
D. KENT,	J. J. O'KELLY,	S. T. O'KELLY,
J. DOHERTY,	DR. CROWLEY,	P. SHANAHAN,
S. O'FLAHERTY,	THOS. DERRIG,	MRS. CLARKE,
MRS. PEARSE,	P. J. RUTLEDGE,	MADAME MARKIEVICZ,
SEAN O'MAHONY,	H. BOLAND,	E. MURPHY,
LIAM MELLOWES,	T. MAGUIRE,	MISS M. MacSWINEY,
DR. CUSACK,	S. McENTEE,	D. O'CALLAGHAN,
F. FAHY,	DR. FERRAN,	DR. ADA ENGLISH,
A. STACK.	JAS. DEVINS,	PROF. W. STOCKLEY—(57).

Ald. T. Kelly was absent through illness. Mr. P. Drohan had resigned. The Speaker (Mr. Eoin MacNeill), being in the Chair, did not vote.

AFFECTING SCENE

Mr. De Valera Shows Signs of Emotion

PLEA FOR UNITY

The National University, Earlsfort Terrace, was the centre of affecting scenes last night on the announcement of the division of Dail Eireann on the Anglo-Irish Treaty, although there was nothing in the nature of a demonstration.

The decision was received in the Chamber with practical silence, but a touching incident was witnessed when Mr. De Valera, after addressing a few words to the Assembly, became overcome with emotion, and having to resume his seat. He buried his face in his hands, but only for a few seconds, when he regained his composure.

Outside the building a great volume of cheers went up from the vast throng that had congregated there awaiting the result, and as the Deputies left they received enthusiastic receptions.

MR. ARTHUR GRIFFITH, WHO MOVED THE MOTION FOR RATIFICATION.

THE HONOURED SIGNATURES.

(CONTINUED ON PAGE FIVE.)

Figure 4: The *Sunday Independent* front page from 8 January 1922 indicating the results of the Dáil vote on the Anglo-Irish Treaty.

on the events of the civil war, though it black-bordered its front page twice in August 1922, to mark the deaths of Arthur Griffith and Michael Collins, the latter also being accorded a full page of photographs of all aspects of his life.[31] Similarly, the paper, again unlike its sister daily title, did not engage in any sustained editorial advocacy on the issue of indecent literature during the 1920s or on the Spanish civil war in the 1930s.[32] It welcomed the advent of radio broadcasting in the Free State but noted, somewhat self-interestedly – given the importance of advertising revenue to newspapers – that 'radio users do not want and will not have announcements for this, that, and something or somebody else. If such a thing were tolerated, sooner or later the whole business would degenerate into an advertising scheme.'[33]

NATION-BUILDING

While the *Irish Independent* was hugely supportive of (though never tied to) the pro-treaty faction of the independence movement that coalesced into Cumann na nGaedheal (and later Fine Gael) and was hugely critical of the anti-treaty faction that eventually formed itself into Fianna Fáil, the *Sunday Independent* was devoid, for the most part, of the animated political positioning and editorial advocacy that characterized the daily title. Indeed, sometimes its political coverage caused disquiet within Cumann na nGaedheal. When, in 1924, it reported that the party was split on whether to admit members of the Southern unionist community into its ranks the story was hotly denied by the party, which was anxious not to hand the mantle of nationalism to the anti-treaty side.[34] The *Sunday Independent* did, however, editorially support Cumann na nGaedheal in the first of the two general elections in 1927, noting that the choice facing electors was between Fianna Fáil, 'whose set purpose it is to repudiate the Treaty', and Cumann na nGaedheal, which sought 'the aggregate happiness of all classes of citizens, which is, or ought to be, the aim and end of all government'.[35] In the 1932 election it did not take sides, though its 'Political Notes' column listed a speculative Fianna Fáil cabinet some days after polling day.[36] On the transfer of power, it noted that to Éamon de Valera and 'to every member of his Ministry is due the support and co-operation of the people, so long as the acts and decisions of the rulers are in accordance with the letter and the spirit of the Constitution'.[37]

31 *SI*, 13 Aug. & 27 Aug. 1922.   32 But see *SI*, 27 May 1928 & 30 Aug. 1936. For more on the *II* and the Spanish civil war see Mark O'Brien, 'The best interests of the nation: Frank Geary, the *Irish Independent* and the Spanish civil war' in O'Brien & Rafter (eds), *Independent Newspapers*, pp 81–93.   33 *SI*, 27 Dec. 1925   34 *SI*, 21 Dec. 1924 & *IT*, 27 Dec. 1924.   35 *SI*, 5 June 1927.   36 *SI*, 21 Feb. 1932.   37 *SI*, 13 Mar. 1932.

It was de Valera's replacement of the 1922 Constitution with his own document in 1937 that prompted the most animated attack on him by the paper. Describing de Valera's document, in a banner page-one headline, as the 'As You Were Constitution', its editorial criticism left nothing to the imagination:

> The first and vital fact to be noted in regard to the draft Constitution is that it does not add an iota to the nation's rights or liberties. Nor does it provide any new or effective method of dealing with such a grave national problem as the removal of partition. Why, then, should this document be produced at all? It is simply a belated attempt by the leader of the Fianna Fáil party to get himself in some way or other associated with the political achievements of his predecessors, whose constructive work in building up the State he spent many years endeavouring to impede. He lacked the vision and the foresight that inspired Griffith and Collins to seize the opportunity that came their way in 1921. The same qualities sustained their sussessors and enabled them to consolidate and extend the gains won by their dead colleagues. They toiled, in spite of desperate opposition, till they made the people of the Saorstat complete and absolute masters in every affair of State. Now when the fruits of their sacrifices and labours have been garnered, Mr de Valera wishes to identify himself with the finished result.[38]

The antagnoism worked in both directions. Having established the *Irish Press* to counter the hostility of the *Irish Independent* and the *Irish Times*, Fianna Fáil politicians often, and without any sense of irony, accused the Independent titles of being the mouthpiece of Fine Gael. There was no love lost on either side. In 1939, the minister for finance, Seán MacEntee, sued the *Sunday Independent* for defamation after it published a report that he had 'suppressed in some underhand way a meeting of the Dublin University Commerce and Economics Society in order to prevent criticism of his policy'. The alleged libel was, MaeEntee held, 'plastered all over the *Sunday Independent*'.[39] The story had appeared on page one under the banner headline 'Trinity College Meeting Suppressed' and alleged that a meeting of the student society had been called off 'following representations privately made, or caused to be made, by a Government Minister to a friend of his in TCD'. In an editorial, the paper noted that MacEntee had been invited to the meeting and so was in a position to refute any criticism of government policy. It was, the paper concluded, 'a scandalous state of affairs that any attempt should be made to gag a citizen'.[40] On the day the case was to be heard, the paper settled with MacEntee.[41]

38 *SI*, 2 May 1937.   39 *IT*, 10 June 1939.   40 *SI*, 13 Nov. 1938.   41 *IT*, 28 June 1939.

At this stage the *Sunday Independent* remained the only Irish Sunday news-paper, with a December 1937 circulation figure of 175,676, and so competed alone against the multitude of British Sunday titles that circulated in Ireland – competition that intensified in the early years of the Second World War, as the latter titles were not subject to the press censorship imposed on Irish newspapers in the furtherance of its neutrality.[42] This, according to its editor, Thomas O'Donnell, constituted an unfair competitive environment. In a letter to Michael Knightly – a former reporter who had worked with O'Donnell on the *Irish Independent* but who was chief press censor 1939–45 – O'Donnell noted that the *Sunday Independent* had been instructed not to print a story about an Irish officer in the Royal Air Force who had been awarded the Victoria Cross. O'Donnell was annoyed that the story had been included in the Radio Éireann Saturday-evening news bulletin and was also annoyed that it had appeared in that week's British Sunday newspapers, which circulated in Ireland. Such an occurrence, O'Donnell asserted, was 'to the detriment of Irish newspapers'. It put the *Sunday Independent*, he continued:

> in a very unfavourable light before the public, who, finding that certain information is available through the Irish broadcasting service and the English newspapers, may naturally conclude that our news service is incomplete or our methods inefficient. Neither conclusion would be in accordance with the facts, but it is grossly unfair to us that there should be a possibility of its arising.[43]

Knightly replied that the issue of 'Irishmen serving with the British Forces is causing us endless trouble' and that on 'learning that Radio Éireann had men-tioned a matter the publication of which was prohibited in the newspapers, representations were made to them and this item was eliminated from the sec-ond news broadcast'.[44]

Matters did not improve when, the following week, the censor stopped a *Sunday Independent* report of a speech by Thomas O'Higgins TD, which was reported on by Radio Éireann and was used as the front-page story by an English Sunday newspaper. As O'Donnell saw it, there existed 'a different standard of censorship for the Irish newspapers and for the Irish radio [and] a different standard for Irish papers and for the English papers coming into this country'.[45] In reply, the controller of censorship, Joseph Connolly, noted that often, in relation to Radio Éireann, 'a speaker is giving a talk and he either

42 *II*, 18 Jan. 1938.   43 NAI, 93/1/102 (no. 88), letter dated 10 June 1940.   44 Ibid., letter dated 15 June 1940.   45 Ibid., letter dated 19 June 1940.

goes beyond his script or is speaking impromptu' – a rationale rejected by O'Donnell.[46] Another issue of concern for O'Donnell was when a story broke at the weekend and the censorship authorities decided to delay publication 'in the public interest', or until the Government Information Bureau issued a statement on the issue. Perhaps tiring of the complaints, Knightly retorted that 'if we think it right to stop a story on Saturday night and release it on Sunday we have no alternative but to do so even if the result is to deprive the *Sunday Independent* of a story'.[47] In internal correspondence, Knightly noted that O'Donnell was 'really a good fellow, but very touchy': in another (unsent) note in which Knightly outlined the powers of his office, he asserted that 'we will not hesitate to ask the Government to take over the complete control of newspapers if we find it necessary to do so'.[48]

A NEW EDITOR

As had occurred during the First World War, the paper shrank in size from eighteen pages in 1939 to fourteen pages in 1940. Later, amid severe newsprint shortages, it dropped from ten pages in 1941 to four pages in 1942 and remained, for the most part, at this size until 1946, when it returned to ten pages per issue. It would not return to its pre-war length until mid-1949.[49] News, accompanied by a photograph, continued to appear on the front page, and in mid-1940 a new editor, Hector Legge, arrived to steer the paper's development over the following thirty years. Born in Kildare in 1901, Legge had joined the Irish Volunteers in 1920, before embarking on a career in journalism by joining the *Catholic Herald* in Manchester later that year. In 1922 he joined the *Irish Independent*, rising over the years to the position of chief sub-editor. A biographical essay (based on his personal diaries) described Legge as 'a devout Catholic – a regular mass goer and a frequent confession goer – who had been educated by the Christian Brothers and who held the order in high esteem. He was also distinctly Fine Gael-leaning in his politics, and was personally close to a number of leading party figures, in particular James Dillon.'[50] The first issue Legge had to deal with as editor was the continuing press censorship. In an attempt to 'smooth relations for the future', Joseph Connolly initiated a meeting during which he informed Legge of 'the delicacy of our position as neutrals and that we had to be careful lest we provide any of the belligerents with an excuse, which under

46 Ibid., letters dated 28 June & 1 July 1940.   47 Ibid., letter dated 6 Aug. 1940.   48 Ibid., notes dated 9 & 8 Aug. 1940.   49 Paper size is measured at end of Jan. each year.   50 Kevin Rafter, 'A tale of womanly intuition: Hector Legge at the *Sunday Independent*, 1940–70' in O'Brien & Rafter (eds), *Independent Newspapers*, pp 119–32 at p. 123.

certain circumstances any of them might be seeking, to question our neutrality'. In a record of the meeting Connolly observed that Legge 'accepted the position and seemed to appreciate our point of view'.[51]

But when Legge had to decide between publishing a breaking story or submitting it to the censor and possibly losing the opportunity to publish, he chose the former every time. In 1942 he published a front-page story headlined 'Detective shot dead in Dublin' that prompted a telephone call from the assistant controller of censorship, Thomas Coyne.[52] In a report, Coyne declared that Legge was 'unrepentant and what he said amounted to this: that as regards what was published, it was a case of his judgment against ours and that he preferred his own judgment'. Legge told Coyne that the report had arrived at the *Sunday Independent* at 3.00 a.m. and he had wondered about 'what sort of a ruling could he expect to get from an official who had been aroused at that hour of the morning and was only half-awake'. Concerned that the story would have been held over or stopped, Legge would have missed his chance at publication and so had decided to publish. The minister with responsibility for censorship, Frank Aiken, instructed Coyne to extract an assurance from Legge that such an occurrence would not happen again.[53] Having telephoned Legge, Coyne received this assurance from Legge, who also stated that the censor's office was 'not giving the *Sunday Independent* the service they were entitled to as we closed down the Censorship Office much too early on Saturday nights [and that] he could not expect to get the same service from a man who had been awakened out of his sleep in the middle of the night who was neither mentally nor physically in a condition to give a matter of business the calm and careful consideration which it merited'. Coyne noted that he had to 'admit that there was something in this' but he baulked at Legge's suggestion that the censorship office should remain open until the paper went to press at 3.00 a.m.[54] For the duration of the war, relations between Legge and the censor's office remained strained: in June 1943 the chief press censor, Michael Knightly, warned Legge that if he persisted in publishing censorable material without reference to the censor's office, an order would be served on the paper to submit each edition in full prior to publication. In reply, Legge simply claimed that he did not 'seek to publish anything that would not be passed by [the] Censor'.[55]

Among the columnists hired by Legge was the writer Frank O'Connor, who, in Legge's words, 'was at war with the Catholic Church and the Catholic Church was at war with him ... he was banned on Radio Éireann'. O'Connor

51 NAI, 93/1/102 (no. 88), memo dated 24 Oct. 1940.   52 *SI*, 25 Oct. 1942.   53 NAI, 93/1/102 (no. 88), memo dated 27 Oct. 1942.   54 Ibid., memo dated 30 Oct. 1942.   55 Ibid., letters dated 7 & 8 June 1943.

was given a pen name ('Ben Mayo') because, recalled Legge, 'at that time there were people in power in Independent House who were more Catholic that the Pope himself'. The pen name was Legge's invention, as he liked short pseudonyms: he had already created 'Andy Croke' for a GAA columnist. Driven to secrecy by what Legge referred to as 'the barbarians of the time', he used to meet O'Connor at a café on Grafton Street on Tuesdays to discuss that week's column before picking it up from him on Fridays.[56] O'Connor's columns on topics such as education, the Irish language, public monuments and Irish history regularly prompted letters condemning and supporting his stance. As well as introducing new columnists, Legge initiated greater use of photographs on the front page and the paper now carried a weekly crossword with a prize of £500. It also had a new competitor, the *Sunday Press*, which was launched in 1949 and which would beat Legge's paper in the battle for circulation between 1949 and 1989. In 1955 the figures were relatively close, with the *Sunday Press* selling 383,716 copies a week to the *Sunday Independent*'s 380,995, and Legge was behind some the biggest scoops of the 1940s and 1950s.[57]

In September 1948, the *Sunday Independent* revealed that the inter-party government planned to repeal the External Relations Act 1936 and declare the twenty-six counties a republic.[58] Writing many years later, Legge declared that the story arose out of 'journalistic intuition' as Fine Gael, when in opposition, had been 'charging that de Valera was living a lie'. Now that the party was in government Legge felt they 'were not going to go on living the lie … it was as simple as that'. It was, he continued, 'sheer chance that the Head of the Government, John Costello, was in Canada' when the story broke. For his part, Costello was convinced that the story 'was the result of a leak from some person with inside knowledge', but he was later informed by Legge that there had been no such leak.[59] However, the 'intuition' rationale for the story has always been questioned – with many civil servants and historians identifying the cabinet leaker as either James Dillon or Seán MacBride.[60] Two years later, the paper broke the news of Noel Browne's plan to revolutionize maternity care. Under the front-page headline 'Free maternity and child welfare services' it reported that 'the service will provide free medical and hospital care for mothers before, during and after the birth of children, and free care for children's health up to their teens', and concluded that 'its adoption by the Dáil seems to be assured, for such a scheme was envisaged in the Health Act passed by the previous Government'.[61] When the ill-fated scheme was defeated by the combined opposition of the Catholic Church and the medical profession and

56 *SI*, 25 Sept. 1983 & 13 Apr. 1969.   57 *IT*, 25 Mar. 1955.   58 *SI*, 5 Sept. 1948.   59 *IT*, 7 Jan. 1976.   60 See Rafter, 'A tale of womanly intuition', p. 120.   61 *SI*, 3 Sept. 1950.

health minister Noel Browne resigned, the paper, along with all titles in the Independent Group, refrained from commenting editorially on the controversy. While it might have been expected that the titles would – as they always had – row in behind the Catholic hierarchy, it just so happened that Browne was the adopted son of major shareholders in Independent Newspapers and so editorial silence on the saga was maintained.[62]

In 1957, amid the IRA's border campaign, the paper published an account of the conditions endured by internees at the Curragh Camp. Under the headline 'Inside the Curragh Concentration Camp' it noted that 114 men were being detained in two huts built to accommodate 80 men and that the roofs were leaking. Oddly, under the three-column piece were the words 'Issued by the Publicity Committee, Sinn Féin'.[63] The piece caused quite a stir in the department of justice, which despatched an assistant secretary, P.M. Clarke, to the camp to meet with senior military officials. At the meeting Clarke declared that Taoiseach de Valera had 'instructed that a statement should be urgently prepared for issue by the Government Information Bureau in rebuttal of the Sinn Fein allegations'. A later memo to the department's secretary general, Peter Berry, outlined the changes that had been made to alleviate the overcrowding.[64] In 1963, in an editorial innovation to help counter the impact of the *Sunday Press*, the *Sunday Independent* introduced a colour magazine. Published between November 1963 and May 1964, the magazine lost £4,000 a week because it could not attract sufficient advertising.[65] Among the prominent display adverts that appeared in the *Sunday Independent* around this time were those for Cleary's department store, Cadbury's milk chocolate, Kodak cameras, Ribena, Uno paint and Lux soap. In late 1964 it published an 'unqualified apology' to justice minister Charles Haughey after he claimed he had been libelled in one of the paper's cartoons. The cartoon satirized Haughey's love of horses and the revelries of a hunt ball, showing a procession of figures emerging from the back of a Garda van, with sergeant yelling 'Come on out, you tally-hoing, hunt-balling pack … Oh, sorry Mr Minister, I didn't see you there!'[66]

By the late 1960s Legge's religiosity was beginning to look out of place in a changing Ireland, though it still delivered the occasional scoop courtesy of the Catholic hierarchy. In February 1966 Bishop Michael Browne addressed a Saturday night public meeting in Galway at which, in the presence of the minister for education, Fianna Fáil's Jim Ryan, he lambasted the government's plan to close a number of one- and two-teacher schools. Denouncing the move

62 John Horgan, *Irish media: a critical history since 1922* (London, 2001), p. 65. 63 *SI*, 18 Aug. 1957. 64 NAI, JUS/8/1056, memo dated 5 Sept. 1957. 65 Hugh Oram, *The newspaper book: a history of newspapers in Ireland, 1649–1983* (Dublin, 1983), pp 293–4. 66 *SI*, 9 & 16 Aug. 1964.

as 'illegal and unconstitutional', Browne then announced that, owing to the 'lateness of the hour' he needed to leave and could not remain to hear the minister's response. Knowing how 'the lateness of the hour' would cause difficulties for the Sunday newspapers that would no doubt wish to report his speech, Browne had taken the trouble to send it in advance to the religiously sympathetic *Sunday Independent* – but not to the Fianna Fáil-supporting *Sunday Press*. The *Sunday Independent* duly ran the story under the attention-grabbing page-one banner headline 'Bishop Attacks Minister'.[67] As John Healy of the *Irish Times* observed, Browne 'knows his way about the press offices and no mistake. The *Sunday Independent*, unlike the *Sunday Press*, could be depended upon to accept a manuscript and not ring the minister to say what was in it.'[68] A year later the *Sunday Independent* was exclusively chosen by Dublin's Catholic archbishop, John Charles McQuaid, as the vehicle to deliver a pastoral on 'the teachings of the Catholic Church on education', with specific reference to 'the ban on Catholics attending Trinity College'.[69] This edict followed an *Irish Times* editorial that had accused McQuaid of pursuing a policy of 'spiritual apartheid' by perpetuating the ban.[70] The following year again, Legge and his paper were denounced at a Labour Party meeting. The speaker, Jim Downey (later an *Irish Times* and *Irish Independent* columnist), declared that 'the current hysteria in certain high places about an alleged Red Menace' was farcical, and that its proponents – James Dillon, Liam Cosgrave, the bishop of Galway and the editor of the *Sunday Independent* – were 'simply not living in the same year AD as the rest of us'.[71] Downey's retort came after Dillon had denounced Trinity College in the Dáil as a hot-bed of communism, and Legge had published a front-page editorial – 'Plain words to Trinity students' – in which he declared that 'the minority group of irresponsibles in Trinity College better get to know quickly that their nonsense, their threats to the good name of Ireland, will not be tolerated by the Irish people'.[72] Their outbursts followed a minor protest by students outside Trinity as the king and queen of Belgium visited the college. Reviewing these events, John Healy of the *Irish Times* pointed out that the two men were good friends, Dillon seemed obsessed with identifying communists at Trinity and the disturbances, as described in the *Irish Independent* and condemned in Legge's *Sunday Independent*'s front-page editorial, were 'a creation of Independent House to some degree'. He also noted that following Legge's front-page editorial, students had marched from Trinity College to Independent House and burned copies of the *Sunday Independent* in Abbey Street.[73]

67 *SI*, 6 Feb. 1966.   68 *IT*, 19 Feb. 1966.   69 *SI*, 12 Feb. 1967.   70 *IT*, 6 Feb. 1967.   71 *IT*, 30 May 1968.   72 *SI*, 19 May 1968.   73 See *II*, 16 May 1968 & *IT*, 25 May 1968.

Towards the end of his thirty-year editorship, Legge declined to publish what undoubtedly would have been the biggest scoop of his career. Amid the emerging Arms Crisis of 1970, which involved the resignation and sacking of several government ministers, the *Sunday Independent*'s political correspondent, Ned Murphy, was given sight of an anonymous letter received by opposition leader Liam Cosgrave. The letter, on official Garda Síochana paper, stated that ministers Neil Blaney and Charles Haughey were involved in 'a plot to bring arms from Germany worth £80,000 for the North' and urged Cosgrave to ensure that the affair was 'not hushed up'. Having written what the *Sunday Independent* later referred to as 'what would have been one of the most sensational stories in the history of Irish journalism', Murphy had to accept Legge's decision not to publish.[74] The following week, once the affair had become public, the paper published the story of its knowledge of the affair under the headline 'The scoop we didn't publish'. Acknowledging that Murphy's account 'was a factual account of events afterwards borne out by statements in the Dáil' and that the story might have brought down the government, it explained that Legge had agonized over where his duty lay – 'to his country or to his profession'. According to the article, Legge had decided that 'the proper place to have the matter raised was in the Dáil'.[75] However, in subsequent years, Legge maintained that his decision not to publish was prompted by his desire to avoid defamation cases being taken against the newspaper.[76] Later that year, Legge retired as editor, though not before offering – with the approval the board of Independent Newspapers – the editorship to *Irish Press* editor Tim Pat Coogan, an offer Coogan turned down.[77]

JOURNALISTIC HEYDAY

Legge was instead succeeded by Conor O'Brien, who had begun his career at Independent Newspapers in 1951 before joining the *Evening Press* at its start in 1954. He succeeded Douglas Gageby as editor of that title in 1959 when Gageby left for the *Irish Times*. Having received a muted response to his plan to re-organize the Press titles, O'Brien returned to Independent Newspapers as editor of the *Sunday Independent* in 1970.[78] By this time the circulation gap between the two Irish Sunday newspapers had widened: in 1969 sales for the *Sunday Press* hit 420,000 per week compared to 331,000 for the *Sunday Independent*.[79] Among the paper's columnists at this time were Joseph O'Malley (politics), Colm Rapple

74 *SI*, 8 June 1975. **75** *SI*, 10 May 1970. **76** *SI*, 15 June 1975. **77** Tim Pat Coogan, *A memoir* (London, 2008), p. 164. **78** Mark O'Brien, *De Valera, Fianna Fáil and the* Irish Press: *the truth in the news* (Dublin, 2001), pp 131–2. **79** *IT*, 13 Mar. 1971.

(business) and Ciaran Carty (cinema). In many ways, O'Brien's six-year editorship of the paper represented its journalistic heyday. Investigative journalism was at its peak elsewhere, with the *Washington Post* revealing the Watergate scandal in the US and the *Sunday Times* exposing the thalidomide scandal in the UK. At the *Sunday Independent* O'Brien had a journalist, Joe MacAnthony, whose investigations delivered a series of scoops for the paper – and which discommoded those under scrutiny.

In January 1972 MacAnthony revealed that the Garda Special Branch (tasked with combating subversive crime) was operating a telephone-tapping operation 'in an unmarked set of offices over a fashionable Dublin shoe store'. Among those tapped were ex-cabinet ministers, a well-known auctioneering firm, a one-time television personality, a county councillor, a foreign businessman, a trade union leader, an ex-army officer, the chancellery of an embassy in Dublin and the headquarters of one of the country's political parties. He further revealed that the Special Branch had acquired expensive equipment that circumvented the scrambling security feature on ministerial phone lines. The story was accompanied by an early morning photograph of a post office official leaving his house to go to work. The named official was identified in the caption as the person who liaised with the Special Branch in its tapping activity.[80] The following March, MacAnthony exposed the stroke pulling involved in the appointments to positions in local authorities when he revealed that Dublin County Council had voted to appoint two brothers of sitting councillors and the son of a Fianna Fáil constituency organizer to posts within the council. He revealed that these appointments came 'as a result of a deal' between Fianna Fáil and Fine Gael to share out the posts between the two parties.[81] Later that year, the paper noted that while legislation had been introduced 'to abolish the system of appointing rate collectors by political patronage', it was regrettable 'that the politicians had to wait until the *Sunday Independent* exposed the unfairness of the system before they decided to act'. Had it not published the story, it concluded, 'the reader could rest assured that the mutual back scratching and political fixing connected with these jobs would still be a part of local politics'.[82]

At some point in 1972, O'Brien asked MacAnthony to look into the Irish Hospital Sweepstakes – a government-sanctioned lottery run by the McGrath family, ostensibly for the benefit of hospitals. As recalled by MacAnthony: 'Conor suggested that I do a story on the Sweeps. I think Conor had a whiff of something though he never said anything, or gave me anything.'[83] MacAnthony's story – under the front-page headline 'Where the Sweep millions go' and beside a photograph of Sweepstake chief executive Joe McGrath and his wife – was

80 *SI*, 9 Jan. 1972. 81 *SI*, 19 Mar. 1972. 82 *SI*, 26 Nov. 1972. 83 *Irish Echo*, 18 Feb. 2011.

groundbreaking. Describing McGrath as 'one of the richest men in Europe as a result of his work in the Irish Sweeps', MacAnthony revealed that Irish hospitals received less than 10 per cent of the value of the tickets, with the other 90 per cent disappearing in 'expenses'. He also revealed that hospitals received only 75 per cent of the sum described as the 'Hospitals Fund', as taxation was collected from the hospitals, not the organizers, and that the organizers were involved with a bookmaking group in buying ticket shares that, ultimately, allowed them to win their own prizes.[84] As recalled by MacAnthony, 'Conor read the story and immediately passed it to the paper's lawyers. The lawyers said we could run it if we were certain that we had all the facts straight.' On 21 January 1973 the paper published the story over three pages. As remembered by MacAnthony, 'We were planning to run the story over two Sundays, roughly 4,000 words in each story. But Conor said that we would never get the second part out. It would be stopped. So he decided to the run the whole story at once'.[85] There was, *Hibernia* magazine noted, 'scarcely a single parallel in Irish journalistic history'. In the *Hibernia* press awards of that year MacAnthony won the award for best investigative article and Conor O'Brien, who 'originated the idea and showed the courage to publish', received a special mention.[86]

The following year, an investigation by MacAnthony and Paul Murphy into planning motions at Dublin County Council revealed that county councillor and North Dublin TD Ray Burke had benefited to the tune £15,000 after a parcel of land in his constituency was rezoned, against the wishes of planners. In the Companies Registration Office, MacAnthony had discovered a memorandum of agreement that included a fee of £15,000 to Burke under the heading 'professional fees'. When contacted for comment, Burke declared that he regarded the zoning motion and the payment as 'entirely unrelated'.[87] As an investigation got underway, the document on which the story had been based disappeared. When interviewed by the detective investigating the affair, MacAnthony was told that, most likely, the investigation would go nowhere.[88]

By this time Independent Newspapers had undergone a change of ownership prompted in large part by the negative reaction from the higher echelons of Irish society to MacAnthony's stories.[89] The Tony O'Reilly era was about to begin and his emphasis was, as he put it himself, 'primarily commercial'.[90] Stories that antagonized the business community and advertisers would have no place in the new dispensation. Ultimately, MacAnthony received kind

84 *SI*, 21 Jan. 1973. 85 *Irish Echo*, 18 Feb. 2011. 86 *IT*, 18 Jan. 1974. 87 *SI*, 23 June 1974. 88 Interview of Joe MacAnthony conducted by David Manning and Miriam Cotton, dated 15 Apr. 2008, available at www.mediabite.org. 89 See Mark O'Brien, *The fourth estate: journalism in twentieth-century Ireland* (Manchester, 2017), pp 173–6. 90 *IT*, 19 Mar. 1973. 91 *Irish Echo*, 18 Feb. 2011.

'words of advice from Conor O'Brien that I should go and find my future elsewhere'.[91] In October 1974 MacAnthony emigrated to Canada, where he worked as an award-winning producer-director with the Canadian Broadcasting Service. Conor O'Brien's career also suffered. In February 1976 he was 'moved upstairs' as editorial manager, and he died in 1985 at just 57 years of age. But his six years at the helm had moved the paper away from the stuffy confines of the Legge era. In one of his last editorials he condemned the Vatican for its stance on matters sexual, a stance described by the editorial as being 'founded on such men as St. Paul and St. Jerome whom most psychiatrists would now regard as being in need of treatment'. The following week the paper carried a letter from the bishop of Ardagh and Clonmacnois (and later cardinal) Cahal Daly, who asked O'Brien to 'withdraw this disgraceful and offensive remark'.[92] O'Brien's obituary – published in the *Sunday Independent* and the *Irish Independent* – noted that 'his innovative and courageous editorship made an influential impact on Irish journalism'. Neither obituary made any reference to the Sweepstakes story.[93]

FATIMA SECRETS

The editorship of O'Brien's successor, Michael Hand, was very different. From Drogheda, Hand had worked for numerous media outlets, including the *Argus*, the Irish News Agency, the *Sunday Review*, and the *Sunday Press*. Prior to becoming editor he was contributing a popular diary page, entitled 'Michael Hand's People', to the *Sunday Independent*. Almost as soon as he took over he faced new competition in the form of the *Sunday World*. While in 1974 the respective sales of the *Sunday Independent* and the *Sunday Press* stood at 330,000 and 430,000, by 1977 the respective sales stood at 272,359 and 381,611, with the *Sunday World* reporting sales of 293,000 copies per week.[94] In 1980 another Irish Sunday title, the *Sunday Tribune*, arrived. Within this changing market there was much soul-searching about what direction the *Sunday Independent* should take. One journalist, Vincent Browne, drafted a plan, which he discussed with Tony O'Reilly, for how the paper might develop.[95] The only idea that was part-implemented was Browne's suggestion that the 'Wigmore' miscellany column (which had been initiated by Conor O'Brien) be moved to the back page and taken over by an investigative team. While the column moved, the investigative team never materialized. Browne's 'Wigmore' column was dropped in October 1976 after it levelled a

92 *SI*, 18 & 25 Jan. 1976.   93 *SI*, 10 Feb. 1985 & *II*, 11 Feb. 1985.   94 *IT*, 25 May 1974 & 31 Aug. 1977.   95 Browne later stated that his plan eventually materialized as his version of the *Sunday Tribune*: *IT*, 16 Apr. 1983, p. 14.   96 *SI*, 24 Oct. 1976.

series of charges against Taoiseach Liam Cosgrave following the resignation of President Cearbhall Ó Dálaigh.[96]

While Hand recruited popular columnists such as Hugh Leonard, Trevor Danker and Ulick O'Connor and facilitated John Devine in his award-winning reporting on Northern Ireland, he also seemed to be caught between two powerful men – the proprietor of Independent Newspapers, Tony O'Reilly, and a politician who was rebuilding his political career and whom Hand admired, Charles Haughey. In the first instance, coverage of O'Reilly's other business interests proved challenging. One such business interest was Atlantic Resources, an oil-exploration company that was publicly floated in April 1981. While the initial shareholders, including O'Reilly, had paid 50p a share, the public flotation saw share prices quadruple, netting the initial shareholders a substantial profit on a company that owned no oil – it owned a 10 per cent stake in an American company that was due to begin drilling off the west coast.[97] As one commentator noted, 'the prices of the shares depended on speculation in the newspapers, and O'Reilly owned many of them'.[98] Two months later, the *Sunday Independent's* business correspondent, Martin Fitzpatrick, interviewed the new president of the Irish Stock Exchange and found the latter 'critical of the recent trend in the Atlantic Resources share price'. When Hand heard this, he declared his intention to edit the interview. As remembered by Fitzpatrick, because of past assurances that O'Reilly's business interests should have no special protection, the issue immediately became a matter for the National Union of Journalists (NUJ), a mandatory meeting of which disrupted production of the paper. While that week's paper was published, the interview at the heart of the dispute was not.[99] The NUJ later received 'assurances from management that they had freedom to write about companies in which the newspapers' directors had interests on the same basis as any other company'.[100]

The following year, Hand refused to publish an investigation into the activities of justice minister Sean Doherty. The story, written by *Sunday Independent* news editor Kevin O'Connor, related how charges against Doherty's brother-in-law were dropped after the Royal Ulster Constabulary detained the main witness in Northern Ireland at the request of the Garda Síochána. It also told how Doherty had unsuccessfully attempted to have a sergeant in his constituency transferred after he raided a pub owned by a friend of Doherty's and had resisted pressure from Doherty to drop charges against those found drinking after-hours. Even though the paper's legal team passed O'Connor's story Hand refused to publish it. When O'Connor argued for publication, Hand told him

97 *IT*, 7 Apr. 1981. 98 Fintan O'Toole, 'Brand leader', *Granta*, 53 (1996), pp 47–74 at 64. 99 Correspondence with Martin Fitzpatrick, 18 Mar. 2018. 100 *IT*, 1 June 1981.

he was 'crucifying the minister on flimsy evidence'. The following week Hand
suspended O'Connor as news editor. In later years, O'Connor established that
Haughey had asked a government minister to contact Hand to get the story
spiked, and Hand had acceded to the request.[101]

There were, however, lighter moments. Hand was probably the only editor
in the Western world who could have claimed to have a direct link to the Fatima
apparitions of 1917 and the diaries of Adolf Hitler. In 1981 an Aer Lingus flight
was hijacked at Le Touquet airport in France and the hijacker, an Australian
ex-Trappist monk, demanded that the 'third secret of Fatima' be published in
the *Sunday Independent*. Having been sent to represent the Irish government at the
scene, minister for transport Albert Reynolds contacted Hand, who arranged
for a special edition of the paper to be flown to Le Touquet. When the hijacker
opened the door of the plane to receive the paper, French troops stormed and
secured the plane.[102] Two years later, when German magazine *Stern* announced
that it had purchased the diaries of Adolf Hitler and was selling serialization
rights worldwide, Hand secured the Irish rights. As publication day neared the
paper ran adverts on RTÉ radio announcing its scoop. But with just hours
to publication, the diaries were revealed to be an elaborate hoax. While the
paper was hastily re-made *sans* the diary feature, and as RTÉ news reported the
worldwide hoax, the radio adverts continued to be aired. Hand's attempts to get
the station to stop airing them went nowhere: he was told that the advertising
executive with the authority to stop the broadcast was not working that weekend.[103] While the paper most likely received a refund from *Stern* (as the London
Times did), in November 1983 it was announced that Hand intended to resign
as editor and become editorial advisor to the managing director.[104] Sometime
later he moved to the rival *Sunday Tribune*, penning a variety of features, one of
which, on the Rwandan genocide, won him an award in 1994.[105] His successor
as editor of the *Sunday Independent*, Aengus Fanning, would go on to reinvent the
title beyond all recognition.

101 Kevin O'Connor, *Sweetie: how Haughey spent the money* (Dublin, 2009), pp 28–9. 102 Albert
Reynolds, *My autobiography* (Dublin, 2009), pp 122–4. 103 *SI*, 13 July 1997. 104 *IT*, 16 Nov.
1983. 105 *IT*, 15 July 1997.

4 / The *Sunday Press*: de Valera's 'Irish-Ireland' weekly

RAY BURKE

The *Sunday Press* was the best-selling newspaper in Ireland for one-third of the twentieth century and it was the country's foremost quality title for forty years. It was 'read in two out of every three households in the Republic' and 'by three in every four adults' during the third quarter of the century, reaching a total of well over 1.3 million adults each week.[1] For nearly half of its 46-year lifespan, between 1949 and 1995, the paper's founder, long-time controller and effective editor-in-chief, Éamon de Valera, was either head of state (president) or taoiseach and the political party that he established and led, Fianna Fáil, was almost perennially in government.

The launch of the *Sunday Press* – on 4 September 1949 – was described in its first editorial as 'an event of national importance, whether considered socially, culturally or politically'. Like its sister papers – the *Irish Press*, founded eighteen years earlier in 1931, and the *Evening Press*, first published in 1954 – the *Sunday Press* was launched when Fianna Fáil was out of government and, also like both its sisters, it quickly helped the party return to power. However, its social and cultural influence was no less significant than its political impact.

EARLY DAYS

The *Sunday Press* was an immediate success editorially and commercially, with sales exceeding those of its nearest rival, the *Sunday Independent*, by more than 100,000 copies each week for much of the following four decades. Its first editorial, headlined 'Ourselves' and running the full length of the front page, pledged: 'Nothing that is of current interest in the life of our people, from sport to politics, from cinema to theatre, from farming to the cost of living, will be overlooked.' It declared that its policy would be 'in keeping with 'the nationalist tradition' of Theobald Wolfe Tone, Davis, Mitchell and Lalor – 'embodied forever in the Proclamation of Easter Week'. It continued:

1 *SP*, 2 Mar. 1969; 20 May 1973.

We stand for the fullest national independence and for democratic government based on Christian principles over every inch of Irish soil; for
the restoration of the language; for the broadest tolerance in public
affairs; for the rights of the weakest sections of the community; and for
all that will help to preserve and to sweeten the traditional Irish mode
of living.

A box in bold type on the front page proclaimed: 'We invoke The Most Holy
Trinity to guide and direct our endeavour and our work.' The front page also
carried in bold type the text of a telegram in Irish from Éamon de Valera,
who was attending a Council of Europe meeting in Strasbourg. He regretted
that he was unable to be present to see the first copies coming off the presses,
but he wished the enterprise 'rath Dé' (God's blessing and grace) and added
that he hoped that the paper would prosper forever for its workers and for the
nation.

The first issue, comprising twelve pages and costing 2*d.* (two old pence),
carried on its masthead the two rubrics that appeared under the masthead of
the *Irish Press* from its first edition: 'The Truth in the News' and 'Do cum Glóire
Dé agus Onóra na hÉireann', the latter copied from the dedication in the *Annals
of the Four Masters* in the seventeenth century. The first editorial also declared:

> Our message to the Irish people, in this our first number, is to hold
> steadfastly to the ideals and principles which have carried them trium-
> phantly through so many periods of stress and anxiety. At all moments
> of national crisis the *Sunday Press* will give them every support that lies
> in its power.[2]

The symbolic locking of the plate of the first front page on the compositor's
'stone' (bench) was performed by Senator Margaret Pearse, a sister of Easter
Rising leader Pádraig and a daughter of the woman who had pressed the button
that started the presses rolling for the first *Irish Press* in 1931. Patriotic continuity was also highlighted in a lengthy editorial in the *Irish Press* on the eve of the
launch. It noted that the new paper would 'come to occupy the same high place
in Sunday journalism that the *Irish Press* occupies in daily journalism' – as 'an
Irish-Ireland organ' – and that 'it will have, as its main concern, Irish life, Irish
interests and Irish aspirations'.[3]

News stories, including one in the Irish language on the front page, filled
four of the twelve pages produced during the paper's early years, combined with

2 *SP*, 4 Sept. 1949.   3 *IP*, 2 Sept. 1949.

three pages of sport and five pages of features. The features section included full pages of fashion and crossword competitions, a page of cartoons and a page on books, the theatre and the cinema. The initial crossword prize fund of £1,000 was quickly increased to £1,500 with £1,000 going to the overall winner. The main fashion competition prize from 1950 was usually a family car or a trip to Paris or Rome. In early 1951 it was 'the prize you've waited for' – a week in New York for St Patrick's Day – where 'you may join the Broadway Parade – the biggest Irish procession in the world'.[4]

Four separate editions were usually produced – Britain and Streets, Country, Northern and City Final (Blue Spot) – involving multiple page updates and re-plates during a print run that continued from about 7.30 p.m. on Saturday to the early hours of Sunday. The first editor (1949–62) was Lieutenant Colonel Matt Feehan, from Clonmel, Co. Tipperary, a de Valera friend who had been a businessman before joining the army. 'It was de Valera who asked me to take the job (of editor)', he recalled later, 'I told him I didn't know the first thing about newspapers, good, bad or indifferent.'[5] There to support Feehan were newly installed Irish Press Ltd managing director Seán Lemass and a young deputy editor, Douglas Gageby. A special emphasis was put on distribution to ensure that the paper was delivered early enough to enable early mass goers to buy it. This strategy paid off: a front-page editorial in the first issue of 1953 describing the paper as 'the infant prodigy of Irish journalism' also observed that it had gained 'a gigantic readership' of hundreds of thousands of people in its first three years. It said the reasons for its success were simple: 'It was pledged to the people of Ireland and everything that was Irish. It had faith in the people and they will continue to have faith in it', adding:

> We are essentially a NEWS paper. It is our duty to give all the news ALL the time. This we will do. We have our staff reporters. We have correspondents in every part of the country and, through the agencies, are linked with every part of the globe. They will continue to give you everything that is worthwhile. IF IT HAS HAPPENED YOU WILL READ ALL ABOUT IT IN *THE SUNDAY PRESS*.[6]

Book serializations were the mainstay of the feature pages each week. These were almost invariably war of independence or Easter Rising memoirs that, in the words of the first editorial, were 'in keeping with the nationalist tradition ... embodied forever in the Proclamation of Easter Week'. A de Valera

4 *SP*, 11 Feb. 1951.   5 *IT*, 19 Mar. 1984. See *IT*, 12 Oct. 1990 for Feehan's obituary. Feehan was succeeded as editor by Francis Carty (1962–7).   6 *SP*, 4 Jan. 1953.

confidante, Robert Brennan, formerly of the IRA, the IRB and the *Irish Press*, and latterly of the Irish diplomatic service in Washington and Radio Éireann, set the tone in only the third issue. Opening the serialization of his memoir *Allegiance*, he traced his radicalization to seeing Maud Gonne play the title role in the W.B. Yeats/Lady Gregory play *Cathleen Ni Houlihan*, and he added: 'To the question which Yeats asked 36 years later – "Did that play of mine send out certain men the English shot?" – I can without hesitation answer "Yes".'[7]

The serialization of *Allegiance!* – the title carried an exclamation mark in the *Sunday Press* – was followed over several weeks by *Guns on the Asgard*, by Mary Spring Rice, one of the four people on the yacht that ferried to Howth in 1914 the Irish Volunteer guns that would be used in the Easter Rising, and later by the memoirs of a Kerry republican, Seamus O'Connor, and subsequently by *The four glorious years* by David Hogan, who was introduced to readers as someone 'whose stories of the War of Independence are well known'. (David Hogan was the pseudonym of Frank Gallagher, the first editor of the *Irish Press* and director of the Government Information Bureau between 1951 and 1954, when the series was published, but readers were not told his real identity until after his death in July 1962.) *The four glorious years* (the definite article was dropped when the series was later published in book form) ran in the *Sunday Press* from May 1951 to October 1952. It was introduced as follows:

> The period from 1917 to 1921 was the most dramatic and the most tense in the modern history of Ireland. For those four years, the Irish people, inspired by the Rising, faced the greatest empire in the world, and despite the rigours of a full-scale military repression, remained unsubdued to the end. It was a period rich in every kind of excitement and daring; and in an effort to transmit some of this to the reader of to-day (and to recall it for the veterans), David Hogan, whose stories of the War of Independence are so widely known, has written a series of articles for the *Sunday Press*. 'In many a city parlour, or farmhouse kitchen', he writes, 'when the night grows old and men have time to talk, minds go questing to those years when Ireland was in revolt. That Ireland of theirs lives again and around that fire the younger ones share, wide-eyed in the tumult and the daring, the heroism and the humour of it all. So in this series will my mind go in and out among the events of the Four Glorious Years, and what will come will, I hope, bring the thrill and the triumphs of it all to the generation too young to have borne its own brave part.'[8]

7 *SP*, 18 Sept. 1949. 8 *SP*, 29 Mar. 1951.

In the final instalment, eighteen months later, Hogan/Gallagher wrote:

> No word that has been written here has been set down to recall the bit-
> terness of those days or that any should taste again the hot anger of that
> time. It is recorded so that the present generation and those who come
> after them will always remember how nobly Ireland was served during the
> Four Glorious Years – and after.[9]

Midway through the serialization, the memoir of another IRA veteran – *Guerrilla
days in Ireland*, by Tom Barry – headed a list of books that 'every young man and
woman in this country should read'. The list was published on the books page
after the literary editor asked seven people ('an educationalist, two librarians,
two publishers, a writer and a bibliophile') to nominate the top twenty books
that should be readily available to the public.[10] And just over a month after the
Allegiance! serialization ended, the front page promised in capital letters 'OUR
GREAT NEW SERIAL *No Other Law*, the story of General Liam Lynch, Chief
of Staff of the IRA, told by one of his comrades-in-arms for the first time'.
The blurb added: 'You must not miss this story. It will give you a new insight
into the character of Ireland's fighting men during the War of Independence.'[11]
(When *No other law* was published in book form eighteen months later, the
Sunday Press described it as 'a great, necessary and moving book which should
be in every home'.)[12]

Second World War memoirs of German and British officers were serialized
during 1953 and 1954, before an August 1955 front page proclaimed: 'And now the
Sunday Press gives readers the greatest story of them all ... the story of the great
raids of the I.R.A. and the gallant men who planned and took part in them.'
Introducing the series (not published in book form until nearly three decades
later) the front-page piece added:

> On Sunday week we start this new gripping serial written by Commandant-
> General Ernie O'Malley, one of the greatest Irish Guerrilla leaders and
> author of the bestseller *On Another Man's Wound*. These tales of epic battles
> are true down to the smallest detail. They tell a tale of courage ... the
> valour and heroism of great Irishmen who had little else but their own
> inexhaustible courage to pit against the might of an empire. They will take
> you back over the paths trodden by Ireland's greatest fighting men ... in
> them you will smell the smoke of battle and meet heroes who today are
> living ordinary lives. *On Another Man's Wound* moved the nation two years

9 *SP*, 5 Oct. 1952.   10 *SP*, 23 Dec. 1951.   11 *SP*, 11 Nov. 1952.   12 *SP*, 23 May 1954.

ago with its vividness. This second series by Ernie O'Malley is an even greater story. It is the story of the men who defeated the Black and Tans. YOU just can't afford to miss it.[13]

The O'Malley serialization began when the *Sunday Press*, which was not yet 6 years old, had already achieved 'the greatest net paid sales ever attained by any newspaper in Ireland' — average net paid sales of 405,922 copies per week during the first six months of 1955.[14] It now commanded just over 51 per cent of all Sunday-newspaper sales, and its short history had been 'a story of lightning growth to its present position of being the greatest newspaper ever in Ireland', readers were told on the day the serialization began.[15] A month later they were informed that *World's Press News* had hailed the *Sunday Press* as 'the first Irish newspaper to sell more than 400,000 copies'.[16]

The 400,000-sales milestone had been reached on 30 May 1954, when, as that year's Irish Press Ltd AGM was told, 'the *Sunday Press* had the honour to publish a four-colour, half-tone picture of His Holiness Pope Pius XII ... the first time such colour work had appeared in any Irish newspaper'.[17] The papal photograph was published just one week after the paper recorded the general-election result in which de Valera and Fianna Fáil again lost power after being back in government for less than three years. The defeat was acknowledged in the front-page editorial, 'Our View', which stated: 'Fianna Fáil goes out of office, but it remains representative of the people as a whole, not merely of sections.' It pointed out that the party had garnered almost 600,000 votes, adding: 'Fine Gael never came near that total and never will.' The Labour Party's poll, it noted, was a quarter of Fianna Fáil's, while the combined total votes of the two smaller Clan parties hardly came to one-tenth of Fianna Fáil's.[18]

One week after the papal issue, the number of pages was increased from twelve to fourteen and readers were told: 'Your favourite paper will be not only bigger, it will be better.'[19] The sustained success of the Sunday title also enabled the directors of Irish Press Ltd to announce three weeks later that they proposed to launch a new evening paper. And a few weeks after that, at the beginning of August, the *Sunday Press* reported that 'in the biggest property transaction of its kind to take place in Dublin in recent years' its directors had purchased the landmark Elvery's Elephant House building at the corner of O'Connell Street and Abbey Street as its new headquarters. The original building, mentioned in *Ulysses*, was destroyed in the 1916 Rising and its replacement dated from 1921. 'This fine building, situated as it is at the centre of Dublin's

13 *SP*, 21 Aug. 1955.   14 Ibid.   15 *SP*, 28 Aug. 1955.   16 *SP*, 18 Sept. 1955.   17 *SP*, 27 June 1954.   18 *SP*, 23 May 1954.   19 *SP*, 6 June 1954.

main thoroughfare', the report added, was 'one of the finest in Dublin, both in construction and architecturally'.[20]

The move to the prestigious new headquarters building (although editorial and production staff remained at Burgh Quay), and the 'spectacular and immediate success' of the *Evening Press* (average daily net sales reached 103,377 in its first month of publication), confirmed the commercial prosperity of de Valera's newspaper group.[21] He addressed the twenty-fifth annual general meeting of Irish Press Ltd in June 1956, six weeks after the nine-month serialization of Ernie O'Malley's IRA Raids in the *Sunday Press* had been followed immediately by 'another scoop' — jail escapes: 'our men battling against the Empire in our fight for freedom'. Now midway through a period on the opposition benches, de Valera, who was given no title other than 'Mr de Valera' in the *Sunday Press* report, told the meeting:

> The newspapers were founded to voice the national ideals and give expression to the views of the vast majority of the people. At the same time the company was a business concern and had to survive as such. Its success as a business had brought it to its present position and the 25th annual general meeting was a natural occasion for rejoicing.[22]

A full-page advertisement a month later in the *Sunday Press* hailed the latest circulation figures for the three Press titles as 'striking evidence of an event unparalleled in the history of journalism — the building up of a great national group of newspapers in so short a time'.[23] And a news report later that year stated that the *Sunday Press* 'goes all over the world' to thousands of subscribers: Irish missionaries, nuns and priests, Irish embassies, exiles, libraries and educational institutions in Iraq, Australia, Amsterdam, New Zealand, Honolulu, Thailand, Toronto, South Africa and Iceland.[24]

Ireland's exiles were acknowledged as emigration peaked during the 1950s (and the population of the republic fell by more than 140,000 between the censuses of 1951 and 1961). Having reported without comment in its first month of publication that 'Since last September sixty young people have emigrated to America from Aran's north island (Inishmore) ... The total gone to Britain is much greater', the paper dispatched reporters Terry Ward and Kevin O'Kelly to Birmingham and Glasgow, respectively, in August 1951 for articles 'spotlighting the conditions under which thousands of our disorganized brothers and sisters must work after emigrating from Ireland'.[25] In September, under the heading

20 *SP*, 1 Aug. 1954.   21 *SP*, 10 Oct. 1954.   22 *SP*, 24 June 1956.   23 *SP*, 5 Aug. 1956.   24 *SP*, 7 Oct. 1956.   25 *SP*, 25 Sept. 1949; 26 Aug. 1951.

Figure 5: The first edition of the *Sunday Press* on 4 September 1949.

'Exploitation', it published 'a flood of letters' from emigrants.[26] The Donegal writer Peadar O'Donnell was commissioned to write about emigrants in 1957, and Northampton-based Domhnaill Mac Amhlaigh became a regular contributor following the publication of his *Dialann deorai* (literally 'the diary of an exile', but translated in 1965 as *An Irish navvy*). Reporter Terry O'Sullivan spent three months in the United States at the beginning of 1953 among the Irish diaspora in Boston, New York and Philadelphia. Soliciting the addresses or telephone numbers of emigrants, he wrote:

> I am going as a personal messenger between family and family, between brother and brother, friend and friend. The places and centres I will visit will be dictated by you, the readers of the *Sunday Press*, for I'll go wherever you say, to see your friends and give them your special greetings.[27]

Approaching its tenth birthday at the end of the 1950s, the *Sunday Press* was firmly established as Ireland's bestselling newspaper, by a distance; its founder was beginning a fourteen-year term as head of state; the political party he founded was securely restored to power for the foreseeable future; and control of the Irish Press Ltd had been seamlessly passed to the founder's eldest son, Vivion.

CHANGING OF THE GUARD

The succession was recorded in the same issue of the *Sunday Press* that carried a full-page report and pictures of Éamon de Valera's inauguration as president on the previous Wednesday – headlined 'Crowning Event of an historic week' – and a front-page editorial, 'Our View', headlined, 'An Taoiseach Sean Lemass', which welcomed his election in the Dáil on the day before the presidential inauguration. On page three of the same issue, the final paragraph of a report on the annual general meeting of Irish Press Ltd, held the previous day, stated: 'At an extraordinary general meeting held earlier in the Shelbourne Hotel, Dublin, Major Vivion de Valera TD was appointed Controlling Director. He was proposed by the chairman, Mr J.E. MacEllin, and seconded by Dr R. Farnan, Director.'[28] Vivion de Valera had been appointed to the company board at the age of 22, shortly after the launch of the *Irish Press* in 1931. He was a major in the Irish army during the Second World War and he was a backbench Fianna Fáil TD from 1945 to 1981. 'In choosing to take on the arduous responsibilities of Managing Director and Editor-in-Chief in 1951, he was effectively writing

26 *SP*, 2 Sept. 1951.   27 *SP*, 25 Jan. 1953.   28 *SP*, 28 June 1959.

finis to the advancement which would undoubtedly have been his in the political sphere,' wrote *Sunday Press* editor Vincent Jennings in an obituary.[29] 'There is', Jennings added, 'a certain, and necessary, tension between the politician and the journalist and to combine the two in one person might seem an almost impossible feat. Vivion de Valera recognized the problem and it is doubtful if anyone else could have coped with it better.'[30]

An earlier paragraph on the 1959 AGM, as distinct from the EGM, quoted chairman McEllin as follows:

> Our thoughts today will be with our founder and first controlling director who is now no longer with us in this company. Mr de Valera now occupies the highest office in the land and it would not be proper for me to enlarge on what we feel. Nevertheless, I will ask you to join with me in congratulations and a heartfelt Beannacht Leat!

Readers were not told, however, that the seamless succession of control of what was now the country's most successful media company had taken place only after all the political parties in the Dáil except Fianna Fáil had voted to censure de Valera for retaining the position of controlling director of Irish Press Ltd throughout his time as taoiseach. The Dáil vote followed an acrimonious debate spread over three days in December 1958 and January 1959 during which the *Sunday Press* was accused of running articles 'glorifying the gun'.[31] The Dáil censure vote was reported on when the *Sunday Press'* cadre of regular columnists included the 'well-known economist and lecturer', and future taoiseach, Garret FitzGerald, a son of Desmond FitzGerald, who had been in the GPO in Easter Week 1916, and who had excoriated de Valera in the Dáil in 1933 over his control of the newspaper company through an injection of cash originally donated by Irish emigrants in the United States for the establishment of an Irish republic and through a golden shareholding based in the secretive US state of Delaware.[32]

The 1959 changing of the guard at Áras an Uachtaráin, at Government Buildings, in Fianna Fáil and at Irish Press Ltd did not alter the successful *Sunday Press* template. Sport – principally Gaelic games, rugby, soccer and horse racing – covered four or five full pages and was often flagged on the front page; book reviews, crossword and spot-the-ball competitions, cartoons for adults and children and, increasingly, business and show-business matters, filled most of the other non-news pages. Photographs – especially those by the outstanding and prolific Colman Doyle – were used prominently and liberally.

---

29 Jennings had succeeded Francis Carty as editor in 1968. 30 *SP*, 21 Feb. 1982. 31 DÉD, vol. 171, col. 2186 (12 Dec. 1958). 32 DÉD, vol. 48, col. 1758 (27 June 1933).

Aside from de Valera, the name associated for longest with the paper may have been that of a Jesuit priest, Robert Nash, whose weekly column ran from 1951 until 1985. The series, usually across four columns on page two, was promoted as 'quite unique in Irish journalism', and as part of the paper's striving to fulfil its 'Do cum Glóire Dé' motto. 'His are no ponderous sermons but rather chats which have established themselves as one of the outstanding features of your paper,' readers were told at the beginning of 1953.[33] In the final column, in July 1985, Fr Nash wrote:

> Countless messages were relayed to me, in the mail and the spoken word, assuring me of many blessings in the spiritual and material order, which came through this weekly reminder. I cannot doubt that it is an apostolate, which is what my vocation as a priest is about.[34]

Another page-two fixture from the mid-1950s was an Irish-language column by the journalist and broadcaster Breandán O hEithir. Titled 'Tus an Pota' (the top of the pot), the column ran until 1963 and O hEithir continued thereafter to write frequently for the paper as a book reviewer and feature writer until his death in 1990.

The pages aimed at women readers were augmented from the early 1960s by the recruitment and long service of Bronwyn Conway, Terry Keane and Angela MacNamara to write on beauty, fashion and personal relationships, respectively. MacNamara was introduced in February 1963, under the heading 'Youth and Love', as follows: 'A mother of four children, she has a modern outlook and lectures to girls in convent schools on youth problems. She has written extensively on these problems and has appeared on TV. Her first column, headed 'Keeping the Rules', began:

> The world today mocks marriage vows. Do we join in this mass mockery which hits the foundations of society, or do we stand out on our own? Christian courtship and marriage are suffering severe blows and the result is chaos. Shocking figures show an increase in sexual promiscuity. Daily papers, Sunday papers and magazines speak in headlines of the grave moral laxity in Britain, calling it a national scandal … In America 25% of marriages end in divorce.[35]

Her first 'Questions Answered' column began in October of the same year and continued until 1981, when she quit on doctor's orders after becoming 'burned

33 *SP*, 4 Jan. 1953. 34 *SP*, 21 July 1985. 35 *SP*, 24 Feb. 1963.

out'.[36] About 400 questions and answers were published annually during the 1970s and she was sending 3,000 personal replies to readers – the 'tip of the iceberg' in 'a vast tide of large and small tragedies to which she has devoted herself', the paper declared.[37] A column in 1966 was headlined 'You won't find a husband in a dancehall' and an opinion piece in 1974, flagged on the front page, was headlined 'Saint Patrick would be ashamed!'[38] Bronwyn Conway, 'beauty consultant and TV personality', wrote weekly from December 1963 and Terry Keane, 'Ireland's leading writer on fashion', joined in August 1968.[39] More than a dozen years later, at the beginning of the 1980s, a front page proclaimed: 'Terry Keane, Bronwyn Conway and Angela MacNamara head the best women's section in Irish newspapers.'[40]

Women readers, particularly 'the housewife', had been sought from the first issue. Within a year of the paper's launch the top prize in the weekly fashion competition was a Morris Minor, 'a family car with low running' costs. Readers were invited 'to exercise their skill and judgment by placing the above eight dresses in order of merit'.[41] In February 1954 'another scoop' introduced the serialization of the story of Sybil Connolly, 'the Irish gown designer who rocked the world of fashion last year with her Irish creations and is now one of the world's foremost fashion authorities'. The front-page blurb added: 'She was the first Irishwoman to "make" the front page of the American magazine *Time* with its global influence ... she has made history'.[42]

The ideal woman for readers – female and male – may have been the Irish-American actress Grace Kelly, who became Princess Grace of Monaco, and the paper's 'Woman of the Year' in 1956.[43] Her marriage ('the Wedding of the Century'), her pregnancies (and even her rumoured miscarriages), her children's first photographs, her Irish visit and her attendances at gala balls were regularly chronicled in words and pictures, usually on the front page, until her death in a car crash in 1982.[44] Princess Grace and Jackie Kennedy (later Onassis) were covered in a way that mirrored Fleet Street's coverage of the British royal family. But visits to Ireland by Britain's Princess Margaret, a sister of Queen Elizabeth II, to stay with her mother-in-law at Birr Castle, in county Offaly, were reported minimally on inside pages, and there were no other mentions of the British royal family and very little reference to British politics (apart from the Suez crisis).

In contrast to the saturation coverage of the Easter Rising and war of independence, the contemporaneous First World War – in which nearly 50,000

36 *SP*, 31 Jan. 1982. 37 *SP*, 27 Apr. 1974. 38 *SP*, 11 Sept. 1966; 17 Mar. 1974. 39 *SP*, 1 Dec. 1963; 18 Aug. 1968. 40 *SP*, 24 Feb. 1980. 41 *SP*, 3 Sept. 1950; 6 Jan. 1952. 42 *SP*, 21 Feb. 1954. 43 *SP*, 30 Dec. 1956. 44 *SP*, 29 May 1960.

Irishmen were killed – was ignored. The first acknowledgment of the conflict did not come until September 1966, six months after coverage of the Easter Rising culminated in a twelve-page 'Special Commemorative Issue' and a front-page editorial entirely in Irish headed 'Athnuachan' (renewal).[45] A single-column item on the bottom of page nine, headed 'Mass for Prof Tom Kettle', gave notice of the fiftieth anniversary of the death of Kettle, 'a former member of the Irish bar and son of a founder of the Land League'. The second paragraph stated: 'Professor Kettle, a member of the Irish Party, was killed in the First World War, during the Battle of the Somme, in September 1916.'[46] (The item appeared underneath a report about the annual commemoration of IRA man Liam Lynch, also scheduled for the following Sunday.)

'Glorification of the gun', whether real or imagined, was not, however, confined to the pre-independence era. Brendan Behan, himself a 1940s IRA Volunteer, quipped that his first reflex on opening the pages of the *Sunday Press* during the 1950s was to duck lest he be hit by a stray bullet.[47] And editor Lieutenant Colonel Matt Feehan signalled the end of the working day by telling staff: 'Wipe your bayonets lads – you've killed enough.'[48] The report on the obsequies of one of those killed in the IRA's 1950s border campaign was headlined 'Limerick's Greatest Funeral'. The report began: 'Fifty thousand people from all over Ireland witnessed the biggest funeral ever seen in Limerick city when the remains of Sean South, 28-year-old clerk, Henry Street, Limerick, who was killed during a raid on Brookeborough RUC barracks, Co. Fermanagh, were removed from the church of St Michael, Denmark St, to Mount St Laurence Cemetery, yesterday.' Alongside was another report noting that Ennis Urban Council and Dublin County Council had passed votes of sympathy with the parents and relatives of South and Fergal O'Hanlon, who also died in the raid.[49]

Circulation peaked at over 500,000 at the end of 1963 when the paper included a four-page, full-colour souvenir supplement on John Fitzgerald Kennedy. The Kennedy visit in June and the summer papal succession had boosted weekly sales to an average of just under 390,000, but the 22 December issue set a new record. Considerably more than half-a-million copies of the paper were printed and distributed, but even this huge production – by far the greatest in the history of the *Sunday Press* and the greatest single issue ever produced by an Irish newspaper – was not sufficient to meet the demand,' the following week's front page recorded, adding: 'In many cases agents were sold out within an hour and many thousands of latecomers were disappointed.'[50]

45 *SP*, 10 Apr. 1966.   46 *SP*, 4 Sept. 1966.   47 Behan, cited by former *SP* deputy editor Emmanuel Kehoe in *SBP*, 6 Mar. 2011.   48 *SP*, 7 Oct. 1990.   49 *SP*, 6 Jan. 1957.   50 *SP*, 29 Dec. 1963.

Average net sales continued to grow steadily in the decade following the Kennedy visit and assassination, due partly to the worsening Troubles in the North. Sales during the second half of 1972 reached 442,817, an increase of 36,331 copies per week on the first half of 1971, and the highest average circulation of any Irish newspaper over a six-month period.[51] During 1972 – the worst year of The Troubles for deaths and destruction – stories relating to the North provided the front-page lead for thirty-one of the fifty-three issues and they abounded elsewhere on the front and inside pages. A two-paragraph, single-column story on the bottom of the front page of the first issue of 1972 showed how the violence had escalated. Under the headline 'Over 1,000 North Blasts', it reported that:

> There were more than 1,000 explosions in the North last year and gun-men stole more than £300,000 in 436 armed robberies, according to figures issued by the British Army last night. During 1971 there were nearly 7,000 security incidents, August being the peak month with 1,073. A total of 114 civilians, 43 soldiers, 11 RUC men and 5 Ulster Defence Regiment men were killed. The figures exclude what is called 'normal crime'.[52]

The first issue after Bloody Sunday in Derry (which occurred on 30 January 1972) carried a front-page note stating that 'by special arrangement today's issue contains material from the *Sunday Times* ... generally regarded as the British paper with the least prejudiced attitude to Ireland'. As well as flagging the articles reprinted from that day's *Sunday Times*, the front page also pointed to page three where 'Vincent Browne reconstructs the Derry massacre in frightening detail'.[53] In the shock and outrage that followed Bloody Sunday, the paper reprinted in full Thomas Kinsella's lengthy poem 'Butcher's dozen' in April.[54]

A hurried rejig of the front page followed the first Dublin city-centre bombing arising from the Troubles. This occurred at 1.25 a.m. on Sunday 26 November 1972, when more than forty people were injured, some seriously, at a late-night cinema exit on Burgh Quay, almost on the newsroom's doorstep. Reports and pictures of the aftermath dominated the front page of the final edition, but all of page three carried a report on the special criminal court trial and conviction that week of IRA chief of staff Seán Mac Stiofáin, and most of page two was devoted to an interview with his wife, Marie. Reports on the jailing of RTÉ (and former *Sunday Press*) reporter Kevin O'Kelly – for refusing to identify Mac Stiofáin as a source – the resulting sacking of the RTÉ

51 *SP*, 4 Feb. 1973.   52 *SP*, 2 Jan. 1972.   53 *SP*, 6 Feb. 1972.   54 *SP*, 30 Apr. 1972.

Authority and subsequent temporary blackout of RTÉ broadcasts were moved
to the back page.[55]

Mac Stiofáin was one of several IRA leaders whose activities and pronounce-
ments featured prominently throughout the 1970s. A profile of Provisional IRA
leader Joe Cahill in 1971 was headlined 'Is he the Collins of the North?' and
a picture of him with his wife and six young daughters at home in Belfast
was published on the first Sunday after his release from Portlaoise Prison in
1975.[56] Another IRA leader, Dáithí Ó Conaill, was quoted on a front page in
December 1974 saying that the IRA was 'still investigating' the Birmingham pub
bombings of the previous month – the biggest IRA massacre in Britain – and
front-page space was also given later in December to the death of erstwhile
IRA leader Stephen Hayes, who had been chief of staff from 1939 to 1941. The
three-column report also noted that Hayes had been secretary of the Wexford
GAA county board for ten years and had represented Wexford at inter-county
level.[57] (Sport and politics were entwined in soccer coverage too. The Northern
Ireland international soccer team was constantly referred to as the 'Six Counties
XI' or the 'IFA XI' until 1974, some sixteen years after it had become the first
team from Ireland to qualify for the World Cup finals.) In January 1976 a front-
page report stated authoritatively that Seamus Twomey was still chief of staff
of the IRA.[58]

'Dev's Farewell' was the front-page lead story headline on 24 June 1973 – de
Valera's last day in public office. The strap above the headline – 'Many historic
occasions recalled' – and the large picture of a smiling de Valera below showed
that Fianna Fáil's loss of power for the first time in almost two decades earlier
that year had not lessened its founder's sense of entitlement regarding Leinster
House and the national parliament. In bold type, the first paragraph of the
front-page lead story declared:

> The Dáil chamber was silent yesterday as its most famous figure ever took
> the Taoiseach's seat. But he could have filled the other one hundred and
> forty-three seats many times over with memories. For it was the President,
> Mr de Valera, smilingly meeting cameramen's requests to resume his old
> seats on the Government and Opposition sides of the House.[59]

Elsewhere on the front page, a box headlined 'A Tribute', also in bold type, indicated that there were pages inside of words and pictures from de Valera's fourteen

55 *SP*, 26 Nov. 1972.   56 *SP*, 15 Aug. 1971; 26 Jan. 1975.   57 *SP*, 1 Dec. 1974; 29 Dec. 1974.   58 *SP*,
15 Feb. 1976.   59 *SP*, 24 June 1973.

years as president, and 'a special tribute by Lord Longford'. This full-page piece was headlined: 'Greatest statesman I have known'. The paper also reported that de Valera, whose term of office expired at midnight, 'will be feted in Dublin today when thousands of admirers from all parts of the country will arrive by rail and road to give him a rousing reception'. The report noted that extra road and rail services were being laid on to bring people to Dublin to witness the presidential parade, organized by Fianna Fáil, from Áras an Uachtaráin to the city centre.

THE DECLINE OF THE *SUNDAY PRESS*

De Valera's retirement from public office (after almost sixty years) came shortly after the midpoint in the lifespan of the *Sunday Press*. His death just over two years later was followed by two decades of continuous circulation decline, at first gradual but eventually precipitous. The colour tabloid *Sunday World*, launched in 1973, eroded circulation at the bottom of the market, and then two new broadsheet titles, the *Sunday Tribune* (launched in 1980 and relaunched in 1983) and the *Sunday Business Post* (founded in 1989), fragmented the quality end.

The first sign of decline appeared just days before de Valera's death. The Audit Bureau of Circulations (ABC) average net paid weekly sales during the first half of 1975 fell below 400,000 copies for the first time in a dozen years. Sales averaged 393,602 copies per week during the six months, which was still 104,815 copies per issue ahead of the *Sunday Independent*, but the peak had passed and weekly sales exceeded 400,000 copies only one more time – and then only marginally and briefly – when they averaged 403,695 during the second half of 1975, boosted by the commemorative 21 August issue marking de Valera's death. In the first half of 1976 average sales were back down to 393,540, and a year later they had fallen to 381,611.[60]

Certified ABC sales figures were published on the front page every six months from 1954 until 1982, the year that control of the newspaper and its sister titles passed to the third generation of a branch of the de Valera family – to Major Vivion de Valera's only son Eamon. (It was also the year that the brash nine-year-old tabloid *Sunday World* eclipsed the *Sunday Press* to become the biggest-selling newspaper in Ireland, obliging the new boss to replace the decades-old stamp that appeared beside the masthead proclaiming 'Biggest sale in Ireland' with one that said '1.1 Million Readers Every Sunday' and later 'Over A Million Readers Every Sunday'.)

Dr Eamon de Valera was introduced to readers in May 1982, in a two-column photograph over a caption that described him as 'the controlling and managing

60 *SP*, 28 Aug. 1977.

director'. The holder of a doctorate in electrochemistry from University College Dublin, he had been appointed to the company board in 1978 and named as 'a full-time executive' two years later when his father became ill. (Staff who had been used to referring to Vivion as 'The Major' immediately dubbed their new boss 'Major Minor' and the sobriquet stuck.) Tensions between politicians – particularly Fianna Fáil politicians – and *Sunday Press* journalists, and between management and journalists bedevilled Dr de Valera's control of the company almost from the start. Fissures within Fianna Fáil dating back to the outbreak of the Northern Troubles and the Arms Crisis damaged the traditionally symbiotic relationship between the party and the Press newspapers at the same time that journalists and other staff were revolting over the changed work practices being demanded by the advent of new technology. The *Sunday Press* failed to appear twice in December 1981 and once again during the following May, after Dr de Valera addressed his first AGM as 'controlling and managing director'. It then missed four issues in July 1983, when journalists stopped work after forty-six of them had their pay cut for attending a mandatory trade union meeting.

Fianna Fáil's simmering troubles erupted at the beginning on 1983 when the newly installed Fine Gael-Labour government disclosed that ministers in the previous Fianna Fáil government had ordered the illegal tapping of the telephones of journalists, including that of the recently appointed *Sunday Press* political correspondent Geraldine Kennedy. 'How they tried to silence me' was the headline over Kennedy's front-page lead story on the Sunday after the revelations.[61] The scandal was also covered on three inside pages, including in an editorial across all eight columns at the top of page four signed by editor Vincent Jennings and headlined: 'Now is the time for all good men'. In the editorial, Jennings declared that:

> Fianna Fáil is in trouble; Charlie Haughey is in trouble, and both facts are sad, but not nearly as sad as the fact that the country is in serious trouble. There are some politicians who would find the distinction between party and country distasteful: that's their problem. The suggestion was made on Friday that the national emblem be changed from the shamrock to the banana. A sick joke, no doubt, but then so was Mr Doherty as Minister for Justice. The parallels to the Nixon White House are uncomfortably close and to the point. Wall-to-wall distrust and paranoia: anyone who disagrees with the leadership is an enemy, or worse – anti-national. Get them, the expletives deleted. What is Fianna Fáil going to do? Which may or may not be the same question as asking what will Mr Haughey do.

61 *SP*, 23 Jan. 1983.

Sean Doherty is gone: Ray MacSharry is gone: the public image of the party is at its lowest point ever. Mr Haughey is so isolated that he must ask himself whether it is in the country's or the party's interest that he remain as leader ... One of the most frightening aspects of last week's revelations was the apparent inability of some Fianna Fáil politicians to understand the dimensions of what had happened. The naivety – not to say stupidity – of Padraig Flynn and Michael Woods going on television and attempting to defend the indefensible boggled many minds. Were they so worried about their own political skins that they could not see that what is the basic institution of any State had in this country become a party plaything? ... Fianna Fáil has to quietly set about uniting its dispa-rate parts: the alternative is disintegration. The damage that has been done is great. It is not irreparable ... If there is any comfort out of last week, it is in our ability as a people to be shocked still by a slippage in high public standards. It's worth holding on to.[62]

The front-page lead on the following Sunday, again written by Geraldine Kennedy, was 'Haughey Digs In', and the attempted heave against him was the front-page lead in the next issue too, this time accompanied by a photograph across four columns of Haughey at his home (in the Gandon mansion in Kinsealy) proffering to the camera the front cover of a hardback book entitled *Lion of Ireland*.[63]

If Fianna Fáil was in decline, so too was the *Sunday Press*. ABC figures were published on the front page only once more, in September 1984. They showed that the paper's latest net paid sales had fallen by 100,000 since 1981, to 281,992. This compared to 227,003 for the *Sunday Independent* and 93,175 for the *Sunday Tribune*. (*Sunday World* net sales, which at this time exceeded 340,000 a week, were studiously ignored).[64] More lasting damage was sustained in the following summer when the management shut down the paper and its sister titles for six weeks, and laid off all 1,000 employees, after the printers (actually hot-metal typesetters and page compositors) refused to agree to change work practices for the introduction of new technology.

Michael Keane succeeded Vincent Jennings as editor at the end of 1986, but sales continued to fall apace, despite the introduction of full colour on

62 *SP*, 23 Jan. 1983.   63 In between the 23 January and 30 January issues of the *Sunday Press* the *Irish Press* had published a notorious double-page spread of articles and pictures looking back on Haughey's career that was seen by many as a premature political obituary – he continued to lead the party and to be re-elected taoiseach for most of the next decade, during which time the *Sunday Press* sought to balance its coverage with almost-weekly praise of Haughey in the anonymous 'Gulliver' column.   64 *SP*, 30 Sept. 1984.

many pages and the forgoing of a price rise.[65] The stamp beside the masthead that had proclaimed 'Biggest sale in Ireland' was changed to 'The only million reader quality Sunday' at the beginning of 1988 and dropped altogether in March of that year. By 1989 the circulation of the *Sunday Independent* surpassed that of the *Sunday Press* for the first time. Another threatened closure in 1990 was only averted by an eleventh-hour intervention by future Taoiseach Bertie Ahern. But the decline was terminal, hastened by haemorrhaging sales, worsening management-staff relations and a disastrous partnership with a US newspaper publisher, Ralph Ingersoll III. Readership figures were published for the last time in March 1995, showing 645,000 adult readers per week, fewer than half the heyday total and signifying sales of little more than 150,000.[66]

The Ingersoll partnership had soured quickly and had broken down publicly within 30 months.[67] It was terminated by the Irish supreme court in May 1995, calamitously for the de Valera side. The last *Sunday Press* was published on 21 May 1995, four days before the supreme court ruling. Journalists stopped work on the day of the ruling after one of them was sacked peremptorily for publicly criticizing de Valera's controlling shareholding and 'management culture'.[68] The non-appearance of the paper on 28 May led management to predict, correctly, that 'the position could become irretrievable if the *Sunday Press* were to miss another publication'.[69]

Attempts to stem the paper's sales and reputational decline in its final years had included the hiring of the renowned Yorkshire-based Republic of Ireland international soccer manager Jack Charlton as a columnist for £500 a week. An advertising campaign was devised around the slogan 'He manages one team; he writes for one newspaper – the *Sunday Press*'. But when Charlton, a member of the England team that won the 1966 World Cup, was asked which newspapers he read, he replied. 'If I'm in Ireland I buy a few of the Irish papers – I do a column for one of them but I can't remember its name.'[70]

65 For an account of Michael Keane's time as editor see Ivor Kenny, 'Michael Keane – the *Sunday Press*' in *Talking to ourselves: conversations with editors of the Irish news media* (Galway, 1994), pp 298–319. 66 *SP*, 5 Mar. 1995. 67 *SP*, 2 Feb. 1992; 19 Dec. 1993; 26 Dec. 1993. 68 *IT*, 24 May 1995. 69 Ray Burke, *Press delete: the decline and fall of the* Irish Press (Dublin, 2005), p. 216. 70 *Guardian*, 30 May 1994.

5 / The people's paper: the *Sunday Review*

JOE BREEN

Even by the standards of that depressed and depressing decade, it was a low-key launch. The *Irish Times* had managed to rustle up a minor public figure to do the honours, and so on Saturday evening, 2 November 1957, the lord mayor of Dublin, Councillor James Carroll TD, pushed the button in the Fleet Street machine room to start printing the first issue of the *Sunday Review*. The *Irish Times*, the *Review*'s senior stablemate, on the following Monday, in a caption to a modest page-seven photograph of Councillor Carroll starting the presses, reported that the issue was sold out: 'In Dublin, most suburban newsagents had sold all their copies before midday. In towns and villages in the country people waited in the streets for an early edition, and there was keen competition to buy the first copy.'[1] The caption added that 'the composing staff welcomed the newspaper with the traditional "knock-down" – one of the noisiest ever heard in a Dublin newspaper office'.[2] The welcome was likely more grounded in hope than expectation. The *Review* was the first Irish Sunday tabloid newspaper – 'as different from the *Irish Times* in style and content as is possible to imagine', and a daring and desperate leap into the unknown for its staid and increasingly financially pressed publishers.[3] The printers would have understood that the success of the new venture was critical to the company's future and, by extension, their own. They were to be disappointed. The *Sunday Review* would last a mere six years before closing in November 1963.

This chapter is divided into two sections. In the first section the idea to develop and publish the *Review* is sketched out against the backdrop of the dire financial position of the *Irish Times* and of the republic as a whole. What prompted a company struggling with a moribund circulation of its major title to suddenly change tack from its paper-of-record instincts and invest in a new and irreverent Sunday tabloid and, shortly after, buy the *Evening Mail*, then already in its death throes? It would, of course, end badly. In unpublished excerpts from a

---

1 *IT*, 4 Nov. 1957.   2 Printers performed a 'knock-down' to mark special events such as retirements. It involved banging a piece of cold metal type or metal ruler on any surface to create a short intense barrage of noise. More recently, the practice has been adopted by journalists in some Irish newspapers.   3 Mark O'Brien, *The* Irish Times: *a history* (Dublin, 2008), p. 159.

2008 interview a year before he died at 86 years of age, Major T.B. McDowell, who became chief executive of the *Irish Times* in 1962, stated that the closure of the two titles was absolutely necessary. 'Yes, they were killing the *Irish Times*. It was going bankrupt at a rate of knots ... keeping them alive was killing the *Irish Times*'.[4] The second section explores the actual newspaper through its six-year publishing history under the direction of five different editors, one of whom, John Healy, would serve in the chair twice. Was the 'brash and breezy Sunday tabloid' ahead of its time?[5] After all, ten years after the *Review* closed the equally brash and breezy tabloid the *Sunday World* was launched into a much changed and more receptive Ireland.

KEEPING THE *IRISH TIMES* IN BUSINESS

The Ireland of the 1950s was a grim place. While much of the rest of Europe enjoyed a post-war boom, in Ireland paltry economic growth, allied to a shrinking agriculture labour sector, resulted in too few jobs and an over-whelming reliance on the valve of the emigration boat. Mary Daly states that the decade after the end of the Second World War was the period when Ireland became most out of step with Western Europe: 'At a time when other countries were enjoying full employment, a rapid rise in living standards, a post-war marriage boom and an expanding urban population, Ireland only experienced these forces vicariously, through the net emigration of 500,000 young men and women to Britain.'[6] Patterson argues that the census of 1956 was a shock to the country's system. It revealed that the population, at 2,894,822, was the lowest ever recorded for the state, having declined by 65,771 since 1951.[7] The year of the fortieth anniversary of the foundational event of the Irish State, the Easter Rising, was one in which the *Irish Times* could editorialize, in response to the census figures, 'If the trend disclosed ... continues unchecked, Ireland will die – not in the remote unpredictable future, but quite soon.'[8]

The survival of the *Irish Times* was uppermost in the minds of the directors and staff in the late 1950s. In 1956, sales of the *Irish Times* were 36,267 compared to 182,650 for the *Irish Independent* and 132,318 for the *Irish Press*.[9] Crucially, the other two news groups also published highly successful Sunday and evening newspapers. John Horgan believes that the major problem faced by the *Irish*

---

4 Unpublished excerpts from interview with then *Irish Times* editor Geraldine Kennedy.   5 Dermot James, *From the margins to the centre: a history of the* Irish Times (Dublin, 2008) p. 158.   6 Mary E. Daly, *Sixties Ireland: reshaping the economy, state and society, 1957–1973* (Cambridge, 2016), p. 2.   7 Henry Patterson, *Ireland since 1939: the persistence of conflict* (Dublin, 2006), p. 109.   8 *IT*, 2 June 1956.   9 Conor Brady, *Up with the* Times (Dublin, 2005), p. 109.

Times was the narrowness and vulnerability of its operations.[10] It had only two other small publications. One was the weekly *Irish Field*, a niche publication that catered for the horse-racing and horse-breeding industries. The other was the *Times Pictorial Weekly*, which had been started in 1941. Interestingly, the '*Pic*', as it was known, would provide a platform on which to build the *Sunday Review*.

Dermot James, a former company secretary of the Irish Times Ltd, outlined the situation facing the directors in the late 1950s: 'Profits were, at best, around the lower end of five figures in the better years and, during those other years (about one in every three or four), simply non-existent.'[11] The *Irish Times* had long identified with, and reflected, the interests of the 'economically significant minority' of the Protestant communities in Ireland, as d'Alton observes, adding that 'long practice playing to a prosperous and literate constituency bore dividends. Even as the proportion of Protestants in the upper economic echelons declined from the 1920s, the newspaper astutely marketed itself towards those who took their places – the Catholic middle classes.'[12] But that was a rosy future an era away from the gloom of the 1950s. Horgan states that the board in the 1950s consisted of a small number of 'Protestant businessmen who controlled all the voting shares: when one of their number died or wished to resign – which was infrequent – the remaining directors habitually purchased his shares, and redistributed them to the next Board appointee.'[13] This had its advantages. Many leading Dublin businesses were owned by Protestants and they advertised consistently in the *Irish Times*, to an extent, observes Horgan drily, 'probably not warranted by the paper's circulation'. But given commercial realities this support could not be relied upon into the future.

As such, when the directors came across entrepreneur J.J. McCann in late 1954/early 1955, they may have believed that he represented a possible uplift in their fortunes. According to the board minutes of 11 February 1955, they agreed to buy new type at a cost of £160 in order to print McCann's *Radio Review*, a profitable radio-listings weekly that was the precursor to the *RTÉ Guide*.[14] Certainly by 19 July 1957 matters had progressed to the point where McCann was appointed a board member and joint managing director (with Frank Lowe). In addition, the *Irish Times* bought the *Radio Review* for £45,000.[15] A month later, 19 August, the board was told that Austin Walsh was to be editor of the new

10 John Horgan, *Irish media: a critical history since 1922* (London, 2001), p. 63.   11 James, *From the margins*, p. 197.   12 Ian d'Alton, 'A Protestant paper for the Protestant people: the *Irish Times* and the southern Irish minority', *Irish Communications Review*, 12 (2010), 65–73 at 66.   13 Horgan, *Irish Media*, p. 63.   14 *Irish Times* minute book, Dec. 1954–July 1974, 11 Feb. 1955. The minute book rarely records boardroom discussions but decisions, and details such as staff pay rises and the ongoing company overdraft, are recorded.   15 The *Radio Review*, which had ceased publication, was sold to Radio Éireann for £10,000 in Oct. 1961: Minute book, 2 Oct. 1961.

Sunday paper, at a salary of £25 per week with Ken Gray, assistant editor of the *Pictorial*, appointed assistant editor at a salary of £17 17s. per week. Clearly much had happened in the interim.

Dermot James places the Sunday project in McCann's hands. He states that the success of his *Radio Review*, essentially an Irish version of the BBC's *Radio Times*, tempted him 'to try his luck at entering into the Sunday newspaper market. The outcome was a deal agreed between him and the paper's directors whereby they took over the radio publication and agreed to print and publish the proposed Sunday paper.' James records that considerable, if muted, antagonism was directed both towards McCann and the staff he brought into the company. It did not help that:

> the door which, as long as anyone could remember, had a notice stating 'Board Room', was suddenly changed to 'J.J. McCann, Managing Director'. Clearly, he wanted everyone to know who was now in charge, and began with a gross act of philistinism by dumping the entire set of bound volumes of the *Irish Times*, running from 1859 to 1956, because he needed the admittedly large room space for more practical purposes.[16]

The cost of the project was immediately evident. Apart from staff wages, the board was told on 9 September 1957 of additional expenses such as a Press Association service that would cost £3,000 a year.[17] By 16 December, the company's overdraft was running at a daunting £134,095.[18] On 13 January 1958, accountant Bartle Pitcher was appointed *Irish Times* general manager.[19] Presumably he was asked to steady the company's finances, which continued to deteriorate at a serious rate. By 24 February the overdraft had swollen to £161,592 and the board decided to increase the price of the *Irish Times* to 4d. and cease publication of the *Pictorial*.[20] In truth, the launch of the *Review* had signalled the end for the *Pictorial*. What is often termed the 'golden era' of photojournalism was coming to an end; in Britain the once hugely successful *Picture Post* closed in 1957. While the *Review* and the *Pictorial* were distinctly different publications – the new Sunday prided itself on its news edge, whereas the *Pictorial* mainly consisted of image-led soft features – they were both strong visually and shared the same

---

16 James, *From the margins*, p. 157. The company did not get a replacement set until 2006, when journalist Peter Murtagh, acting on behalf of the newspaper, bought a bound collection from the UDA-associated People's Museum in Belfast for £9,300, or €14,800. The collection, with some gaps, covers the years 1894 to 1985.   17 Minute book, 9 Sept. 1957.   18 Ibid., 16 Dec. 1957. This figure today would be over €3 million (source: www.cso.ie).   19 Pitcher would leave the company within months and move to Independent Newspapers, later INM, where he would rise to the position of CEO.   20 Minute book, 24 Feb. 1958.

tabloid format. Essentially, it could be argued that they were competing in the same space. Something had to give and it was the much-loved *Pictorial* that gave way to the brash new taste of the future. But all was not well. James notes that 'as more and more money continued to be directed at the troubled tabloid, there was growing animosity among members of the staff of the *Irish Times* who now feared that McCann's paper was not only likely to fail, but could drag the daily down with it'.[21]

A NEWSPAPER IS BORN

It had all seemed so much brighter a few short months earlier when, as James observes, the new tabloid got off to an encouraging start with sales of 100,000 copies.[22] Even the *Irish Times*, which generally ignored its less reserved stablemate throughout the *Review*'s six-year history, save for incongruous weekly promotional advertisements, was caught up in the excitement of the launch, albeit in the informal social space of the 'Irishman's Diary':

> Not many journalists get the opportunity to assist in launching a brand-new newspaper. The staff of the *Sunday Review* will have that unusual experience when the first issue of their paper comes off the presses in the basement of this building in the early hours of Sunday morning.[23]

The article, bylined as ever by the anonymous Quidnunc, noted that the editor of the new paper, Austin Walsh, was born in London 'with, as it were, printing-ink in his veins'. His father had worked in the *Daily Express* newsroom and his mother, whose family owned the *Donegal Vindicator*, was 'attached' to the *Catholic Herald*. Walsh was 'educated in Dublin at the Catholic University School. He worked for *Irish Digest* and other magazines before joining *Radio Review*, where he spent the last five years as assistant editor.'[24] The 'Diary' also offered snapshots of key members of Walsh's staff: 'His assistant, Ken Gray, is an old St Andrew's boy who has been in the *Irish Times* organization since he left school.' He had moved to the new paper from the 'post of assistant editor of *Irish Pictorial*'. The features editor, Jim Edwards, had made the same journey.

The implicit balance in these senior appointments is important: Walsh, Catholic and an *Irish Times* outsider but with a journalistic pedigree, would have

---

21 James, *From the margins*, p. 158.   **22** Ibid. In fact the ABC-audited sales for Jan.–June 1958 were 190,222 per week.   **23** *IT*, 2 Nov. 1957.   **24** The main writer of the 'Irishman's Diary' through this period was Seamus Kelly, a journalist, drama critic and sometime actor who appeared in John Huston's 1956 film *Moby Dick*. John Moran sketched out his colorful life in 'An Irishman's Diary', *IT*, 25 Aug. 2010.

been McCann's choice, clearly underlining that this was his project. Edwards and Gray, who would later enjoy an illustrious career in the *Irish Times*, were there to reflect and protect the interests and values of the parent organization, not least its Protestant heritage.[25] If those staff appointments would not cause undue concern in the hearts of loyal *Irish Times* readers, then the balance struck in the next two appointments might have raised eyebrows. Under the subhead, 'Travelled Men', the article outlined the contrasting histories of the news editor and the chief sub-editor, two pivotal positions:

> The news editor and the chief sub-editor must be two of the most widely travelled of Irish newspapermen. Liam MacGabhann, news editor, comes from Valencia Island, Co. Kerry, and he was a national teacher before joining the *Irish Press* in 1932. He spent most of the next 20 years at Burgh Quay, apart from a year working for *An Poblacht* [sic], the organ of the Republican movement, under Mr Sean MacBride, and a year in the I.T.G.W.U. under another distinguished chief, Mr Cathal O'Shannon. In 1952 he became Irish representative of the *People*. He has travelled, he thinks, in nearly every European country, from Madrid to Moscow, as well as the USA. Donagh MacDonagh, the chief sub-editor ... is, like Austin Walsh, the son of a newspaperman. His father, George MacDonagh, was editor of the *Limerick Leader* and the *Carlow Nationalist* before coming to Dublin as chief reporter of the *Irish Independent*. Donagh was a reporter in the *Independent* until 1943 when he joined Reuter's newsagency as a war correspondent, and was promptly sent to Burma to report the war with the Chindits. [He then worked in Reuter's offices in Singapore, Manila and Tokyo before returning to London and then Dublin.][26]

Again there is a balance struck. MacGabhann's career suggests a left-leaning republican – hardly then a natural fit in the *Irish Times* building – while MacDonagh's odyssey with a British news agency, including a stint reporting on the Second World War, suggests someone more amenable to an *Irish Times* view of the world. The same would be true of sports editor Eddie Boyle, who had spent fifteen years with the *Scottish Daily Express* and five years in the RAF. The section of the 'Diary' dealing with the *Review* ends with a veritable mission statement from the editor: 'Austin Walsh says that the new paper will combine a Sunday picture paper with full news coverage and a full sports service.

25 Ken Gray would later become an *Irish Times* director and deputy editor of the *Irish Times*. 26 *IT*, 2 Nov. 1957. Burgh Quay was the headquarters of the Irish Press Group; Cathal O'Shannon Snr was the father of Cathal O'Shannon, later an outstanding journalist on the *Review*, the *Irish Times* and RTÉ.

Figure 6: The *Sunday Review*'s first edition on 3 November 1957.

"We intend it to be bright, but without sacrificing decent standards. It will be very much a people's paper. We hope that people will let us in on their worries, and write plenty of letters to us.'"[27] The reference to 'decent standards' reflects the chilling effects of the predominant Catholic morality that dominated Ireland from the 1930s through to the 1960s. O'Brien quotes journalist Michael O'Toole's observation that up to the 1960s journalists were generally a 'docile lot, anxious to please the proprietor, the advertiser, the prelate, the statesman'.[28] In fairness, proprietors also lived in fear of clerical condemnation; operating in a society dominated by the Catholic Church, no publication could afford to offend it.

FIRST EDITION

The first edition of the *Sunday Review* (3 November 1957) exhibited all the nerves and missteps of an under-rehearsed debut production, albeit one with drive and conviction. The 'Irishman's Diary' of the day before had warned that the publication of a new paper was not just a matter of writing a few articles and getting them printed: 'It involves a considerable feat of organization in news services, distribution and so on. Besides, however well organized you are, the dress rehearsal is never quite like a first-night. That's why all the *Sunday Review* team are waiting, as eagerly as anyone else, to see their first issue off the press.'[29] If the newspaper was not exactly an object of beauty, with a random selection of fonts fighting a losing battle with quirky, ungainly layout to convey some sense of style and order, it was already indicating that it would be the 'hard-hitting, tough little paper' remembered by one of its contributors, Donal Foley.[30]

This first edition deserves detailed examination as the tone, the content and the look (later tidied up into a recognizable pugnacious popular newspaper personality) set the pattern for Walsh's editorship, which would last until October 1959. The launch paper was twenty-eight pages and it cost 4*d.* As it was printed on the *Irish Times* broadsheet press, the size of the paper only could increase or decrease by four pages (i.e. two sides of a single broadsheet). There was a healthy stock of display advertising, but an insignificant amount of classified advertising, which was a big earner in all newspapers. The two-line masthead was ranged left in a sans serif casual script font not unlike a heavier version of Comic Sans, with the 'Sunday' in white reversed out of a red background and 'Review' in white reversed out of a black background, the

two words separated by a dateline, volume number and price. The impression
was friendly, informal, modern. In the absence of any definitive information
to the contrary we can presume that Gray was the designer. He had become
a gifted visual journalist working on the *Pictorial* and would be key to direct-
ing the *Review's* energetic tabloid presentation, not least the use of innovative
layout tools such as edgy typefaces, graphics and dramatic images. At a time
when newspapers were staid and conservative in appearance, the *Sunday Review*
screamed for attention, splashing pictures and headlines with a determination
to be different and to be seen.

   The newspaper fell into the category of 'emphatic tabloid', as described by
Kevin Barnhurst and John Nerone:

> The tabloid's map of the social, although perhaps less nuanced and intel-
> ligible than the broadsheet's, was more morally charged, full of heroes
> and villains ... where the reserved broadsheet form told readers what was
> important, the emphatic tabloid told readers what was evil.

They also argue that the emphatic tabloid was the dialectical twin of the broadsheet. They believed that tabloids existed only in markets already served by a
conventional broadsheet, as 'They presupposed their broadsheet rival and more
or less yielded to it the role of prime mapper. This left the tabloid free to
pursue fun, blood and moralism.'[31] The *Sunday Review* was entering a market well
served by the two dominant indigenous titles, the *Sunday Independent* and the
Sunday Press, plus a plethora of British imports. It had to create its own space, its
own identity. Similarly, Martin Conboy, referring to the multimodal meanings
of newspapers in general, notes that the inter-relationship between a newspaper's writing and its typographical features, layout and pictures combines to
present an identifiable community of appeal: 'The choice of language as well as
its layout is always significant in this process.'[32]

   This creation of its own identity to an 'identifiable community of appeal' was
no simple matter. The other Irish Sundays had daily titles (the *Irish Independent*
and the *Irish Press*), and if in both cases the Sunday was not simply a seventh
day edition but a newspaper in its own right, there was a degree of continuity
and shared identity – in terms of news values and visual appeal. This was not
the case with the *Irish Times* and the *Sunday Review*. Apart from house advertisements promoting either title, there was little visual coherence, editorial overlap
or indeed evident interest from either party. The *Irish Times* archive records a

31 Kevin G. Barnhurst & John Nerone, *The form of news* (Guildford, 2001), p. 252.   32 Martin Conboy,
The language of news (London, 2007), p. 12.

paltry number of editorial mentions for the *Sunday Review* during its publication life. The Sunday title was equally uninterested in the work of the daily, with some notable exceptions such as when they shared Cathal O'Shannon's news reports from the Congo during the crisis in 1961. They may have operated from the same building but they had little else in common. Everything was a mark of difference: what they covered, how they reported it, the language they used, how their respective papers looked and who read them. To add further spice to what must have been an uneasy journalistic melting pot, the brash newcomer's use of scarce resources was perceived, as already stated according to James, as putting the venerable daily at risk.[33] As such, the *Review* was very much a standalone publication, isolated, a part of the *Irish Times* family but also apart from it. Perhaps this gave the newspaper some of its gritty character, its sense of defiance, its pugnacity.

Certainly, from the first edition, the *Review* sided with those on the losing side of Ireland's economic divide, notwithstanding the jarring social columns soft-focusing on the rich and famous and features aimed at women that championed middle-class preoccupations with fashion, cooking and home hints. The first lead is a classic tabloid human-interest story: 'Red tape may split a family'. The accompanying posed image of a boy and girl embracing ('This may be goodbye – Twelve-year-old John Beirne weeps with the girl he called "sister" … six-year-old Bernadette Joyce') drives the un-bylined story by acting out the event of a separation. The lead in bold type speaks to the image:

> 'A little boy and his "sister" weep and cling to each other every time a car stops anywhere near their home at Churchboro', Ballinlough, Co Roscommon.

'FOR THEY BOTH FEAR THAT IT MEANS THEY WILL BE PARTED'

The story sounds typical of the time. The 15-month-old boy was boarded out to a farmer and his wife by the local council. Six years later the wife gave birth to a girl. As they grew up the two children became 'inseparable', but then the wife fell ill and died. Now, because there is no woman in the house, the boy must return to care.[34] The children are victims of circumstance. And if there are victims there are also invariably villains, namely the power behind the red tape. The language is simple and direct, fuelled by indignation and a crusading spirit. The combination of image and text demands an emotional response

---

33 James, *From the margins*, p. 158.

from readers. It would be the model for many such lead stories over the next six years. As Donal Foley remarked of the paper's news values: 'If you had a good story you hit the reader with it by professional use of print and clever illustration. And you were not afraid to say what you meant.'[35]

Two other stories on the crowded first front page reflect the grim social world of the 1950s. Headlined 'Stay at home pleads priest', the text was typically direct: '"Don't come to London. There are no jobs for you". So warned Fr Tom McNamara, Chaplain of London's Irish Centre last night. He was pleading with intending Irish immigrants.'[36] This is one of seventeen stories dealing with emigration in the first edition, reflecting the enormity of this issue. At the bottom of the page was more evidence of poverty and the dearth of social support services. Headlined 'Dad gives up 4 children', the text baldly stated:

> Corporation lorry-driver John Kavanagh (30) had to take a heart-breaking decision yesterday and send four of his five children to institutions. His wife, Mary, disappeared from their home in Ballyfermot on October 15. He told the *Sunday Review*: 'I had to stay out of work to care for the children. I can't afford to do so any longer'. One child, a boy of four, is being cared for by Mrs Kavanagh's parents.[37]

Another report raises issues of temporality. 'Cyclist is killed by Govt. car': 'A man was killed yesterday by a car in which the Minister for Lands, Mr E. Childers, was a passenger.' The report names the dead man and the Wicklow location of the accident and notes that neither the minister nor his driver was injured. It then states that 'at an inquest the jury recorded a verdict according to the medical evidence'.[38] On the face of it this represented a remarkable feat of efficiency; that an inquest jury could be assembled to deliver a verdict on the same day that a man died. The newspaper also thought it unusual and signalled this by printing the inquest paragraph in bold. Perhaps there was a more simple explanation – that the accident had not taken place 'yesterday' but some days earlier and that the report was filed 'yesterday' after the inquest. What is interesting is the use of a typographical element (bold type) to signify something unusual: novel use of type, borders, panels, images, pull quotes and graphical devices of striking invention would become part of the newspaper's armoury and identity over the next six years.

The tone of the coverage is concerned and rooted in the everyday. An underlying theme is poverty, with the lead story and the report on children sent

34 *SR*, 3 Nov. 1957.   35 Foley, *Three villages*, p. 113.   36 *SR*, 3 Nov. 1957.   37 Ibid.   38 Ibid. Erskine Childers was, ironically, a regular contributor, mainly on travel.

to 'institutions' clear evidence of societal malfunction and bureaucratic indifference, while the priest's warning on jobs in London further underlines the issue of unemployment in Ireland. Pages two and three offer further evidence of social pressures: a photograph on page two shows 'a family of ten' waving to friends and family before departing for the boat to Britain, while on page three a headline over another photograph states 'Taoiseach's cousin an emigrant'. This showed Owen Coll (aged 40), his wife and eight children boarding a flight to Canada 'to give them a future'.[39] On the same page a report headlined 'Our bravest boy emigrates' tells how Brendan Merriman (aged 16), who had received a medal for saving a young woman from drowning, had, along with his family, 'gone from the once-booming but now depression-hit town of Ballyshannon'.[40] The underlying message is that nobody, neither the powerful nor the heroic, is exempt from the scourge of emigration.

The structure and pagination of the newspaper also remained remarkably consistent. As stated, as a tabloid, it could rise or decrease in size only in numbers of four. The standard size was twenty-eight pages, which would fall to twenty-four in the slow advertising months post-Christmas and during summer and increase to thirty-two when advertising was strong; in its final year the paper would experiment with supplements in an attempt to boost circulation. Within the twenty-eight-page configuration, news would typically occupy pages one to eight, features pages nine to twenty-one and sport pages twenty-two to twenty-eight; as with its Irish competitors, there was no dedicated business or finance coverage (in time a column dealing with finance and investments would be added). Later, this configuration would be adapted slightly to reserve the back page for a social diary and news stories, but the allocation of space remained broadly consistent. This pagination compared with the eighteen to twenty broadsheet pages of the *Sunday Independent* and the market leader, the *Sunday Press*.

Sprinkled throughout the news, features and sports pages were a range of opinion columns, social diaries and advice features on fashion, cooking and home hints. The latter were unabashedly aimed at women in the home; the mainstreaming of feminism was some way off. It is important to note that the *Review* started out, like most newspapers of the time, as a gendered publication – written and produced, mostly, by men for men. Over the six years of its publication life, however, a more assertive female view became apparent. Opinion columnists like Jane Beaumont, suspected to be a pseudonym, emboldened by the winds of change, social and economic, blowing through the republic, asked on page eleven of the 21 March 1963 edition, 'wouldn't it be awfully good for

39 *SR*, 3 Nov. 1957.   40 Ibid.

their [men] over-inflated ego if they had to ponder such articles as "what does she see in you?"'

There was a strange duality of purpose at play in the social diaries, particularly in the early years of Walsh's editorship. One diary, under various headlines and bylines, chronicled in slavish prose the lives of the elite, a combination of the remnants of the old aristocracy and the new rich. The other, again under a range of bylines and headlines, but initially titled 'Dublin after Dark – Around the City with Colm Kelly', related in more demotic language the parties, anniversaries and events taking place in Dublin. Later, a 'John Gunn', probably another pseudonym, would take over the main social diary of the great and the good, with Patsy Dyke, a young English journalist who had married *Irish Times* reporter Cathal O'Shannon, producing a more countrywide social diary that typically was allocated a double-page centre spread.[41] That duality was also evident, for example, in the choice of standalone images to illustrate pages. It was the convention then to use wedding pictures for illustration – there was an endless supply and they were cost-free. But while the bulk of the news stories reflected working-class hardship and struggle, the images tended to convey a message of middle-class bliss. The early editions also included 'Social & Personal' notices – likely lifted from the *Irish Times* – which struck an equally incongruous tone. Page five of the inaugural edition included a 'Social & Personal' notice that 'the artist, Derek Hill, who has been staying in the Royal Hibernian Hotel, has returned to Co. Donegal'.[42] On the same page, 'Hubbies cause big scandal' told how 'desertion of their wives and children by emigrant Irishmen has become a major national scandal, according to social workers here and in Britain. More than 2,000 deserted their families in the past 18 months.'[43]

If the news pages betrayed some tensions, the features section was more emphatic in its purpose. 'The Story of Mama Kevina' was spread across pages eight and nine. It was the first instalment of a serialized account of the life and work of a Franciscan missionary sister, Mother Mary Kevina, who came from near Arklow, Co. Wicklow.[44] In the introduction to the un-bylined article, the local Ugandan king is portrayed as primordial evil incarnate and his world as a place beyond civilization:

> The death drums stampeded the jungle into screaming life. And danger
> lurked in every echo ... It was into the land of this strange neurotic

41 Patsy Dyke later was a well-known social diarist at the *Sunday Press*. 42 *SR*, 3 Nov. 1957. 43 Ibid. 44 Ibid. Serialized stories were common in all Irish Sunday newspapers of the time; they were believed to encourage repeat sales.

man – at once a devil and a divine – that Mother Mary Kevina from the County Wicklow led her loyal little band. All of them were dedicated in their mission unto death. They endured rigours and suffered tortures and torments with superhuman fortitude … It is a story packed with adventure and laughter and tears. It is a story that you will want to continue next week and the week after. The story of the 'Black Martyrs', the devil cults, the tribal wars, the fights against enemies white and black, within and without, THE STORY OF MAMA KEVINA and the Franciscan Missionary Sisters of Africa who blazed the golden Light of the World across the Dark Continent.

The crude racist stereotyping would not have surprised readers; while the concept of afrophobia in Ireland would become clearer with the actual arrival of African migrants during the Celtic Tiger period, the Ireland of the 1950s would have been at ease with what is now known as 'old racism'. Lucy Michael states that 'old racisms usually refer to the way in which black people or other non-white ethnic groups were perceived as racially biologically inferior, and framed within a binary logic of black and white'.[45] This othering approach is particularly evident later, in the coverage of the Congo civil war in 1960, when nine Irish soldiers serving as UN peacekeepers were killed in an ambush.

The sports pages in the first edition were relatively standard though here again there were signs of duality – the ambition might have been to produce a 'people's paper', but journalistic choices suggested a more elite agenda. While GAA and racing were well covered and, interestingly, Irish soccer received greater prominence than the game in Britain, the two codes given pride of place on the back page were hockey and rugby, hardly games that would excite a working-class readership. Sport occupied roughly the same amount of space as news and was evenly balanced between match reports, previews and features. This reflected the sporting timetable and also how important sport was in driving circulation. Most non-GAA matches took place on Saturday afternoon, making essential the Sunday newspaper report. GAA games took place on Sundays; as such, the generous allocation of space to GAA games was taken up in features, previews and columns. Paddy Downey, recruited from the *Gaelic Echo* magazine, was deputy sports editor while doubling as the *Review*'s main GAA correspondent.[46] Sports editor Eddie Boyle doubled as soccer correspondent.

There was, of course, no mention of sex, before, during or after marriage in any section of the newspaper. And, surprisingly, little mention of Northern

---

45 Lucy Michael, *Afrophobia in Ireland* (Dublin, 2015), pp 5 & 7; static.rasset.ie/documents/news/afrophobia-in-ireland.pdf.   46 Downey would later enjoy a long career as *Irish Times* GAA correspondent.

Ireland other than in sport. Foreign news coverage was also token, mixed in with general news coverage – though, later, foreign news would get its own section. There were, however, lots of columns. Columnists have a key role in print journalism, especially Sunday newspapers. It must be remembered that, unlike daily newspapers, Sundays had no ready-made diary of events, such as the courts and the Dáil, with which to generate news stories. A liberal sprinkling of columnists helped anchor the various sections in the newspaper, providing personality, continuity and content, without the need for major internal editorial direction – columnists were, and are, generally self-starters. They also were mostly freelance contributors and, as such, cheaper and more expendable than staff.

Prominent columnists on the *Review* included the colourful Eoin 'Pope' O'Mahony (1959–62), a quixotic barrister, journalist and broadcaster whose weekly writings seemed overly personal and bloated. In his *Dictionary of Irish biography* entry, Charles Lysaght describes O'Mahony as an 'errant scholar' whose *Sunday Review* columns were 'less inspired' than his regular newspaper letters and book reviews.[47] Other sometime columnists included the novelist Kate O'Brien, RTÉ broadcaster Ciaran MacMathuna, the pseudonymous Sadlier Keogh, Dublin GAA luminary Kevin Heffernan and Northern Ireland soccer legend Danny Blanchflower.[48] Reporters and regular freelancers included later RTÉ executive Mike Burns, future *Sunday Independent* editor Michael Hand, future government press chief Eoin Neeson and feature writer Marion Fitzgerald.

ROOTED IN SOLIDARITY

As the newspaper bedded in over the following weeks, its appearance and content became more consistent and structured but the voice of the newspaper remained dramatic and rooted in solidarity with the less fortunate. On 4 November, under a banner headline on page eleven, 'Could you live on 45s a week?', the unnamed writer stated in short staccato paragraphs:

> Over 166,000 pathetic people – 7,500 of them blind – are living on the verge of starvation in Ireland today.
>
>   They are members of the great army of the Forgotten.
>   They are old-age pensioners.[49]

47 Charles Lysaght, 'O'Mahony, Eoin Seosamh' in *Dictionary of Irish biography* (dib.cambridge.org).   48 Named after two disreputable nineteenth-century Irish parliamentarians, William Keogh and John Sadleir (correct spelling), the erudite and humorous column shared page two with Backbencher's 'Inside Politics'. It was written by *Irish Times* literary editor Terence de Vere White.   49 *SR*, 24 Nov. 1957.

By 1 December the masthead had turned to a blue backdrop. There was now a leader column and the first topic was the finger-wagging 'Child Crime', which noted that 'Too many children of today regard obedience as a vice, private property as a joke, kindness and courtesy as effeminate.'[50] Features included 'Man against the jungle – True-life adventures of a big game hunter'; 'Confession of a con-man' and Winston Churchill's butler on life with the great man. But social concern continued to be represented by articles such as 'Traders in Poverty', which explored the world of hire-purchase and moneylending in graphic terms.

Walsh was producing a lively alternative to the *Independent* and the *Press*, and the impressive Audit Bureau of Circulations figure for January to June 1958 of 190,222 copies reflected this.[51] However, all was not well on the financial front. The overdraft was now running at roughly £160,000. By 9 July the board heard 'that a number of economies to reduce the expenses of the *Sunday Review* were outlined by [general manager] Mr Pitcher including the dismissal of circulation representatives and five members of the editorial staff'.[52] In addition, the board decided that unsold copies (known as 'returns') 'would only be accepted on the basis of 50 per cent credit'. All three actions would hobble the growth of the newspaper and the paper did begin to lose some of its early energy.

The second set of ABC figures for 1958, from July to December, showed a fall to 183,936. This dismal trend continued into 1959 with January–June (176,283) and July–December (170,597). The good news was that the cutbacks had helped trim the overdraft to £104,826. McCann, presumably frustrated and under pressure as his pet project declined, resigned on 13 April 1959. The board members now looked elsewhere for someone who might light their fire. Their spotlight fell on Douglas Gageby, *Evening Press* editor and former editor-in-chief of the Irish News Agency. He was appointed to the board on 1 May and as joint managing director (with George Hetherington) from July. On 12 October 1959, Gageby told the board that he had informed Walsh a change of editor had been agreed upon: 'Mr Walsh agreed to accept one year's salary and cease at once. Accordingly, a cheque for £1,325 was handed to him. The £25 was in respect of the current week's salary.'[53] The board also approved the appointment of chief sub-editor Donagh MacDonagh as editor at a salary of £1,550 a year.

Walsh was under pressure with the falling circulation and always had been on borrowed time once his patron, McCann, left. MacDonagh managed to inject some badly needed new life into the paper and the circulation slide

50 *SR*, 1 Dec. 1957. 51 ABC.org.uk 52 The board minutes of 22 July record that 'it was decided that the notice given to Mr [Donal] Foley (London) should be rescinded'. How different would the history of the *Irish Times* have been if the future news editor, who would play a key role in Douglas Gageby's remodelling of the newspaper, had been let go? 53 Minute book, 12 Oct. 1959.

slowed to under 1,000 copies in the January–June 1960 total of 169,215. It helped
that that first six months was a busy news period – the Congo crisis kicked
off in July – but the new editor also brought a sharp sense of modernity to
bear. On 24 January 1960 the issues of gender equality – 'Why can't she hold
the kitty?' (relating to female bank managers) – and apartheid – 'Colour bar:
Irish boycott call' – in South Africa were highlighted.[54] On 31 January Liam
MacGabhann, in his biting column 'Candidly Speaking' on page two, headlined
'Is no comment the only answer?' states: 'Keeping things in the dark has become
a national pastime in Ireland.'[55] On 27 March, a leader headlined 'A Tragedy'
states that: 'Mr Aiken [minister for external affairs] spoke for every decent Irish
man and woman when he said we were shocked at the recent tragic happenings
at Sharpeville, South Africa.'[56] Another part of Africa was also set to shock
Ireland. On 24 July, the front-page banner headline asked: 'Will our boys have
to fight in the Congo?' On page two, a 'special correspondent' replied: 'Yes, if
the need arises.' On the same page, under the headline 'A Call To Arms', the
leader writer struck a stirring note: 'The call to Ireland to send troops to the
Congo will have brought a thrill of pride to her people ... Should our soldiers
go into action there will for us be no material gain. We want no empire and we
seek no domination of any people of any colour.'[57]

In the same month, for reasons unspecified, MacDonagh, too, resigned.
Initially his deputy, Ken Gray, took over. Gray, whose design work had earned
him a prestigious award from *Printing World* in London the previous November,
was then replaced by John Healy, a 30-year-old reporter from Charlestown,
Co. Mayo, who was appointed editor in December 1960, after three months as
acting editor.[58] Healy, who agreed a salary of £1,352 a year, was most definitely
Gageby's man; they had worked together in the Irish News Agency and later at
the *Irish Press*. The Congo, specifically the Niemba ambush in which nine Irish
soldiers died, would produce the first memorable front page of Healy's editorship. On 20 November 1960 page one was dominated by a photograph of a
coffin being unloaded from a plane at Baldonnel Aerodrome, with the heading:
'The Grief and the Glory – an Irish soldier comes home'.[59] Healy may have
known little about the mechanics of newspaper production, editing or design,
but he knew how to make an emotional impact.[60]

Healy's tenure was a rollercoaster ride at a time when the *Irish Times* was
going through something similar. In September 1959 it had explored buying the

54 *SR*, 24 Jan. 1960. 55 *SR*, 31 Jan. 1960. 56 *SR*, 27 Mar. 1960. The Sharpeville massacre occurred
on 21 March 1960 when police opened fire on anti-apartheid protestors, killing 69 people. The day is
now a public holiday in South Africa. 57 *SR*, 24 July 1960. 58 The board gave Gray a £25 bonus
in recognition of the award. 59 *SR*, 20 Nov. 1960. 60 James Downey, *In my own time* (Dublin,
2009), p. 81.

Evening Mail. The *Mail* was a tired but venerable Dublin newspaper that was being rapidly eclipsed by the dynamic duo of the *Evening Press* and the *Evening Herald*, but the *Irish Times* board wanted an evening paper to complete its stable of products and be on a par with the Press Group and Independent Newspapers. By July 1960 the board had made the fateful decision to buy the *Mail* for £217,000. The *Irish Times* would not have to wait long to regret it. The purchase prompted something of a game of musical chairs in editorial control. Alan Montgomery, then chief reporter (i.e. news editor) of the *Irish Times* was appointed managing editor of the *Mail* in September 1960. But in November 1961 the then editor of the *Irish Times*, Alec Newman, was let go — referring to the directors he said that 'the bastards got me'.[61] He was replaced by Montgomery who, in turn, was replaced at the *Mail* by Healy. Healy's deputy, Ted Nealon, a fellow young western journalist and future television presenter and Fine Gael politician, took over at the *Review*.

FLAIR FOR TABLOID JOURNALISM

But before all this change, Healy made his mark. In his first year or so at the helm of the *Review*, his flair for tabloid journalism — sometimes crass, always colourful — halted the circulation slide, with the figures for January–June 1961 showing a gain of over 5,000 copies in the total of 169,850 (the figures for July–December were a disappointing 6,000 fewer, at 163,674).[62] Once his position as editor had been made permanent — the announcement was made on page fourteen in the 1 January edition — Healy set about stirring up as much mischief as possible. The 1 January front page, under a headline 'We must do this more often — Margaret', featured a half-page photograph of Princess Margaret and her then husband, society photographer Tony Armstrong-Jones, being greeted at Shannon Airport after they arrived for a short private visit.

> And there smack-bang in the middle of them was The Man from the *Review* – Liam MacGabhann – the man from the rebel Kingdom of Kerry. With cameraman Jack McManus he joined the flight in London yesterday to bring you in the usual vivid style an exclusive report on THAT VISIT.[63]

The report continues: 'Has Mrs. Armstrong Jones and her husband been deliberately diverted to Shannon Airport so that they can steal, unwelcomed, into

61 Vincent Browne, 'Undermining trust', *Magill*, 6 Dec. 2006: magill.ie/archive/undermining-trust.   62 Over the history of the *Sunday Review*, the July–Dec. figures were always weaker than the preceding six months; this is attributed in part to the July–August period when circulation slumps as people go on holidays.   63 *SR*, 1 Jan. 1961.

Ireland, the Land of the Welcomes?' And then under a subhead 'Tradesman's entrance', it asks, 'Has 700 years of British rule here stripped from us the hallmark of this ancient nation: hospitality? ... Is someone afraid she'll see the General Post Office where a handful of men with little more than a dream challenged her grandfather's Empire and showed him, and the world, how men could die bravely? And why shouldn't she see Mr de Valera, the Irishman above all others now living, who played so great a part in wrenching Ireland from Britain?' Clearly even in the young republic the hold of the British royals on the popular imagination remained strong though the subsequent reader response in the letters column was mixed. This report followed the previous week's front page with a splash headline: 'WHO is keeping Margaret outside the Pale?' By-lined 'By the Editor' and illustrated by a large side-profile image of the princess by her husband, the text strikes a myriad of provocative buttons, from the privileging of a British royal to republican bluster.[64]

In the depth and tone of the coverage Healy was staking a claim for the *Review* to be different, to be relevant, and even, to a degree, irreverent, to ask the hard questions in demotic language to which readers could relate. He was asserting the right of the *Review* to speak for the ordinary citizen. He was also careful to balance his championing of a royal visit, though in a private capacity, with fawning recitation of the republic's foundation myth. This was reinforced by his refusal to use Princess Margaret's title in the 25 December front-page text (save for the caption), even going so far as to call them 'the Joneses'. There is also a degree of fun at play, testing the limits of nationalist tolerance while playing to a suspected subliminal monarchist sympathy – and all in a tone of bemused innocence. It was also his way of exploiting celebrity culture – a key weapon, then as now, in the armoury of a popular newspaper. Healy had clearly taken to heart Lord Northcliffe's advice to tabloid journalists: 'Never lose your sense of the superficial.' It is also notable how Healy's editorship, where possible, privileges the role of the image, particularly on the front page. This was before the age of television in Ireland. Photographs are used as evidence of objective truth; they provide witness and they demand a response.

This was especially true of the front page of 8 January 1961. 'The Face Of Famine' features a young emaciated African boy staring out into the distance. There is no caption but there is a cross reference to more photographs and a report on pages twelve and thirteen.[65] However, this striking and innovative use of an image was clearly not enough for someone because to the right of the boy's head is a 'Government Notice', or advertisement, seeking medical

64 *SR*, 25 Dec. 1960.   65 *SR*, 8 Jan. 1961.

personnel to go to the Congo. It is a bizarre decision that undercuts the emotional impact of the page when its aim, presumably, was to enhance it. But in a way this error was typical of Healy's editorship. He was a brash young man in a hurry, full of ideas and energy, making up the rules as he went along, as with front pages such as that from 12 March 1961. Labelled 'Sensation', the banner headline shouted: 'Girl buried 30 years ago comes back'.[66] Of course, she had not been physically buried but courtesy of a bureaucratic mix-up she had been registered as dead; the story inside the paper clarified this. But such treatments of similar stories are analogous to the derided website clickbait of today – irresistible fare for the curious and the gullible.

Throughout this first period with Healy as editor, the paper retained its core shape from inception, with some tinkering around the edges. For instance, foreign news was allocated its own defined space, albeit under ever-changing – and ever-more-ridiculous – nameplates, including 'This Small Small World'.[67] But arguably the most important innovation was Healy's own column, written under a pen name. Introduced as 'The newest feature in Irish journalism', 'Inside Politics by Back Bencher' made its debut on 16 July 1961.[68] The first column was innocuous fare dwarfed into insignificance by the lavish coverage afforded to the John XXIII's encyclical on social justice, 'Mater et Magistra', which was splashed across the front page, with the full text of the document squeezed into eight pages inside.[69] However, Backbencher (the byline settled on this compound form after various iterations) would enjoy a long and lively life in the *Review* and later in the *Irish Times*. It was 'the most influential political column of the 1960s [and was] distinctive in that it often contained information, sometimes on government policy, sometimes political gossip, derived from Healy's large circle of sources and it was written in an irreverent style'.[70] Terence Brown describes Healy's writing as striking 'a note of self-confident omniscience' and he notes Healy's predilection for referring to Charles Haughey in glowing terms, notably as the 'golden boy of Irish politics'.[71] Healy also used the leader column to praise the future Fianna Fáil leader, such as on 24 February 1963, when Haughey's 'zeal for work and reformation' in the department of justice was cited.[72] Former *Irish Times* deputy editor James

66 *SR*, 12 Mar. 1961.   67 *SR*, 29 July 1962.   68 *SR*, 16 July 1961.   69 The importance of Catholicism was reflected in a four-page pullout supplement and lavish front-page treatment on 18 June 1961, to mark the visit of the papal legate, 'His Eminence Cardinal Agagianian'; the previous week the nearest thing to Irish royalty, Princess Grace of Monaco, also received a four-page pullout when she paid an official visit.   70 Mark O'Brien, 'Sources say ... political journalism since 1921' in Mark O'Brien and Donnacha Ó Beacháin (eds), *Political communication in the Republic of Ireland* (Liverpool, 2014), pp 79–96 at 84.   71 Terence Brown, *The* Irish Times: *150 years of influence* (London, 2015), pp 246–7.   72 *SR*, 24 Feb. 1963.

Downey, who worked on the *Sunday Review*, believes that Ted Nealon deserves
equal credit for the column: 'It is not too much to say that between them they
transformed political coverage.'[73]

Healy's time at the *Mail* was short; he took over as editor in November
1961, and the paper's final edition was published on 10 July 1962. The previous January, the paper had been relaunched as a tabloid against a backdrop of
financial peril – the company's overdraft had soared to £262,173 in December
following the purchase of the *Mail*. But the change in format did not result
in a change in fortunes. In May 1962, a nervous *Irish Times* board enlisted the
help of a business consultant, Major T.B. McDowell, 'to advise on methods
whereby an improvement could be made in the affairs of the company'.[74] He
was invited to join the board as vice chairman at a salary of £2,000 a year. This
caused some friction with Gageby, who feared the appointment would undermine his authority as managing director. However, both men met the unions to
discuss the closure of the *Mail* and both men then decided to reinstate Healy
at the *Review*.[75] Nealon could consider himself unlucky: he had tried to follow
Healy's lively script but the paper lacked the same brio. Readers were voting
with their money and the circulation for January–June 1962 fell to 159,771 – a
loss of almost 4,000 copies. The next six months continued the trend with the
July–December 1962 total down to 154,551. On 19 November, the board decided
to give the *Review* one more year, 'the company to be worse off to an amount
of £35,000 so as to make sure of exploring every avenue of putting it on a
firm basis for the future'.[76] Some measures were outlined to boost circulation,
including the insertion of an eight-page comic supplement. But even without
the *Mail*, the overdraft remained a daunting £193,456.

THE CLOCK IS TICKING

If the *Irish Times* was still in the mire, the country was showing signs of finally
emerging from it. The Economic and Social Research Institute reported that
1963 showed 'satisfactory growth for the Irish economy'. Gross national product rose by about 4 per cent.[77] Emigration, while still a serious issue, was not
consuming the country; J.J. Lee states that the total population, which fell
from 2.96 million to 2.82 between 1951 and 1961, had risen to 2.98 million by
1971.[78] Unemployment was still rife, 'squalor and neglect in the midst of a new-
found opulence', but that sense of the country turning a corner for the better

73 Downey, *In my own time*, p. 81.   74 Minute book, 21 May 1962.   75 Ibid.   76 Ibid., 19 Nov.
1962.   77 C.E.V. Leser, *The Irish economy in 1963 and 1964* (Dublin, 1964). See esri.ie/pubs/GRS21.
pdf.   78 J.J. Lee, *Ireland 1912–1985: politics and society* (Cambridge, 1989), p. 360.

permeated the *Sunday Review*.[79] On 9 December 1962 the paper carried on page fifteen its first colour advert – for Cadbury's Irish Roses. And Healy introduced his own idea of colour into the editorial pages. Columns on knitting and nature and advertisement-supported supplements on topics such as home baking sought to widen the paper's appeal.

The growing fascination with the 'space race' between the two Cold War superpowers, the US and the USSR, was reflected in a picture-led front-page splash on the 'Agony of Anna – a brave wife' on 28 January 1963. 'For four fateful hours yesterday, Mrs Anna Glenn, wife of 40-year-old astronaut Lieutenant Colonel John Glenn, sat magnetised by a battery of TV sets as she followed with the whole world the drama of heartbreak Cape. The slim dark-haired woman listened to the call-off announcement without any apparent trace of emotion. She planned to get some sleep after all the tension.'[80] In other words nothing happened, but the heightened personalization of the news-agency story fed into the tabloid's human-interest frame; here, surrounded by modernity, was a quiet, faithful wife playing a role steeped in time. On page fourteen, in 'The day I met Spaceman Glenn', John Bowman, later to become a prominent RTÉ journalist and historian, seems mesmerized by his experience at the US space centre in Cape Canaveral, Florida: 'Just an ordinary superman. That's the most apt description I can think of for Lieut-Col John Glenn.'[81] On 11 March 1963, in an 'exclusive' 'Face-to-Face' interview, Elvis Presley tells entertainment journalist Adrian MacLoughlin that a recent biography was 'the true story of my life … maybe it was slightly overdone. I wasn't exactly a dead-end kid headed for skid row. I was driving a truck, sure, but lots of guys raise families driving trucks.'[82] The newspaper was showing an increasing interest in popular culture, particularly from abroad. This was driven by many factors, including the increasing influence of television; RTÉ had been broadcasting since December 1961. Sex was becoming a topic, albeit still constrained by Catholic morality, and photographs of women, especially foreign actresses, seemed a little more suggestive and a lot more prominent.

Healy was hugely impressed by the US, though conscious of its downsides: 'It is at once the most unselfish country in the world, where some of the most selfish men in the world live; it is, too, the most democratic country in the world where the most undemocratic things can, and do, happen.'[83] He had spent four months there in 1957 working on a now defunct New England evening paper, the *Holyoke Transcript-Telegram*, as part of a US state department programme – 'a trip I might not have made but for the generosity of my schoolfriend, neighbour

79 Diarmuid Ferriter, *The transformation of Ireland, 1900–2000* (London, 2004), p. 536. 80 *SR*, 28 Jan. 1963. 81 Ibid. 82 *SR*, 11 Mar. 1963. 83 John Healy, *Healy, reporter* (Achill, 1991), p. 129.

and colleague, Ted Nealon, who gave me the price of a one-way ticket to New York'.[84] The influence of brash American newspapers, such as the *New York Post*, was evident in the increasingly confident *Review*. In addition, the rise of Irish-America, epitomized by John F. Kennedy, made the US a vicarious Irish success story. This would reach its zenith in the *Review* in the coverage of the JFK visit and that of his assassination.

As the joy and validation of JFK's June visit ('Wonderful, Wonderful!' sang the headline of the 30 June 1963 leader comment) gave way to the grey autumn, the clock was ticking for the *Sunday Review*.[85] The overdraft was now running at £177,754. An 11 September 1963 board meeting was told that Healy and Gageby had put together a plan aimed at increasing the circulation to 185,000 by October, 195,000 by November and 200,000 by December. The centrepiece of the plan was the launch of a centre section entitled 'Women's Review'. It was a last desperate throw of the dice. Gageby told the board that 'Healy was confident that the circulation target would be achieved even with the price increase to 6*d*. A trial period of 8–9 weeks was all that was needed to prove his point.'[86] On 20 September the new twenty-two-page centre section was launched, promising coverage of 'Fashion – beauty – health – good food – travel – motoring – theatre – records – childcare – gardening – books – fiction – shopping – show talk – serial story'. It was innovative, recognizing the importance of women, but flawed in its implementation. Some content was simply repurposed from the main paper. The material aimed at women was a combination of inappropriate American features and fiction and house-produced staples such as fashion, beauty, childcare and health, with general-interest coverage (motoring, theatre, records) filling out the back. The design was modular, with a modern aesthetic, but it was clumsy and type-heavy. It showed signs of having been created in a hurry and on a tight budget while the content betrayed the (likely) male commissioning editor. At twenty-two pages, compared to the sixteen pages of the main paper, it was the tail wagging the dog – the newspaper was unbalanced. The supplement would improve in appearance over the next two months and, though it would continue to be called 'Women's Review', the content would be more broad-based, with the final two covers given to showband star Brendan Bowyer and Irish Sugar Company managing director and war of independence veteran Lieutenant General M.J. Costello.

It did not matter. On 25 November 1963, McDowell told the board the plan had not worked. He said he would ask Cecil King, the British newspaper baron who had grown up in Ireland, if he was interested in taking on

---

84 Ibid., p. 128; this was the same Ted Nealon whom he had replaced as editor.   **85** *SR*, 30 June 1963.   **86** Minute book, 11 Sept. 1963.

the *Review*, 'but if something could not be done quickly it was agreed that the SR should cease publication'.[87] At this stage the *Irish Times* was in its usual flap. Five weeks earlier editor Alan Montgomery had resigned.[88] He was replaced by Gageby. This suited both McDowell and the new editor. Gageby clearly loved journalism and now did not have to worry anymore about being usurped by McDowell, while the latter could now go about the difficult business of modernizing the company unhindered. This odd couple would steer the *Irish Times* into a golden era. On 2 December 1963, McDowell reported to the board that nothing had come of his visit to London. 'It was decided, after further discussion, to cease publication of the SR, the issue of yesterday being the final one.'[89]

The paper went out with the biggest story of its short life – the assassination of JFK. The front page was headlined: 'Mrs Kennedy invites Irish troops for the funeral'.[90] Inside, the 'Women's Review' was replaced by a supplement detailing 'The Life and Death of John F. Kennedy'; the running head, ironic in retrospect, was 'Commemoration Issue'. The supplement opened with a text, presumably written by Healy: 'A monstrous act. A blind, stupid, senseless act, this assassination of a man who had become the strength and hope of the free world.' Within a week Healy and 'Backbencher' had relocated to his 'new pulpit' at the *Irish Times*. He had been editor of two newspapers, both of which were now gone. But, argued James Downey, no slave to the Healy legend, he had been starved of staff and resources by a hard-pressed board. 'These disasters were not of his making.'[91]

CONCLUSION

If timing is everything the directors of the *Irish Times* were sadly bereft of it during the period 1957–63. Already saddled with a huge overdraft, and small profits (if any), they launched a poorly resourced Sunday newspaper in a country already well-served by two indigenous Sunday newspapers and reeling from emigration and unemployment. They made matters worse by buying at a premium price an evening paper that clearly was beyond saving and then relaunching it into a market already well-served by two indigenous titles. The laudable aim, as outlined by John Horgan and Mark O'Brien, was to provide

87 Ibid., 25 Nov. 1963.   88 'Monty', as he was known, was asked to sit in on job interviews for a new Guinness PR chief. He decided the best man for the job was himself and he duly applied. Not only was his new salary a handsome increase but, unlike the *Irish Times*, there was little chance of Guinness going out of business.   89 Minute book, 2 Dec. 1963. The dates are misleading here. The final edition was that of 24 Nov. – the last edition on file in the NLI.   90 *SR*, 24 Nov. 1963.   91 Downey, *In my own time*, p. 84.

protection for the core title, the *Irish Times*. Instead, as Downey and others have stated, they nearly killed it.[92] The demise of the *Review* was particularly unfortunate, especially as, according to Downey, it 'had almost reached the point of turning the financial corner'.[93] According to *Irish Times* managing director Louis O'Neill it suffered from a lack of advertising: 'I think when it closed down it had a circulation of 190,000 … it didn't grab the advertisers, let's put it that way and it just didn't make money at a time when the *Irish Times* didn't have an awful lot of money anyway and couldn't afford to have a further drain on its outgoings.'[94]

But viewed another way, the *Review*, when it closed, had five times the circulation of its parent title. It had managed to survive for six years and its circulation was rising when it was forced to close. The *Review* was a new style of newspaper in Ireland and not just in format. Through layout and language, the newspaper sought to create a new newspaper discourse, sharper, more critical, more empathic with its readers. It was not always successful – a combination of poor judgment and paucity of resources. But Donal Foley's assessment – that it was a 'hard-hitting tough little paper' – is, in general, true, though, like its competitors, it shied away from questioning the power of the Catholic Church, or indeed any church.

Of the five men who served as editor, John Healy emerges as the most dynamic. Reading through the editions one suspects that the greatest sin in Healy's eye was to be boring; so even the most anodyne lead story is turned up full volume, headlines are loud and photographs are generally well displayed. He had a penchant for human interest stories but the weird and the wonderful were balanced with sobering social realism. He understood that Ireland under Lemass was changing for the better, opening up to the world, and his leaders were supportive, if not slavishly so. His blind spot was Haughey. He was not the only one to fall for his mohair-suited soft-talk, but he was among the most steadfast.

Today the *Sunday Review* is a forgotten title. Very few of those who worked on the paper are still around. But it deserves to be remembered because in its short publishing window it framed an important segment of Irish social history through innovative visual journalism and lively reportage and comment. Within ten years the more racy *Sunday World* would fill the tabloid space with great success. Was the *Sunday Review* ahead of its time? Had the *Irish Times* held on for another year would the *Review* have prospered or would it have brought

92 John Horgan, *Irish media*; O'Brien, *The* Irish Times; James Downey, 'Irish Catholics' favourite editor' in Andrew Whittaker (ed.), *Bright brilliant days* (Dublin, 2006), p. 23.   93 Downey, *In my own time*, p. 84.   94 O'Neill cited in O'Brien, *The* Irish Times, p. 161.

the whole *Irish Times* operation down with it? We can never know for sure. What we do know is that McDowell and many others believed it would. And that belief sealed its fate. It would be over thirty years before the *Irish Times* again toyed with the idea of a Sunday newspaper, but that is another story altogether.

6 / 'Are you getting it?' – the *Sunday World*

SIÚN NÍ DHUINN & REGINA UÍ CHOLLATÁIN

> The *Sunday World* is a showband. You know that of course. Well for a start the SW [*sic*] operates on the premise of giving the punter what he – and I mean *he* wants. Or what it *thinks* he wants. Moreover SW is a product of the showband mentality which sprang up in this country during the late sixties and early seventies as a backlash against the cultural force-feeding we'd been suffering for decades at the hands of our elders and betters, who oddly enough also thought they knew what we wanted.[1]

In an era in which showbands were centre stage for Irish entertainment the above quotation aptly describes the often crude 'backlash' that the *Sunday World* engaged in through its reportage of a rapidly changing Ireland. Through broaching taboo subjects its reportage encroached on the long dominant vision of conservative Catholic Irish Ireland as contemporary pop culture gained ever more traction and 'instead of athletic youths and comely maidens, the people of Ireland were looking at comely youths like David Bowie and athletic maidens like Suzi Quatro on *Top of the Pops* and *Like Now*'.[2] This chapter examines the publishing phenomenon that was the *Sunday World*, from its launch in 1973 to its takeover by Independent Newspapers in the early 1980s – essentially the time during which its template as a hugely successful tabloid was created. As noted in the previous chapter on the ill-fated *Sunday Review*, timing and context is everything in the publishing world. And, whereas the *Review* may have been before its time, the *Sunday World* was poised to reap the benefits of the changes that had been sweeping through Ireland since the 1960s. The adoption of free trade had resulted in a booming economy, more women had joined the workforce, RTÉ had begun broadcasting in 1961 and free second-level education was introduced in 1967. The 1970s would also bring change: the Northern Troubles erupted, Ireland joined the EEC (now the EU), the Employment of Married Women Act 1973 removed the prohibition on married women working in the civil service and a report by the first Commission on the Status of Women in Ireland was published.

---

1 *HP*, 21 Sept. 1984, pp 7–10 at p. 7 (interview of *SW* editor Colin McClelland).   2 Ibid.

The significance of the *Sunday World*, what it stood for, and understanding its success, is rooted in understanding the Ireland in which it was published and what the public had been exposed to prior to its publication. If a 'new' Ireland was emerging, the 'old' Ireland had not quite stepped aside: shortly after the *Sunday World* first appeared the *Irish Times* reported on the formation of a 'League of Decency' in Dublin 'to do everything in its power to prevent the major step in the complete demoralisation of our country'. Such 'demoralisation' covered a multitude of issues deemed indecent such as:

> promiscuity, contraception, divorce, abortion, venereal disease, broken marriage, loss of souls, to stamp out pornography, excessive drinking and drug addiction, indecent films, plays, books, magazines, etc.; to restore the dignity of women and respect for them by men and to encourage those who are straying from God, to return to him.[3]

In many ways, the conclusion of Éamon de Valera's second term as president in 1973 signified the end of a period of Irish history that was Catholic, conservative and generous in its censorship of texts by some of its greatest writers. Ireland was a nation struggling to come to terms with its identity. Salacious headlines, photos of semi-nude women, breaking sex scandals and a tagline that asked 'Are you getting it?' which became synonymous with the *Sunday World* thus made parts of Irish society feel uncomfortable. Such 'indecencies' had pride of place on the pages of the paper that marked a radical departure in the realm of the Irish press. The content of the *Sunday World* indicates clearly how it viewed itself as 'a backlash against the cultural force-feeding' that Ireland had experienced. In one interview, *Sunday World* editor Colin McClelland described de Valera's retirement as the end of over half a century of a very different 'vision' for Ireland – an era in which the *Sunday World* would not have been tolerated:

> Ten or twenty years earlier when he had every Parish Priest in the country driving bales of the *Sunday Press* around in the boots of their cars and flogging them outside the church gates, de Valera would have stomped the *Sunday World* out as an obscene publication. Now, all he could do was go home and sit in the porch and listen to the radio.[4]

Indeed, the paper's third issue announced the death of another architect of the Ireland that the *Sunday World* would rail against – Dublin's Archbishop John Charles McQuaid. A very important factor, therefore, in the success of the

3 *IT*, 26 Mar. 1974.   4 *HP*, 21 Sept. 1984, p. 7.

Sunday World was its timing: Ireland was ready for change. The Irish public was hungry for this type of publication, which exuded an air of sensationalism and a sense of the unknown. This was acknowledged emphatically by Gerry McGuinness, who, along with Hugh McLaughlin and Tom Butler, established the paper:

> The timing was spot on. Anybody could have done the *Sunday World* with the right mixture as we got it. Had I launched the same product, as the *Irish Times* did in the late fifties, it would have failed as the *Sunday Review* did … In 1971, Hugh McLaughlin and I felt the time was ripe and the *Sunday World* became a phenomenal success. The worst sale it ever had was 206,000 copies on day one.[5]

Timing was not the only reason for the *Sunday World*'s success though. Access to the colour printing press of the Creation Group, which published several successful women's magazines and in which Hugh McLaughlin was a shareholder, ensured that the *Sunday World* had an edge on its competitors.

Recalling the decision to embark on the venture, Gerry McGuinness remembered an event held by the Marketing Institute in Brighton at which he presented on the irreverent style of the paper:

> The first question I got was, 'What publisher do you style yourself after?' I said, 'Lew Grade'. The questioner said, 'With respect, Lew Grade is an impresario, not a publisher'. I said 'I know he's an impresario – so am I. I get together as he does in the London Palladium on a Sunday night, a TV star and a pop star and a bunch of naked women and a good sports section and a television interviewer and we call the whole mixture the *Sunday World*'. I was delivering to the consumer what I felt the consumer wanted to read and this is why the *Sunday World* worked.[6]

Being particularly shrewd when it came to marketing the paper, McGuinness was fearless in challenging the main institutions of the era, including the Catholic Church. One example of this was the ploy he engaged in to attract the public's attention to this new kind of newspaper. McGuinness pulled what Seán Boyne describes as 'a stroke' in order to increase sales in Cork. He wrote to the local bishop posing as a worried mother of six, asking him to denounce this new publication, the *Sunday World*, as an irreverent rag. He ensured several

5 Ivor Kenny, 'Gerry McGuinness' in *Out on their own: conversations with Irish entrepreneurs* (Dublin, 1991), pp 204–22 at p. 213.   6 Ibid.

of his friends did likewise. The bishop took the bait and criticized the paper from the altar, whetting the congregation's appetite and stealthily invading the nation's conscience via their own moral compass, the Catholic Church.[7]

'WE INTEND TO DIG'

First published on 25 March 1973, the *Sunday World* 'absorbed many insights from its UK competitors, notably a cheeky willingness to engage in sexual innu-endo'.[8] As one commentator noted, its format was 'undiluted magazine: TV, films, music, showbiz gossip, fashion, "girlie pin-ups", lightweight opinion, sports, cartoons and so on. Politics, when it was covered, was treated in a trivial manner.'[9] Recalling the paper's launch, columnist Seán Boyne remarked that 'In the mainly conservative world of the Irish media, it was like no other paper that had been published before'.[10] The first edition of forty pages had a 'colour girl' on its front page and, alongside its news pages, it had seven pages of sport and a 'women's page', and it placed an emphasis on the entertainment world, especially the live music scene. It also carried extensive television listings. It was edited by Joe Kennedy, who had previously been assistant editor of the *Evening Herald*, and the assistant editor was Kevin Marron, formerly of the *Sunday Press*. Its news editor was Liam MacGabhann, who was later succeeded by Eamon McCann. In his inaugural editorial, Kennedy outlined the paper's ethos:

> In this newspaper, common objects like spades will be known as spades. They are used to dig with and we intend to dig. For the news and the facts behind the news ... The Irish media have been much at fault because they have communicated according to their politics and policies. They have been trammelled with strings. They have been manipulated like puppets. We have no strings ... Where we can discover hypocrisy or corruption our job will be to expose it. And we will do this so that it will be easily seen by as many people as possible, written as clearly as we can, graphically and with an economy of words.[11]

As one reviewer noted, the paper 'began to publish stories about bad housing, prison conditions, discrimination against working women, children sleeping rough in Dublin and so on. And for the first time, an Irish newspaper began to air in a frank, explicit manner, subjects like incest, abortion, drugs

7 *40 years of splashes* – anniversary supplement, *SW*, Mar. 2013, p. 2.   8 John Horgan, *Irish media: a critical history since 1922* (London, 2001), pp 108–9.   9 *HP*, 21 Sept. 1984, p. 7; the commentator was John Waters.   10 *40 years of splashes*, p. 2   11 *SW*, 25 Mar. 1973.   12 *HP*, 21 Sept. 1984, p. 8.

and homosexuality'.[12] Instantaneously, and despite costing one penny more than
the *Sunday Press* and *Sunday Independent*, the *Sunday World* was a runaway success in
urban and rural areas and across all social classes.[13] Between July and December
1973 it established weekly sales of 206,442.[14] By 1977 it had overtaken the *Sunday
Independent*, selling 293,004 copies per week compared to the *Independent's* 272,359,
though it remained behind the *Sunday Press'* sales of 381,611.[15] By 1981, the respective figures were 348,343 (*Sunday World*), 281,603 (*Sunday Independent*) and 388,200
(*Sunday Press*).[16]

EDITORIAL ETHOS

In the context of editorial policy, from its inception, the *Sunday World* was not
like other newspapers, nor did it want to be. The first edition's lead story typifies
this, telling of the hunt for Belfast girls who had lured two British soldiers to
their deaths in a flat on the Antrim Road, including as many details as possible.[17]
Seán Boyne describes how the staff of the paper itself intentionally tapped into
something new within Irish readers and worked to carve out this niche:

> Frequently, we chose NOT to join in the consensus dictated by other
> journalists as to what was a good story. It was often a consensus that
> our readers did NOT share. We decided it would be better to do our
> own thing and to follow our own instincts. Other newspapers sent their
> reporters to press conferences. We tended to avoid these events, preferring
> to pursue our own leads and ideas.[18]

This choice not to join in the consensus dictated by other publications brought
its own difficulties, and the paper often found itself in the dock. In September
1975 it published a front-page article headlined 'Find this evil man', in which it
printed a photograph of a man that it described as being a major organizer of
prostitution in Dublin.[19] When the individual sought (unsuccessfully) a high
court injunction to prevent the publication of further stories about him, the
paper admitted that it had 'published extremely defamatory statements' about
the individual and that it 'wished to publish more extremely defamatory statements' as it could 'justify these statements to the hilt'.[20] The paper's lawyer,
Noel Peart, declared that the paper was highlighting 'a matter of great public
importance' that had previously been invisible.[21]

---

13 Horgan, *Irish media*, p. 109. The *SW* cost 6p, while its competitors cost 5p. **14** *IT*, 20 Oct.
1976. **15** *IT*, 31 Aug. 1977. **16** *IT*, 30 May 1981. **17** *SW*, 25 Mar. 1973. **18** *40 years of splashes*, p.
2. **19** *SW*, 21 Sept. 1975. **20** *IT*, 14 Oct. 1975; *SW*, 19 Oct. 1975. **21** *IT*, 14 Oct. 1975.

Sometimes, however, the paper pushed the boundaries too far. In July 1976, editor Joe Kennedy and journalist Eamon McCann were fined £600 and £300, respectively, for contempt of court arising from its reportage of a child custody case that had been heard in the high court and the supreme court. The case had been held *in camera* but, under the headline 'Tug-of-love children involved in tennis-style battle', replete with a photograph of the children, the paper presented the mother's account of the case and declared that the court system and the society it supported were 'hypocritical about motherhood, morality and the family'.[22] This, the supreme court declared, amounted to 'a gross scandalisation of the court'. Chief Justice Tom O'Higgins declared that the paper:

> bore on its face at least the stamp of recklessness ... The aspersions cast on this court and on the administration of justice in it, have not been and could not be, justified. Had the fullest possible apology not been tendered, this court would have felt compelled to visit on these offenders a substantial sentence of imprisonment, both as a punishment and a deterrent.[23]

However, the *Sunday World* was not deterred and continued to challenge beliefs and systems by exposing what was happening at all levels within Irish society. In November 1976 it was back in the high court to successfully fight injunctions from two Dublin 'health centres' that it intended to expose as brothels.[24]

In 1977 Kevin Marron replaced Joe Kennedy as editor and, in a talk to the Publicity Club of Ireland, defined the paper's approach as 'enterprise journalism':

> It didn't wait for things to happen. It made them happen. It goes out there and turns over a few stones and says 'Look what we've found'. It is a time-consuming, expensive, and highly dangerous type of journalism and could teach one an awful lot about our tangled legal system.

Irish newspapers were, he argued, 'snobbish and took themselves far too seriously'. In contrast, the *Sunday World* sought to 'stimulate and entertain [in the] era of gossip journalism'.[25] Shortly afterwards, Marron's deputy editor, Tony Fitzpatrick, left to establish the *Sunday Journal* and was replaced by Colin McClelland, a Belfast reporter who had worked for several music magazines and, later, the Belfast newspaper the *Sunday News*.

22 *IT*, 8 July 1976.   23 *IT*, 26 June & 8 July 1976.   24 *IT*, 18 Nov. 1976; see *SW*, 7 & 21 Nov. 1976.   25 *IT*, 30 Sept. 1977.

McClelland had arrived as chief sub-editor two years previously, having been tipped off about a vacancy by his fellow Belfast-man Sam Smyth. McClelland would, from 1981, edit the paper after Marron retired due to illness. It was under McClelland that the *Sunday World* began to give sustained attention to the areas of crime and law and order. As McClelland recalled:

> Well, the law and order campaign which we got involved with … we thought it was something which was becoming a big worry to the ordinary citizen – that they were just getting scared shitless of going to bed at night in case someone would come along and steal their bed. And drug pushing was just starting to raise its ugly head. And there was crime in the streets. And it seemed to us very few people were saying anything. So we started a law and order campaign and we started to report more diligently on court cases that involved criminals and we did editorials on the legislation that was available to penalise law-breakers. We reckoned that it was a major concern for most of our readers.[26]

But such coverage brought many risks:

> In the middle of the mixture of sex and sport, you have to put in what was always our forte, heavy investigative reporting. We would go out and find the evil men, the drug dealers, the criminals, the guys who were pulling cons, fraud. That was always the *Sunday World*'s big stick. The libel laws have forced us to pull in our horns. We have been punished severely in the libel courts – many times, I would argue, unfairly. Unless you believe what you wrote was absolutely right, you don't go into the High Court with all its costs … We have paid out an awful lot of money. Our teeth have been drawn in going after the criminals. There comes a point in a commercially-driven newspaper like the *Sunday World* where you have to say we can't do this to the same extent any more.[27]

But despite the risks, the arrival of the *Sunday World* changed the game when it came to print media. McClelland and those who went before him (Kennedy and Marron) pioneered a new approach in which they endeavoured to provide the reader with what they thought they wanted, instead of what they needed to analyse what was happening around them. McClelland claims this was a lesson he had learned early in his career and brought with him to the *Sunday World*: 'So,

---

26 *HP*, 21 Sept. 1984, p. 9.   27 Ivor Kenny, 'Colin McClelland – The *Sunday World*' in *Talking to ourselves: conversations with editors of the Irish news media* (Galway, 1994), pp 342–60 at p. 356.

my first lesson was: find your marketplace, understand who it is you are writing for.'[28] The *Sunday World* and its staff made no secret of their non-conformative editorial ethos. In fact, it would appear as one of the traits they most celebrated. In one interview, McClelland claimed that breaking boundaries was one of the reasons the work was so appealing:

> The excitement of working on the paper came from the fact it was colour and it was iconoclastic – it was upsetting all the sacred cows of that time. It introduced an awful lot of things that hitherto had been unthinkable. It became the brand leader, the great paper of the 70s and 80s.[29]

While the *Sunday World* acted on converting the unthinkable into action, this new bold, unapologetic approach to Irish journalism functioned as both a stick and a carrot, paving the way for other publications and challenging, even antagonizing previously conservative, powerful, authoritative institutions.

The maverick status of the publication and its instant success did not go unnoticed and, according to McClelland, it was not long before contemporaries began to copy elements of the *Sunday World*'s format and style. As he observed, 'With the possible exception of the *Irish Times*, every national newspaper in Ireland has stolen some of the *Sunday World*'s magic.' McClelland was more than happy to take the credit for this shift of vision and approach in Irish journalistic forums – which was significantly at odds with the de Valerian vision of what a newspaper should be in the context of developing cultural currency and preserving conservative societal structures. He particularly acknowledges the influence the *Sunday World* had on the *Sunday Independent*, an influence that is still tangible in its current iteration:

> The *Sunday Independent* is the *Sunday World* in a pinstripe suit. That's an over simplification and, of course, they do many things we would never do, but into their mix they have skilfully fed the sexual content of the *Sunday World*. They have also fed in the gossip format and the controversy they did not have previously.[30]

Editors who paid no heed to the seismic changes happening around them did so at their peril; according to McClelland, 'to ignore the *Sunday World* would have been bad business and bad journalism'.[31] In McClelland's eyes, the paper had an advantage over other papers that were in the business of providing similar content, but which were not up front about their motives:

28 Ibid., p. 344.   29 Ibid., p. 353.   30 Ibid.   31 Ibid., p. 354.

Where we score over other papers is we don't pretend to do anything else – we don't say this is a feature about lingerie or about holiday swim-wear. We simply say: here is a picture of a pretty girl, we think she looks smashing.[32]

The *Sunday World* was comfortable in its coverage and content and an inexplicable synergy between reader and paper had been created through its unapologetic, brazen approach. McClelland felt the reader had altered to fit the paper, rather than the other way around. He also believed, rightly or wrongly, that there was a level of acceptance now for this type of journalism:

People have got over the idea of taking the *Sunday World* seriously. They don't say any more that you don't buy the *Sunday World* because it's sexist. They accept the *Sunday World* the way it's presented to them.[33]

One person who took the *Sunday World* very seriously was the majority share-holder of Independent Newspapers, Tony O'Reilly. The *Sunday World* had effectively appeared out of nowhere, had been a huge success, and had pushed the *Sunday Independent* from second to third place in the circulation stakes – with the knock-on effects this would have on advertising rates. It was only a matter of time before O'Reilly, who had acquired Independent Newspapers in 1973, made an offer. By 1976 Hugh McLaughlin wanted to cash in his investment in the paper and in 1978 he and Tom Butler sold their shares (58 per cent of the paper) to Independent Newspapers. While McGuinness initially retained his shareholding, Independent Newspapers completed the acquisition in 1983.[34] By the following year, the *Sunday World* was contributing £1 million per annum to the profits of Independent Newspapers and was a significant cash generator for the group.[35]

POLITICS AND THE NORTH

Newspapers, like theatre and art, reflect society. But newspapers, through report-age, op-eds and letters from the public, are expected to reflect society in a more linear way than their artistic parallels. For many decades there had been some-thing of a 'special relationship' between press and politics, with the Irish Press Group being supportive of Fianna Fáil and Independent Newspapers being sup-portive of Fine Gael. It was into this duality that, in the words of John Bowman,

32 Ibid., p. 355.   33 Ibid., p. 356.   34 Kenny, 'Gerry McGuinness', pp. 210–11.   35 Horgan, *Irish media*, pp 109–10.

Figure 7: The front page of the *Sunday World* on 21 September 1975.

the 'largely apolitical' *Sunday World* appeared.[36] Other commentators questioned the 'apolitical' nature of the paper; John Waters, for example, noted that the paper's two main proprietors, Hugh McLaughlin and Gerry McGuinness, were 'close confidants of Charlie Haughey – if they could do anything in their newspaper to help him out, so much the better'.[37] Indeed, McGuinness was Haughey's next-door neighbour and a regular visitor to his home.[38]

For the most part, however, the paper took a light-hearted approach to politics – an early edition posed the question 'Who's the sexiest man in the cabinet?' – with its two-page spread awarding the honours jointly to Garret FitzGerald and Justin Keating.[39] When, in the early hours of Sunday 17 November 1974, President Erskine Childers suddenly passed away, the paper had already begun its print run and a crucial decision needed to be made. As remembered by Seán Boyle:

> This was one news story we could not ignore – or could we? The *Sunday World* editorial bosses of the day were faced with a tough decision. They could stop the presses and put up a new lead story. Due to the technical limitations that would mean missing delivery deadlines and losing out on sales. Or they could think the unthinkable and just ignore the story. In the end, that's what they did. Rival journalists were outraged. How dare we not cover this big story, it was an insult to the Presidency, etc. But the readers didn't seem to bat an eyelid, and sales were up the following weekend.[40]

The lead story in that week's paper centred on a Garda sergeant who had been victimized and harassed after a raid on a west Cork pub, where a prominent politician had been caught drinking after hours. This type of story, according to Boyle, 'was the kind of injustice that happened from time to time in Ireland and that was traditionally shoved under the carpet'. It was also the type of story that 'helped to establish the reputation of the *Sunday World* as a newspaper that was prepared to fight for the small man against the establishment'.[41] Other coverage that made a mark included the 'Pub Spy' feature, which reviewed public houses and 'did more than anyone has realized to improve hygiene, conditions and service in Irish bars', and a campaign against rogue builders that prompted government intervention.[42]

The Northern Troubles also loomed large in the paper's news agenda, with several of the paper's prominent journalists, including Eamon McCann, Sam Smyth and Colin McClelland, coming from the North. Interviews with leading

36 *IT*, 28 Dec. 1973.   37 *HP*, 21 Sept. 1984, p. 7.   38 Kenny, 'Gerry McGuinness', p. 217.   39 *SW*, 15 Apr. 1973.   40 *40 years of splashes*, p. 2.   41 Ibid.   42 Ibid.

members of the republican movement were common at a time when the Section 31 broadcasting ban meant republicans could not be interviewed on radio or television programmes. The paper also regularly featured interviews and stories with a human element on leading republican figures, which other papers consciously avoided. On one occasion it devoted a full-page photo spread to the wedding in Dundalk of Long Kesh escapee Francie McGuigan, in which IRA chief of staff Seán Mac Stiofáin, himself not long released from incarceration, posed with the happy couple.[43] On another occasion, after loyalist paramilitaries shot and injured Bernadette McAliskey, it was to the *Sunday World* that she gave her first interview while recovering from her injuries.[44]

But reporting the Troubles was dangerous. Before moving to Dublin, Colin McClelland had worked with Jim Campbell, then news editor of the *Sunday News*, and recalled the great, though dangerous, training he received:

> Jim sent me to the worst places in Belfast at the worst times to do the worst stories. He'd send me to Artillery Flats where neither the RUC nor the British Army could enter because the Provos had the place locked up. He'd tell me to go up to the 13th floor to talk to the people about why the lifts were broken and they could not get their prams down. I had to go in cold, nobody to ask for, my only protection was my press card. I found the best time to do it was early in the morning because all the guys who had been out rioting the night before were asleep.[45]

In later years, while editor of the *Sunday World*, McClelland appointed Campbell as the paper's Northern editor because of his reputation for being 'a ferociously good newsman, intrusive and fearless'.[46] The danger inherent in covering the Troubles was brought home to McClelland and Campbell in May 1984 when Campbell was shot by loyalist group, the Ulster Volunteer Force (UVF), for his reporting on a UVF gunman nicknamed 'The Jackal'.[47]

The attack was roundly condemned by journalists, who noted that Campbell's fearless reporting was the reason he was targeted. It was openly acknowledged that his work stood out from the pack, as 'the majority of Belfast journalists failed to investigate and report on dangerous areas, as he had done'.[48] Campbell later returned to work with a bullet in his spine. While McClelland made it clear that he need not carry on the work he had been doing in relation to the paramilitaries, Campbell persisted in his investigations. In October 1984 loyalist paramilitaries placed a bomb (which did not detonate) in the paper's Belfast

43 *HP*, 21 Sept. 1984, p. 8. 44 *40 years of splashes*, p. 2. 45 Kenny, 'Colin McClelland', p. 348. 46 Ibid., p. 357. 47 *IT*, 19 May 1984. 48 *IT*, 24 May 1984.

office. Having moved to Donegal, Campbell continued to write for the paper, the Northern edition of which sold 87,000 copies a week.[49] The Campbell shooting had tragic resonances many years later when another *Sunday World* reporter in Belfast, Martin O'Hagan, was killed by loyalists in September 2001.

THE MALE GAZE

For all its innovation, some aspects of the *Sunday World* require a more sustained critique, most particularly its approach to covering women. For the very most part, Sunday newspapers, up to recent times, were gendered publications, written mostly by men for men, with some minor roles for women, mostly revolving around fashion and beauty. In many ways, the *Sunday World* added to this marginalization of women through its objectification and framing of females as sexualized entities to be admired, though it also promoted frank discussions of issues sexual, which was a novel departure for the Irish print industry.

Somewhat amusingly, its use of photographs of near-nude models led to a successful libel action against the paper. In 1974 one reader, Liam O'Dwyer, sued the paper after it published defamatory letters from other readers in response to his own letter. O'Dwyer had written to the paper to complain about its use of 'a semi-nude picture of a girl'. He had enquired whether the aim of such images was to help 'the paper's sales in Christian Ireland' and declared that 'whoever chose the picture had the sexiest mind in Ireland and should be on the dole'. The paper subsequently published a letter from one 'Fr O'Doherty', which declared that O'Dwyer 'suffered from a form of sexual aberration [and] was the type of individual who specialised in the lowest type of graffiti found on lavatory walls'. During the subsequent hearing, while no such person as 'Fr O'Doherty' could be found, the paper claimed the letter was fair comment and that it could not be expected to authenticate every letter it received. The court awarded O'Dwyer damages of £500.[50] The following year, the paper's images of women again prompted protests. This time posters featuring a model with the words 'Are you getting it every Sunday?' were pasted over with smaller posters emblazoned with the words 'These ads degrade women'.[51]

In a similar vein, sometimes the paper's reportage prompted protests. In February 1984, in a story headlined 'Sexy high jinks in CIÉ', the paper announced that 'attractive bus conductresses' were at the centre of a 'sex shocker' within the company. The report claimed that three unnamed inspectors were having affairs with female conductors, and that one of the women was 'using her body' in the hope of securing promotion.[52] The story prompted a picket at the paper's office

49 *IT*, 14 Apr. 1987.   **50** *IT*, 1 Mar. 1974.   **51** *SW*, 6 July 1975.

by CIÉ workers, who also refused to handle other titles from Independent Newspapers, thus disrupting the distribution of the *Irish Independent* and *Evening Herald*.[53] At that year's annual meeting of Independent Newspapers, one share-holder criticized what he referred to as a 'scurrilous and cheap attack on the sexual morality of an easily identifiable group of women' and another declared that it looked as if the profitability of the company relied 'largely on the sexy presentation of the *Sunday World*'.[54]

There was, however, a dichotomy between the paper's use of cover girls and its frank personal advice column. The column ('Dear Linda') announced its intention to help readers with personal problems. It marked a radical departure – both in terms of the advice given and the frankness with which it was deliv-ered – and contrasted sharply with the column by the *Sunday Press*' agony aunt, Angela MacNamara, whose advice 'was strongly influenced by the Catholic dis-course governing sexuality that emanated from the Vatican'.[55]

But there was no getting away from the paper's gendered approach – a criti-cism rejected by long-time editor Colin McClelland, when he noted that:

> Our readers like to see pictures of pretty girls. If market research showed that people liked to see pictures of baby kangaroos instead of girls, we'd probably run a lot of pictures of baby kangaroos. Market research shows that people don't like looking at pictures of naked men, because the naked male is not a particularly attractive sight … If we felt that there was a market out there – if there was people who wanted to see pictures of men in bathing trunks, we would probably put it in, yeah. I have no feeling that it's taboo or it can't be done. If that's what the people want, that's what the people get.[56]

However, when invited to appear before the Oireachtas Committee on Women's Rights to discuss the portrayal of women in the media, McClelland, alone of all the Sunday editors so invited, declined to appear and instead wrote to state that he 'had no wish to sit in a room and be cross-examined by anyone, even by such an august body as the joint committee on women's rights'. He did, how-ever, take issue with what he viewed as the committee's position that 'there is no difference between men and women':

> My own view is that there is a considerable difference between men and women. They look different for a start, and I firmly believe that a tractor

52 *SW*, 26 Feb. 1984.   53 *IT*, 29 Feb. & 3 Mar. 1984.   54 *IT*, 29 Mar. 1984.   55 Paul Ryan, 'Asking Angela: discourses about sexuality in an Irish problem page, 1963–80' in *Journal of the History of Sexuality*, 19:2 (2010), 317–39 at 319.   56 *HP*, 21 Sept. 1985, p. 10.

adorned by a girl in a bikini is infinitely more pleasing to the human eye than the same tractor adorned by a man in Y-fronts. To me, that's the way God planned it.[57]

This response was criticized by members of the committee as 'appalling, insulting, impertinent and patronizing'. The committee's chairperson, Máire Geoghegan Quinn, Ireland's second female member of Dáil Éireann following Countess Markievicz, observed that the committee had the power to direct people to appear before it. The contents of McClelland's letter were described by Madeleine Taylor-Quinn TD as a continuation of the sexism present in the *Sunday World.* The committee agreed unanimously to attach the letter to the committee's final report as evidence of the attitudes towards women in the media. It was also noted that McClelland's attitude was in contrast with that of his contemporaries who had appeared before the committee.[58]

But such attitudes towards women were not exclusive to the pages of the *Sunday World.* In his *Irish Times* column 'Sounding Off', John Healy suggested that McClelland, editor of 'the tit-and-tickle, weekend biggie' was absolutely right to 'stay at his desk and let our legislators go fish':

> I'd do the same myself and may have to yet if that shower of publicity-seekers decide that writers of political comment should be summoned to explain themselves and their writings before their Dáil betters. The answer from me will be short and sharp and brutally blunt. Two words will about cover it ... As far as I am concerned, it's 'up yours' to any member of that committee wishing to question me on my operation. Maura Geoghegan-Quinn [*sic*] can bleat about insults to the Oireachtas and the rest: I won't lose one minute's sleep of nights [*sic*].[59]

Among those who may have been losing sleep over the portrayal of women in the press and its side effects on society as a whole was the minister for women's affairs, Nuala Fennell. Minister Fennell, speaking at a seminar titled 'Focus on Women' in December 1985, referenced three women who had been murdered in the recent past and linked the portrayal of women as sex objects with their treatment as victims of rape and acts of physical violence. She could not, she noted, 'stress strongly enough the degree of association there was between the image of women as being there for sexual stimulation, and their treatment in every area of life'. She highlighted the *Sunday World* in particular: 'And I single out one Sunday newspaper, the *Sunday World*, as the most pernicious influence in

57 *IT*, 18 July 1985.   58 *IT*, 18 July 1985.   59 *IT*, 22 July 1985.

this regard.'[60] Given that the paper was selling 369,833 copies a week, its circulation, if not its influence, was substantial.[61] All this was taking place at a time when the feminine voice was gradually gaining strength and would culminate in the election of Mary Robinson as president in 1990. In an ironic twist, the paper's discourse, while divisive and very provocative, did serve some purpose in creating a forum of sorts to highlight women's issues, albeit in an often questionable manner. The old social structures in Irish society had ensured that women were not the face of modern twentieth-century Ireland but were more the domestic foundations holding it together. However, the *Sunday World*'s challenging of the old value system that had prevailed for over sixty years helped in ensuring that woman were addressed as political rather than domestic beings. Eventually, even the paper changed: it dropped its front-page cover girl one year after Mary Robinson's election.[62]

DEFYING AUTHORITY

So what contribution has the *Sunday World* made to Irish journalism or Sunday journalism? There is no doubt that its determination to 'discover hypocrisy or corruption [and] expose it' ensured that it broached taboo topics and challenged the norms of Irish society from its first edition. Context is key; due partly to the era in which it first appeared, the *Sunday World*'s reportage often became the news as it reflected a changing Ireland, most particularly the seismic changes in the values of Irish society – a society that was gradually leaving behind the de Valerian era of protectionism, censorship and a strict Catholic sensibility and embracing instead the modern world, with all the complexity – morally, culturally and socially – that that entailed. The era in which the *Sunday World* published its first edition is very different to that which pertains now. In that context it had a role to play in the ventilation of controversial views and the exposure of many hidden aspects of Irish life. At various points its success relied on the guiding principle of defying the authorities of the time. In fact, it did not just report on the emerging cracks; it broadened the chasm, exposing many scandals and events that moulded the changing face of modern Ireland. The view of women that it conveyed remains controversial, and this type of journalism, which highlights the role of women as objects, is the subject of ongoing debate. More than anything else, the *Sunday World* paved the way for a new system of reportage – it opened a window for the Irish Sunday reading public into a new and exciting, albeit sometimes terrifying, world.

60 *IT*, 2 Dec. 1985.   61 *IT*, 25 Mar. 1988.   62 *IT*, 26 Oct. 1991.

7 / The short and troubled life of the *Sunday Journal*

MARY MULDOWNEY

> What had started with some promise as a Sunday farming paper and gone
> adrift had then, under the ownership of motor insurance boss Joe Moore,
> become a mediocre fifth national Sunday paper, never likely to survive in
> a market where it clearly had no place.[1]

This damning indictment of the quality of the *Sunday Journal* was written in
1983, roughly one year after the newspaper was shut down because it had accumulated significant losses and no buyer could be found for it. The first issue
of the *Sunday Journal* was published on 2 March 1980 and its final closure was
announced on 23 June 1982. So, what happened to the early promise? In this
chapter, some memories of former *Sunday Journal* editorial staff are supplemented by contemporary analysis from other journalists in an effort to answer
that question.[2] When it was launched, the paper had a small team of very well
qualified and experienced journalists who were enthusiastic for the new project,
which was aimed at the farming community and agribusiness. The visual appeal
of its colour tabloid format was enhanced by the high standard of its content.
Nevertheless, in the period leading up to its demise, the *Sunday Journal* was
shown to have abandoned its original agricultural focus to such an extent that
one critic, referring to its political content, observed that 'it could nearly have
been written by Fianna Fáil party headquarters'.[3]

CREATING THE TEAM

The original inspiration for the *Sunday Journal* came from former deputy editor of the *Sunday World*, Tony Fitzpatrick. He was one of the co-founders
of Aesthetic Enterprises, the publishing company that would produce the

1 Francis Xavier Carty, *Elections '82: what the papers said: an analysis of press coverage of the two 1982 general
elections in the Republic of Ireland* (Dublin, 1983), p. 28.   2 Interviews were conducted with two editors
of the *Sunday Journal*, the editor of the 'Mainly for Women' pages and an agribusiness specialist. It did
not prove possible to arrange an interview with the managing editor.   3 *EH*, 12 Sept. 1983. The critic
was Francis Xavier Carty; Carty, *Elections '82*, p. 8.

new paper. Financing came from Donegal man Frank McCrossan and British businessman Charles de Selincourt, both based in London. According to an article in the *Irish Times* in December 1979, twenty-seven people were to be employed and Aengus Fanning and Michael Miley would be joint editors.[4] The budget was £350,000 for the first year and £105,000 to be spent between December 1979 and end of February 1980; £35,000 of this would be spent on promotion. Fitzpatrick had a holding of 30 per cent of the company shares and McCrossan and de Selincourt initially controlled the balance. However, McCrossan bought out de Selincourt within months of the launch of the paper.[5]

Tony Fitzpatrick's first task as managing editor was to recruit the journalists who would write for the paper. Michael Miley recalled how he came to be the first editor:

> In the autumn of that year ... I got a call from a friend of mind, who was a PR guru. He said there was a guy called Tony Fitzpatrick looking to talk to me and there was a great opportunity to go in as the editor of a new Sunday newspaper. It turned out that they had proposed and started talking to two of us at the same time, Aengus Fanning and myself, to become joint editors. I met Fanning and I met Fitzpatrick and we agreed. He offered very good terms and of course, Fanning offered his notice to the *Independent* – I think they had a going away party for him and then he decided no. So, I finished up finding myself the sole editor, which at the time kind of pleased me because I thought I'll either sink or swim on my own.[6]

Willie Kealy was working for the Press Group as an agricultural correspondent when he was approached by Tony Fitzpatrick to join the new title. He was told that the *Sunday Journal* was going to be an 'agricultural paper'. He felt it had the potential for success, even though the *Irish Farmers Journal*, which was published on Thursdays, dominated that market:

4 *IT*, 6 Dec. 1979. The editorial titles within the paper were not as clear as at other papers. Fitzpatrick held titles such as managing editor, editorial director and editor in chief, and internally those responsible for producing the paper were referred to as deputy editors but, externally were referred to as the paper's editors. For the sake of consistency, within this chapter, those responsible for producing the paper are referred to as editors.   5 *IP*, 4 July 1980, p. 4; interview with Willie Kealy (editor, Mar. 1980–June 1982), 11 Jan. 2018; interview with Michael Miley (editor, Mar.–Aug. 1980), 8 Feb. 2018.   6 Miley interview; Aengus Fanning (1942–2012) was editor of the *Sunday Independent* from 1984 until his death. He was the farming editor of the *Sunday Independent* when Tony Fitzpatrick tried to recruit him for the *Sunday Journal*.

It was a very good market, there was plenty of advertising in that area and there was plenty of money in agriculture. This was 1980 so the financial benefits of joining the EEC in 1973 were still there, especially in agriculture. I think the *Farmers Journal* at the time was selling about 74,000 copies a week and the *Sunday Journal*, when it started up, was selling about 64,000 so it came quite near to matching them; they did quite well.[7]

Several other journalists were approached to join the team because Michael Miley knew them 'from the circuit'. Jim Aughney was working for *Business & Finance* magazine, reporting on agribusiness affairs, when he was asked if he would like to go 'down to Parliament Street', where the paper's city-centre premises were located. He knew it was a risk because it was a new venture and he had just taken on a mortgage. He remembered meeting Tony Fitzpatrick and being reassured by him:

He was a very suave guy. He had a sort of cast in one eye which made him sort of piratical in appearance, but he was quite a slim, good-looking guy and he was quite dapper. So, he said there was plenty of money to sustain this and all that kind of thing, so I joined up.[8]

Judith Elmes came on board through Fitzpatrick's network. He had been her news editor at the *Sunday World* and she was happy to follow him to the *Sunday Journal* as women's editor. She described him as a 'very appreciative boss', who allowed people to make their own decisions:

It was going to be a 'respectable' tabloid for the farming community, a Sunday tabloid. There were journalists there whom I'd never met before but were great fun to work with, to look after the ag [agricultural] end of things on the paper. I was purely on the women's pages. We obviously had weekly editorial meetings to decide who was doing what and that sort of thing, but my remit was very definitely the women's pages, although on occasion the women's pages would have a slightly agricultural slant.[9]

She does not recall being concerned about the financial security of the paper and was more interested in the challenge presented by being the women's editor, which was a more responsible role than she had played previously, where she

7 Kealy interview. There also existed the monthly agricultural magazine the *Farmer*. It was published between March 1979 and April 1982, by Belenos Publications, owner of *Business & Finance* magazine.   8 Interview with Jim Aughney, 22 Jan. 2018.   9 Interview with Judith Elmes, 19 Feb. 2018.

had worked on news and features without a specific portfolio. Her job as editor of the 'Mainly for Women' pages included writing a weekly column in which she offered her views on 'whatever the news stories were at the time'.

The submission deadline for the Sunday paper was Wednesday evening because several days were needed to plan the layout, given the technology available at the time.[10] Stories were produced on manual typewriters and Judith Elmes recalled that she would push back the typewriter when she had completed an article, remove her copy from it and proofread it herself before passing it on to the layout designer:

> Did it go past Willie for approval? I don't think it went past Willie or Michael. I think it was just they trusted me. It was that open a situation if you like. I suppose that people were less litigious anyway. I wasn't actually going to write anything they would sue me for because it was more my personal comments on issues. So that wasn't generally a problem. The guy who was the designer of my section and for a lot of the paper was Colm McGinty [later] editor of the *Sunday World*.[11]

Colm McGinty edited the entertainment pages as well as doing the layout and worked closely with photographer Dave Cullen. Judith Elmes was impressed by the look of the paper, which had 'plenty of light and space and the colour was good'. Dave Cullen did all the fashion pictures for the paper:

> He and Colm would very often come up with their own ideas, very often from a design viewpoint rather than what the actual fashion was. It was all about making it eye-catching and attractive to look at and they did between them, very much so.[12]

Inspiration for the content of the women's pages might come from book launches or film reviews but Elmes' preference was to take an issue that was currently in the news, find people who were in similar situations, 'talking to them and letting them have their say'. The 'Mainly for Women' pages featured Carmel Redmond as the 'Agony Aunt'. She had been a nun with an English order, living in Ireland, and she was also a trained counsellor. Elmes explained that because the paper never had a huge circulation, the number of letters every week was probably not huge and the 'whole bag' would probably have gone to Carmel Redmond to select what to respond to in print:

10 The paper was printed by Dublin printing firm Richview, Browne & Nolan.   11 Elmes interview.   12 Ibid.

As far as I recall, Carmel was handed the letters that came in and then she would choose them. I was also thinking, when you were asking about her, did I have to run her [appointment] past Willie or Michael or Tony. I think maybe I just said, well I've found somebody who is qualified, and they were fine.[13]

The letters to Carmel Redmond offer an insight into some of the social attitudes and problems of the time. There were regular appeals for advice from people who had concerns about such issues as their sexuality; difficulties with overly controlling parents, especially mothers; women who felt trapped in situations where a mother-in-law was still in residence on the family farm; and men and women who were very conscious of the social scrutiny that they felt was prevalent in small rural communities.

Michael Miley also recruited Willie Ryan, a friend of his who was working with the *Farmers Journal* at the time:

He was very ill at the time and I went to see him in hospital and I said, 'By the way, how are you fixed for a change of direction?' They didn't know what was wrong with him and he said, 'No problem, if I ever get out of here.' There was no more discussion and he rang me from a coin box, I think it was in James's Hospital, a week later and said okay. They'd found out he had some virus, whatever the problem was, and he reckoned he'd be out in two or three weeks. I said, 'You'd better give notice' and he said he'd already given notice to the *Farmers Journal*.[14]

Ryan was one of the journalists who stayed with the *Sunday Journal* until it closed in 1982. His weekly column on the political scene in Ireland was often irreverent and criticized political figures from all parties, with his most pointed comments tending to be reserved for the government of the time.

Other members of the *Sunday Journal* team included Liam Nolan, who became sports editor. He had previously worked with RTÉ's features department before becoming active in sports documentaries. Teresa O'Connor came from the *Farmers Journal* to cover news stories and wrote features on social issues. She had a regular column entitled 'A girl with a mind of her own'. In the first six months particularly, there were many articles in the paper that were sympathetic to the plight of marginalized groups such as single mothers, gay men whose families were unaware of their sexuality and others who were victimized by Ireland's illiberal views on social issues. These articles had no

13 Ibid.   14 Miley interview.

byline but the interviewees thought that Teresa O'Connor would have written them.

Brian Byrne wrote a column called 'Brian Byrne goes down your way to …' in which he presented commentary on villages and towns, with some local history, all illustrated by photographs that he took himself. His visits were not confined to rural areas and there were features on villages that had become part of a conurbation, such as Clondalkin and Swords in the Dublin area. There were other regular columns about angling and gardening and a weekly piece written by Fr Colm Kilcoyne, entitled 'In my view'. Frank Kelly wrote a regular column that seemed to be based on his character, Gobnait Ó Lúnasa who was extremely popular in the early 1980s.[15] In the paper's early issues, the national and local politics of the day were prominently featured. Michael Miley remembered some of the contributors:

> We had some very good political stuff in it. Almost all of it written by outside people. Darach MacDonald used to do some very good profiles. We had some very good political stuff, very 'insider' political people who knew what was going on in politics.[16]

These 'insiders' made their contributions anonymously for a number of reasons – but Miley knew them and he had total confidence in their expertise.

GETTING STARTED

The editorial in the first issue of the *Sunday Journal* made the intention to appeal to a farming readership very clear, with an unequivocal rejection of the government's budget proposal to introduce a new tax on farmers. The measure had come in the wake of the huge PAYE workers' protests against inequity in the taxation system, which had been organized by trade unions in the previous year:

> Last year there was the iniquitous two per cent levy. Now farmers are to have their own special resource tax, in case their income tax returns aren't sufficiently high to placate the Revenue Commissioners and the non-farming lobbies. It seems that in achieving equity, the old maxim of some being more equal than others still applies. And it is Irish farmers who have come out as less than equal.[17]

---

15 Gobnait Ó Lúnasa was one of the many characters created for radio and television by Frank Kelly (1938–2016), who was an actor, comedian and satirist.   16 Miley interview.   17 *SJ*, 2 Mar. 1980.

Jim Aughney remembered how some of his own early stories had come into being:

> Before I joined up, I had planned to go to England to a friend's wedding or something and on the way, I rang up Bord Bainne's subsidiary, Adams Foods in the UK and I got an interview with this guy out in the middle of England and found my way to him and all that. Of course, once I went in to the *Sunday Journal* I said to myself, 'Here's a 1,500-word article I've written on Bord Bainne.' Nobody had really written anything about this and it was a bit of an exclusive and all that.[18]

Teresa O'Connor wrote a hard-hitting article about a Garda probe into corruption in the administration of an agricultural scholarship in Cork where the Fraud Squad was involved in investigating the allocation of the scholarship funds by the Cork County Agricultural Committee.[19] O'Connor also wrote regular stories on agribusiness and issues of interest to the farming community, as well as covering other national news, especially in the political arena.

The front page of the 6 April 1980 issue was dominated by Willie Kealy's story about RTÉ's *Late Late Show* of 29 March, which featured an 'encounter' between farmers and urban dwellers. In the aftermath of the show, the recently elected Irish Farmers' Association (IFA) president, Donal Cashman, complained that the show had been a set-up and farmers were caricatured, rather than enabling a better mutual understanding between city and country people. He was criticized by many IFA branches throughout the country for taking part in the programme, although some branches apparently expressed the view that he had done the right thing by not responding to baiting by some of the *Late Late Show* audience.[20] The *Sunday Journal* editorial expressed concern about the 'fear and ignorance' on both sides in the rift between urban and rural communities. The story, which was spread over several pages, covered the anger that emanated from farming bodies in the aftermath of the show, but also conceded that the PAYE workers in the audience had justification for their resentment of the farmers:

> Urban people think that every farmer drives a Mercedes, makes a fortune and pays no tax. Farmers think the urbanites are lazy, molly-coddled and rampant socialists out to nationalise their land. Neither image is a true one. Farmers are now paying tax in the same way as everyone else,

18 Aughney interview.   **19** *SJ*, 16 Mar. 1980.   **20** *II*, 1 Apr. 1980; *IFJ*, 19 Apr. 1980; *EH*, 26 Apr. 1980.

although for years the way in which farmers were taxed was grossly unjust for the rest of the community.[21]

Michael Miley observed that the strength of the *Sunday Journal* team came from their network of contacts, particularly in the agribusiness industry and in farm organizations. These contacts gave them the opportunity to lead with a lot of stories at a time when 'there was a lot of stuff going on' in the agribusiness sector:

> Larry Goodman, at the time, was beginning to build his empire and we broke a couple of stories on companies that he had bought, and he tried to stop us. I remember there was one particular story and I think we put it on the front page, or page three, that he had bought a plant in Bagenalstown in Carlow and it was totally denied that he did it. I had a very good source and we took a chance and went on it. The guy guaranteed me that he would pay the libel costs if we were sued and it turned out that they had an arrangement with the Haughey government that they would launch the following Wednesday and we blew it on the Sunday.[22]

In the lifetime of the *Sunday Journal*, the Irish Farmers Association was politically split down the middle. Willie Kealy remembered that the *Farmers Journal* supported one faction and the *Sunday Journal* backed the other:

> It was no easy thing taking on the *Farmers Journal*. The *Farmers Journal* was a very wealthy entity and it was run by a trust. But really the man who ran it was Paddy O'Keefe, who was one tough cookie and you didn't lightly take on Paddy O'Keefe. Anyway, as it happens it did work for a while and it could have worked if it wasn't for the falling out among the people who had the money.[23]

The politics of the farming sector caused a further problem for the *Sunday Journal* in early July 1980, when Paddy Lane, former president of the IFA, responded to a report by Willie Kealy that he had drawn £30,000 in expenses during his last year in office. Michael Miley used the headline 'What Lane cost the IFA'. There was no suggestion that any criminal behaviour had been involved but Lane denied the allegations and said he had called an independent auditor to examine his expenses. He called a press conference to announce his reaction and said he

21 *SJ*, 6 Apr. 1980.   22 Miley interview.   23 Kealy interview.

would want the auditor's report to be published in full 'to clear his good name'. Willie Kealy recalled that Lane's faction in the IFA would have been backed by the *Farmers Journal*, while the *Sunday Journal* was allied with the 'other side':

> On the one hand there was Paddy Lane and Joe Rea ... On the other side was Donal Cashman from Cork and the chap from Wicklow, Alan Gillis, who became an MEP afterwards for Fine Gael. We were on the side of Cashman and Gillis. Lane was president and then Rea tried to succeed him, but Cashman won.[24]

The *Irish Times* reported that Paddy Lane had issued writs for libel against the *Sunday Journal*, but Michael Miley denied this had happened. In the long run, he felt that being perceived to have attacked Paddy Lane would not have been beneficial for the paper:

> It was early days and it was a great story. It might not have done the *Sunday Journal* any good because at the end of the day, at that stage farmers would, when push came to shove, they would side with their organisation.[25]

Jim Aughney's view was that the IFA was like the GAA in that most members vote for the incumbent office holder's nominee. When the president steps down 'you always vote for the deputy'. He was very surprised when Cashman beat Joe Rea, who was popular in his own right and had what should have been the advantage of having served as deputy to Paddy Lane.

ENTER JOE MOORE AND PMPA

Willie Kealy remembered that everything was going fine for a while until the money that the backers had put up seemed to run out more quickly than they expected:

> I think they agreed to put up more money, or to put up the next tranche of money earlier than they had planned but I think it was underfunded from there on. Then they just fell out with Tony [Fitzpatrick] and Tony fell out with them. I think they decided that they weren't going to put more money into it. So, they wanted Tony out, Tony said, 'I'm not going out, I've got a contract and it's cast-iron.' They said, 'Well okay, we're pulling out and you can keep it. You can have the lot and good luck.'[26]

24 Kealy interview.   25 Miley interview.   26 Kealy interview.

With the withdrawal of the financial backers by the end of June 1980, staff members occupied the premises in Parliament Street and kept everything going. Short-term finance was sourced, which included contributions from staff members. The National Union of Journalists (NUJ) issued a statement saying staff were trying to continue publication because of their confidence in the viability of the newspaper, if it developed as originally envisaged.[27] Jim Aughney remembered that Teresa O'Connor was the first NUJ mother of the chapel for the *Sunday Journal.* The journalists had several meetings about the problems facing the paper and they decided that if the paper stopped production, it would be finished. They got a lot of advice from union members in other publications about the best way to conduct an occupation of the business premises, in order to keep production going:

> I think somebody said if the ESB comes to the door you tell them that you're occupying the premises and it's a trade union action. The ESB did come to cut us off because the bill hadn't been paid and the guys just turned around immediately when we told them what it was. Somebody minded the door to make sure the wrong guys, the heavies didn't come in and the rest of us just worked away. I remember I had interviewed Hely-Hutchinson, who was the chief executive of Guinness, about a month or six weeks earlier and I rang him up and got us an ad. I think I got a thousand quid ... There was one distributor and I think he was accounting for something like 40,000 copies every Sunday. I think he put up some money to get an edition out. I got the ad, things like that happened and we kept it going for a few weeks and then Joe Moore came in.[28]

Judith Elmes was on sit-in duty in Parliament Street, with another member of staff, when the man had a seizure. One of the subs went with the man to hospital when the ambulance arrived, and Judith stayed in the building because of the anxiety about maintaining the security of the occupation. Judith was a member of the NUJ (she has since been awarded a life membership) and she remembers the sense of solidarity among *Sunday Journal* people and their supporters from other chapels:

> I would say there was quite a sense of team about the *Sunday Journal.* Everybody, by and large, liked each other and got on well and we had loads of fun. We were proud of what we were producing, I think. In my

27 *II,* 5 July 1980.   28 Aughney interview.

view, that was my favourite job. I think in all my career I loved the independence there, the freedom I had to write on what I was writing.[29]

The front page of the 6 July 1980 issue carried a prominent statement, signed by Tony Fitzpatrick as editorial director:

> As many of our readers will have heard, we nearly didn't make it this
> week. I am pleased to say that moves to avert a situation which would
> have prevented the *Sunday Journal* being published today proved success-
> ful. This issue has been brought to you through the unselfish efforts
> of a good many people who put the future of the paper before any
> personal considerations. They believe, as do all members of our edito-
> rial, advertising and administrative staff, that to close the *Sunday Journal*
> is unthinkable.[30]

Joe Moore was approached by Tony Fitzpatrick to become the new backer for the *Sunday Journal* and he came on board at the beginning of July 1980. Moore was a former teacher and civil servant and was elected to the national executive of the Private Motorists Protection Association (PMPA) in May 1952, before being made trustee, honorary secretary and honorary treasurer by March 1953.[31] In 1956 his first attempt to establish an insurance company by raising money from PMPA members failed. In 1958 he formed the Private Motorists Provident Society (PMPS), initially to provide a car-damage scheme, then to exploit the lax regulation of provident societies by expanding into advancing car loans in 1961. In the mid-1970s, the PMPA board give Moore total control over all investment decisions. He then embarked on a series of what were in the long term to be loss-making investments, including McBurney's, the McCairns Motor Group and the *Sunday Journal*.[32]

The PMPA buyout of the paper and the accrued debts was not a straight-forward affair. Initially, the original financial backers refused the PMPA's offer. Ella Shanahan reported on the front page of the *Irish Times* that the *Sunday Journal* was in danger of closing that week:

> The reason is a boardroom battle, with the major financial backer – an
> Irish businessman living in Britain – refusing to continue financing the
> publication without getting more control of the week-to-week running of
> the paper. The paper, which is reported to have a circulation of 50,000 and

29 Elmes interview.   30 *SJ*, 6 July 1980.   31 Terry Clavin, 'Moore, Joe' in *Dictionary of Irish biography* (dib.cambridge.org).   32 *IT*, 20 Oct. 1983.

is aimed primarily at the farming community, has so far cost its publishers, Aesthetic Enterprises, £250,000.[33]

Shanahan went on to note that discussions had taken place between some of the paper's directors and representatives of its rival, the *Farmers Journal*, on a possible takeover. But it seemed that Paddy O'Keefe, the chairman of the IFA's Agricultural Trust and editor of the *Farmers Journal*, rejected any idea of taking on the *Sunday Journal* as a going concern. The *Irish Press* reported on a statement from Michael Miley that the *Sunday Journal* had achieved a circulation of 50,000 but it had lost just over £250,000 since it was launched, and advertising had never reached the level expected by the backers. Nevertheless, staff had only learned how bad things were in the few days preceding an application for a liquidator.[34] Two weeks later, the *Irish Independent* reported that the *Sunday Journal* would not be published on the following Sunday, as the staff had decided not to attempt to publish a third issue on their own. In the meantime, the majority shareholders adjourned the meeting of creditors for a week, while awaiting the outcome of developments. Proposing the motion for the adjournment, Victor Currie, who had been appointed chief executive to replace Tony Fitzpatrick, stated that the assets of the company had been frozen, and they would not be further diluted by waiting another week.

Currie also announced that the company did not feel responsible for the debts incurred by the staff in publishing the paper over the previous two weeks. A second offer, which included the PMPA taking on the *Sunday Journal's* liabilities, was accepted. Tony Fitzpatrick would remain as editor and no redundancies were expected, although the twenty-two staff members would be expected to adapt to the more 'urban oriented' approach that was to be introduced. The paper was to be printed by the PMPA print works in Portlaoise. A few weeks later the *Irish Times* reported:

> The legal formalities concerning the purchase of *Sunday Journal* by PMPA Ltd have now been completed. The former directors have resigned, and four new directors have been appointed. Those are Messrs Joe Moore, chairman, Michael J. Dore, Hugh Sheridan and Seamus G. O'Mordha, secretary. Clearance of the transaction under the Monopolies and Mergers Act has been obtained from the Department of Industry and Commerce and Tourism.[35]

Neither Michael Miley nor Willie Kealy was impressed by Joe Moore's plans for the *Sunday Journal*. As Willie Kealy recalled:

33 *IT*, 3 July 1980.   34 *IP*, 4 July 1980.   35 *IT*, 16 Aug. 1980.

> I remember going to a meeting, when he took over, I went over to PMPA headquarters and went in to a boardroom where he was, and he was telling us how great it was going to be. I wondered was he going to put money into it, was he going to invest in it, is he going to promote it or what's he going to do. I said, 'What is your secret? What are you going to use to see sales maintained or increased?' He said, 'We'll use my charisma' ... Great, I thought. We're home and away. We're going to have Joe's charisma and that was going to be it.[36]

Moore did not want the *Sunday Journal* to continue as a 'farming paper'. His intention was to change its focus to general features, with some news but with a strong motoring emphasis. Sean McGlynn, an operations manager in the PMPA, was appointed as a temporary general manager of the paper until the position could be filled on a permanent basis. His remit was to cut the costs of the *Sunday Journal* and keep them down in the future. Willie Kealy remembered McGlynn as a 'nice man' who did not relish his 'axeman' role and whose job would have been made immeasurably more difficult because whatever chance of survival the paper had in its original focus, it was 'madness' to try to compete with the existing weeklies, particularly the *Sunday World*. Judith Elmes believed that the situation was exacerbated because it was never made clear to the potential readership that the paper had widened its brief and that it was no longer primarily for a farming audience. This had an immediate impact on advertising sales:

> That's why I feel that the general public was never made aware of that; such advertising as there was, was aimed differently and people didn't know what they might be buying if they bought it. In the early issues it was all tractors and feeds and results from the marts around the country.[37]

THE 'NEW' *SUNDAY JOURNAL*

The front page of the first edition under the new management, in July 1980, carried a confident message in full colour:

> We're back! ... with a promise that your favourite Sunday newspaper is going to offer you much, much more in the weeks to come: more news, more pictures, more competitions. There will always be so much more to read in the *Sunday Journal* – the family paper you can feel proud to be seen

36 Kealy interview.   37 Elmes interview.

Figure 8: A typical *Sunday Journal* front page, from the edition of 21 June 1981.

with. Our sincere thanks to the many readers who encouraged us with
their letters and phone calls during the last few weeks.[38]

The message also presaged the new editorial approach, which emerged relatively
soon. The paper was being rebranded as a 'family paper' and this was reflected
in the content. As promised, there were increasing numbers of competitions,
accompanied by the introduction of horoscope pages, a children's section edited
by Pat Ingoldsby, a lot more celebrity gossip and lifestyle features. In 1981 an
eight-page motoring supplement was introduced.

The first indications that the changed editorial policy would be a problem
came in September 1980 when it was reported in other papers that Michael
Miley would be resigning as editor.[39] Willie Kealy had written a story about an
internal Fianna Fáil poll that identified significant concern among party members about the impact of Charlie Haughey's leadership on voters. The story,
headed 'A Poll Shock for Charlie', revealed that 'a secret opinion poll carried
out by Charlie Haughey has backfired disastrously ... for the results show his
popularity at such a low ebb that he has kept them from even his most senior
ministers'. It also revealed that most of Fianna Fáil's parliamentary party was
unaware of the poll having been carried out, and that it showed 'a sensational
dissatisfaction among the electorate with Mr Haughey's leadership of the government'.[40] As recalled by Kealy, 'I wrote the story and Tony said it couldn't go
on the front page. It wasn't that Moore spiked it.'[41] Michael Miley remembered
that it was Tony Fitzpatrick who told him to move the story from the front
page. He did not know for sure whether Fitzpatrick had been approached by
Sean McGlynn, acting on Joe Moore's behalf, but he said that given the precari-
ous situation of the paper in the preceding months, and the hardship endured
by the staff in keeping it going, he decided not to fight the downgrading of
the story from the front page. He did not resign because of it but the incident
certainly contributed to his decision to move on:

> There wasn't really a gap in the market with the *Sunday World*, the *Sunday
> Independent*, the *Sunday Press*, and the *Sunday Tribune* was there at the time. I
> saw this becoming a mish-mash of nothing, not having a clue where it was
> going to be going in the future and I decided to leave ... I had a meeting
> with him [Joe Moore] after that and he brought up the story and he said
> it was only a load of rubbish anyway, no matter what party it was. He
> wasn't going to, he wouldn't credit the story.[42]

38 *SJ*, 27 July 1980. The paper did not publish on 20 July 1980.   39 *IP*, 13 Sept. 1980.   40 *SJ*, 7 Sept.
1980.   41 Kealy interview.   42 Miley interview.

The NUJ chapel members employed by the *Sunday Journal* met management to discuss editorial policy. Joe Moore issued a press statement saying he had nothing to do with the day-to-day running of the paper.[43] Tony Fitzpatrick had close links with Fianna Fáil and particularly with Charlie Haughey. In the 1970s he had worked for Markpress, the public relations firm that the Fianna Fáil government once employed to improve Ireland's image abroad, and he was to become the party's press officer in the 1981 election campaign.[44] Joe Moore was also one of Haughey's supporters. When the PMPA had been set up initially, they had had difficulty getting a licence from the department of industry and commerce and its minister, Jack Lynch. Writing in the aftermath of the PMPA's financial collapse in 1983, Olivia O'Leary considered why Moore was so devoted to Haughey:

> Moore resented the Department's reluctance and that of Lynch. He took it as a personal reflection on himself, and it may explain his subsequent fervent support for Charles Haughey in the 1979 ousting of the Lynch camp.[45]

Willie Kealy continued to lead the remaining team but they were often under considerable pressure. He remembered that there were so few resources that he could often find himself writing half the paper. Jim Aughney had left the *Sunday Journal* not long after the staff's sit-in to keep the paper going, because he was concerned about the financial stability of the company, but he arranged with Willie Kealy that he would continue contributing to the *Journal* with stories about agriculture and agribusiness because 'it was so important'. He said that Kealy and Miley were 'great journalists', not least because they were courageous about telling stories that might embarrass powerful people and organizations. Nevertheless, over the remaining life of the *Sunday Journal*, the substantial news elements of the paper continued to decrease in terms of the number of pages devoted to them, although several major stories were broken about topics concerned with agriculture and agribusiness.

Throughout 1981 there was an increase in the number of freelance writers who contributed celebrity gossip and lifestyle stories. Towards the end of 1981 and into 1982, infomercial features were appearing more regularly, such as a three-part series on industrial progress in the Limerick and Shannon areas.[46] The move away from the serious journalism espoused in the early incarnation

43 *IP*, 13 Sept. 1980.   44 *IT*, 5 Sept. 1981.   45 *IT*, 20 Oct. 1983. For an overview of PMPA see Simon Carswell, *Something rotten: Irish banking scandals* (Dublin, 2006), pp 46–65.   46 *SJ*, 24 Jan. 1982, 31 Jan. 1982 & 7 Feb. 1982.

of the *Sunday Journal* did not have the impact that Joe Moore had expected, and sales figures continued to fall, as did advertising revenue.

In August 1981 a new managing editor was appointed to replace Tony Fitzpatrick, who was taking up the appointment with Fianna Fáil, replacing Frank Dunlop, who had been seconded to the department of education, serving a Fine Gael minister, John Boland. The new managing editor was Dan Carmody, who was also managing editor of the *Leinster Express* (owned by the PMPA) and the *Kilkenny Standard*. In a 'Saturday Column' item in the *Irish Times* about the Fianna Fáil plans to challenge Garret FitzGerald's Fine Gael, Conor O'Clery wrote:

> Tony Fitzpatrick is seen as first and foremost a PR man, personally loyal to Charlie Haughey, rather than the party. The suspicions are backed by one or two incidents during the election campaign, when Tony handled Fianna Fáil's press relations. There was, as one TD put it, 'fierce aggro' over the distribution to the newspapers and RTÉ of scripts of Ministers' and TDs' speeches. Some scripts, it is alleged, were never delivered to newspaper offices.[47]

In December 1981 the *Sunday Journal* carried a two-page spread of predictions for the coming year, none of which concerned the demise of the paper itself or the two general elections that were to occur, in February and November. By January 1982 the paper had been reduced from forty-eight to forty pages and the motoring supplement had been downsized proportionately. Brian Byrne's 'Down your way' column went to the United States on one occasion, resulting in a short feature on the California Highway Patrol.[48] A substantial three-part series on the Irish in Britain began in February, but for the most part, the paper's horizons seemed to be narrowing.[49]

There was little political coverage in the *Sunday Journal* in the lead-up to the February 1982 general election. Willie Kealy's story on the revolt in the Labour Party against then leader Michael O'Leary made the front page.[50] Later in the year, O'Leary resigned from the party and joined Fine Gael. While there was relatively scant coverage of the February election campaign, the paper carried some advertising for Fianna Fáil, and none for the other parties. There was little in the way of examination of the events, personalities and issues of the election.

Writing in 1983, following a claim by Albert Reynolds that the Irish media had been running a witch-hunt against Charlie Haughey, public-relations expert

47 *IT*, 5 Sept. 1981.   48 *SJ*, 17 Jan. 1982.   49 *SJ*, 14 Feb. 1982, 21 Feb. 1982 & 28 Feb. 1982.   50 *SJ*, 31 Jan. 1982.

and academic F.X. Carty's detailed analysis of the newspaper coverage showed that the opposite was the case. His scoring was influenced by the stance of the editorial and other serious opinion columns in the national newspapers, the selection of page-one lead story, the choice of headings, and the emphasis given to issues, personalities and their effects. The results of his research are summarized below, followed by his analysis of the *Sunday Journal's* coverage of the February 1982 election:

Score (out of 100)[51]	[Government]	[Newspaper]
55	Fianna Fáil	*Sunday Journal*
35	Fianna Fáil	*Sunday Press*
35	Fianna Fáil	*Irish Press*
10	Fianna Fáil	*Evening Press*
5	Fianna Fáil	*Sunday World*
5	Coalition[52]	*Sunday Independent*
15	Coalition	*Irish Times*
15	Coalition	*Sunday Tribune*
25	Coalition	*Irish Independent*
25	Coalition	*Evening Herald*

This paper was too obviously Fianna Fáil to be taken seriously in its political comment ... On January 31 it declared that 'the sensible thing would seem to be to vote for Fianna Fáil' and emphasis was laid on Fianna Fáil's merits. February 7 issue was weak on coverage and comment. Nor was there any real attempt on February 14 to cover the election but what was given was weak and generally feeble, superficial and friendly to Fianna Fáil. The editorial was insulting to the readers in its simplicity, giving all the superficial benefits promised by Fianna Fáil, all the soft options with no regard for the deeper issues.[53]

By the time the second general election of 1982 took place in November, the *Sunday Journal* had been closed.

51 Carty gave each newspaper a score 'ranging from 100 (Fianna Fáil) through zero to 100 (Coalition) and then averaged each result'. 52 Fine Gael and Labour. 53 Carty, *Elections '82*, pp 7 and 28.

It would be unfair to describe the *Sunday Journal* as a 'Fianna Fáil paper', although the connections between Joe Moore, Tony Fitzpatrick and the party certainly seem to have influenced its approach to national politics. It is much more likely that the reason for the paper's demise was its lack of clarity about its market. Ireland did not need another national newspaper and given the size of its population it was never going to be sustainable. While the *Sunday Journal* might have prospered if it had stuck to its original plan to be an 'agricultural' paper, in that market there were already major competitors, particularly the *Farmers Journal* and the *Farming Independent*. There was also a transformation taking place in Irish farming when the *Sunday Journal* was launched. Michael Miley noted that the 'gravy train' that had commenced when Ireland joined the then EEC had 'stopped flowing':

> We were starting the oil crisis, interest rates increased rapidly, farmers found themselves caught in a price/cost squeeze. In other words, the prices plateaued, and some prices went down. The costs exploded, and a lot of farmers got into financial difficulties around the very late 70s and into the early 80s. That sadly coincided with the launch of the *Sunday Journal*. If the *Sunday Journal* had been launched maybe four to five years earlier, during the real boom period following EEC membership, it might have had a different history. Leaving aside the fact that its commercial base was poor.[54]

THE END OF THE *SUNDAY JOURNAL*

The last issue of the *Sunday Journal* was published on 23 June 1982. Much of the paper was given over to coverage of the unfolding scandal in Erin Foods. There was no reference to the difficult negotiations that were going on in the background to try to keep the paper going. It was widely reported that the PMPA had lost more than £1 million on its ownership of the paper. The business was thrown open to offers but none of them matched the asking price. According to PMPA sources at the time, bids came from Tony Fitzpatrick, and from businessman Ken Bates, representing a British group. There were also talks with publisher Hugh McLaughlin, who apparently had plans to start an evening newspaper.[55]

There were twenty-five people working for the *Sunday Journal* when it was closed by the PMPA on 24 June.[56] Thirteen of the staff members were members of the NUJ and the remainder were members of the Irish Transport and

54 Miley interview.   55 *II*, 24 June 1982.   56 *IP*, 24 June 1982.

General Workers' Union. They met with management in the aftermath of the closure and a deal was worked out. Redundancy payments were never likely to be significant, given the short lifetime of the paper but Willie Kealy was credited by staff with negotiating the best compensation possible in the circumstances. On 21 October 1983 the high court appointed Kevin Kelly as administrator of the PMPA, following a petition by the minister for industry and commerce, Des O'Malley. Joe Moore was dismissed in the following month, leaving the PMPA in massive financial disarray. The resulting government bailout of the insurance company took over thirty years to complete, costing the Irish taxpayers £230 million (equivalent to 2 percent of GNP). The losses were resolved by the imposition of a levy on all non-life insurance premiums until 1993.

The *Sunday Journal* is not well remembered as part of Ireland's weekly press. It was conceived as one thing and rapidly developed into what Michael Miley described as a 'mish-mash'. Joe Moore's intervention in July 1980 was no doubt welcome to the people working for the paper who had made heroic efforts to keep it running when it was first threatened with closure. Unfortunately, his desire to own a national paper and the self-belief that facilitated his creation of the PMPA also explained his failure to benefit from the expertise of the specialist journalists who were responsible for the initial success of the paper in its intended farming market. Willie Kealy offered one explanation for the dearth of information about the *Sunday Journal*: 'You might find people who were there wanting to forget about it. Who wants to be associated with a failure?'[57]

---

57 Kealy interview.

8 / The *Tribune*'s turbulent times

PAT BRENNAN & BRIAN TRENCH

The *Sunday Tribune*'s thirty-year story starts with *Hibernia*'s demise, as an attempt to continue by other means that magazine's dissenting journalism. Set up by an unlikely partnership of John Mulcahy, proprietor-editor of *Hibernia*, and Hugh McLaughlin, the commercial magazine publisher and *Sunday World* co-founder, the *Sunday Tribune* went through three distinct phases: 1980–2, under the control of McLaughlin, with various associates; 1983–94, under the editorship and partial control of Vincent Browne, with changing investment partners; and 1994–2011, under the effective control of Independent Newspapers, with a succession of four editors. This chapter concentrates on the first two phases, from the founding years through Vincent Browne's editorship. In these thirteen years, the *Tribune* sought to maintain a structure and perspective that was independent and distinct within the mass-market media of the time. We review several key features of the *Sunday Tribune* of that period, and present a portrait of a newspaper that has a particular place in the history of Irish journalism and newspaper publishing. But we also describe the pervasive uncertainty about the *Tribune*'s commercial potential, and even its survival, as investors and senior executives came and went frequently, with unsettling effects on the continuing production of the newspaper.

RAPID RISE AND SELF-DESTRUCTION

The *Sunday Tribune* was launched in November 1980 as the first Irish national newspaper in compact size and with spot colour available throughout the paper. Its content and layout were quite similar to *Hibernia*'s in its last years, not least because the core of the editorial and production team, as well as regular arts and books contributors, came from *Hibernia*. Among the significant additions to this group were Jim Farrelly (ex-*Irish Independent*) as news editor, Mary Holland (ex-*Observer*) as political analyst, particularly of Northern Ireland, Tom McGurk (ex-RTÉ) as magazine editor and feature writer, Geraldine Kennedy (ex-*Irish Times*, later to return there as editor) as political correspondent, and Colm Tóibín, who was to become an internationally renowned author, as radio reviewer. Sport had not featured in *Hibernia* and Mulcahy phoned Seamus Martin, then with the *Evening Herald*, to offer him the position of sports editor.[1] Martin, in turn, recruited reporter Eoghan Corry and columnists Breandán O hEithir, Anthony Cronin and Eugene McGee, and also 'had the "honour" of giving [Eamonn Dunphy] his first regular job in journalism'.[2] According to Dunphy's account, however, editor Mulcahy informed Martin that Dunphy was to be his soccer correspondent and Martin 'appeared to grimace'.[3]

In his first editorial for the *Sunday Tribune*, John Mulcahy declared the new paper's 'aim to hold an independent line in politics and a liberal one in economic and social affairs'.[4] But his partner, Hugh McLaughlin had let it be known there would be no resemblance to *Hibernia*.[5] Some months in, Mulcahy was finding the relationship difficult and he soon left, becoming perhaps the only person, through the sale of his shares to the Smurfit Group, to make a capital gain from the *Sunday Tribune*. Conor Brady, then planning a study break from the *Irish Times*, where he was night editor, records that he received a phone call from McLaughlin, whom he did not know, inviting him to become editor with an 'absolutely free hand in editorial policy'.[6] Within weeks of taking up the position, Brady switched the paper's format to broadsheet, considered more suitable for the 'serious' journalism to which the *Tribune* aspired.

These were congenial times for a newspaper with strong political coverage and keen insight into events in Northern Ireland; the H-Blocks hunger strike had started in October 1980 and it rippled into politics in the republic, as hunger strikers and supporters stood for election in the June 1981 general election – the first of three to take place in less than eighteen months. Geraldine Kennedy frequently supplied page-one leads, including exposés on the alleged tapping of phones at Fine Gael headquarters and on rifts within Fianna Fáil.[7] An exclusive interview in June 1981 with Fianna Fáil leader Charles Haughey, who was then in opposition, was a prelude to many stories based on information from Haughey's opponents within the party, when he was in government. Conor Brady later recorded that he was urged by the former head of a semi-state body to 'curb the activities' of Geraldine Kennedy and that Hugh McLaughlin had a similar approach from 'some people around Haughey'.[8] McLaughlin also had a direct approach from Haughey himself, and in a radio interview following a report by Kennedy on a challenge to his leadership of the party, Haughey said that he would be 'inclined to look after my own future' if he worked

1 Seamus Martin, *Good times and bad: from the Coombe to the Kremlin, a memoir* (Dublin, 2008), p. 55 2 Ibid., p. 56. 3 Eamonn Dunphy, *The rocky road* (Dublin, 2013), p. 254. 4 *ST*, 1 Nov. 1980. 5 *IT*, 12 Sept. 1980. 6 Conor Brady, *Up with the Times* (Dublin, 2005), p. 50. 7 *ST*, 25 Jan. 1981. 8 Brady, *Up with the Times*, pp 192–3.

for the *Sunday Tribune*.[9] Kennedy continued with her critical coverage of Fianna Fáil, including a report on the fund-raisers behind the party and an interview with former minister George Colley, who criticized low political standards and implied he might withdraw support from Haughey's government.[10] Kennedy and her colleague Darach MacDonald reported on phone surveillance of parliamentarians, making their calls accessible to Haughey and others close to his leadership; Kennedy's commentary asked: 'Did Haughey know?'[11] A year later it emerged that Kennedy's own phone was being tapped at the time she was reporting for the *Sunday Tribune* on dissent within Fianna Fáil.

The paper had audited average weekly sales in the first half of 1981 of 110,000, and the print run reached 140,000 during that year. Despite this early and notable success, however, the Smurfit Group withdrew its financial backing due to continuing losses.[12] In an editorial on the parting of the ways, it was claimed that there was 'a certain feeling of relief in both camps' but also – and not for the last time – that 'the future control of the *Sunday Tribune* must remain a subject of some speculation'.[13] The editorial team continued to grow, however; new entrants included Emily O'Reilly, who joined from college as education correspondent, and Deirdre Purcell (billed as 'RTÉ newscaster'), who contributed profiles and interviews. But with Smurfit's withdrawal there was no strong force to restrain McLaughlin as he embarked on a diversification that was intended to support the *Sunday Tribune* as part of a larger stable. Jim Farrelly moved from the *Tribune* to lead a new title, the tabloid *Daily News*; it lasted just two weeks before closing and bringing down the whole enterprise, with debts of £3.5 million, in October 1982.[14]

Senior journalists sought to find alternative backers, approaching the insurance company, PMPA, and the venture capital arm of Allied Irish Banks, among others.[15] But just weeks after the *Tribune* closed, *Magill* editor Vincent Browne secured financial support from Tony Ryan, who had become one of Ireland's richest people through aircraft leasing, to buy the paper's title from the liquidator.

RESURRECTION AND A NEW AGENDA

It took just under six months, including negotiations with several print unions, to prepare the relaunch. Browne recruited Gerald Barry from RTÉ as political correspondent, Paul Tansey from the *Irish Times* as business and deputy editor,

9 Mark O'Brien, *The fourth estate: journalism in twentieth-century Ireland* (Manchester, 2017), pp 189 & 188.   10 *ST*, 9 May 1982 & 6 June 1982.   11 *ST*, 27 June 1982.   12 *IT*, 12 May 1982.   13 *ST*, 16 May 1982.   14 *IT*, 28 Oct. 1982.   15 Martin, *Good times*, p. 60.

and John Kelleher, an old associate, from RTÉ to be managing director. Barbara
Nugent, as advertising manager, and Martin Dobey, as financial controller,
made up the rest of the senior management team.

Browne set out his stall at length in an editorial – 'Where We Stand' – that
committed the paper to support a pluralist society and women's rights, and to
cover Northern Ireland and the economy in depth. The Sunday Tribune declared
its position clearly on several current and conflicted issues: 'We are opposed to
the constitutional ban on divorce, to the present laws relating to contraception,
to the Catholic Church's attitudes on mixed marriages and integrated education ... we are also opposed to the proposed constitutional amendment on the
abortion issue.' At the same time, the editorial insisted that 'it is not fundamen-
tally the editorial views of a newspaper that determine its editorial character,
it is the standards it brings to its journalism'.[16] As we shall see, however, the
themes and positions highlighted in this editorial did very significantly shape
the paper's journalism. The Sunday Tribune was strongly, and unusually, issues-
and agenda-driven.

On page one in the first edition under his leadership, Browne announced:
'It's Great to be Back', firmly linking his project with that of the previous
Sunday Tribune, which 'achieved an authority and credibility unmatched in the
Irish Sunday publishing scene and we hope to advance from there'.[17] Also on
page one, strong stories on Fine Gael's internal divisions over the proposed constitutional abortion amendment and on an IRA vigilante punishment shooting
in Dublin set the tone for what followed.

The constitutional amendment was a gift to the Sunday Tribune that kept on
giving, up to the vote in September 1983 and beyond. There was continuing
coverage of intra-party and inter-party rifts on the issue, including opposition
within Fine Gael to party leader Garret FitzGerald, and divisions within the
Catholic Church on the guidance to be given to voters. In an early example of
the two-page analysis of an issue that became a Sunday Tribune hallmark, Emily
O'Reilly and Joe Carroll examined 'The Pro-Life Campaign – How It Started.
How It Succeeded. The People Behind It'.[18] A month after the vote, Carroll
reported that senior Vatican officials thought the wording of the amendment
was 'unsatisfactory' and the issue too complex to be decided in a referendum;
Carroll explored at length 'Inside the Hierarchy', revealing unseen differences
there.[19]

It was perhaps the Sunday Tribune's attention to these issues that led to a call
coming to the paper on a Saturday afternoon in February 1984 from someone
with first-hand information of a terrible tragedy a few days earlier: a teenage

16 ST, 17 Apr. 1983.   17 ST, 17 Apr. 1983.   18 ST, 24 Apr. 1983.   19 ST, 16 Oct. 1983.

girl and her baby had died following childbirth at a grotto in a Midlands town. The informant gave the name of the town (Granard, Co. Longford) and of the girl (Ann Lovett) and little more. After hurried inquiries and a long discussion about whether to use the girl's name, the *Sunday Tribune* had a report of ten short paragraphs, the publication of which had ripple effects far greater than the size of the report might have suggested.[20] The story was amplified in news media, and later in song and performance, over the weeks and months that followed, as Ann Lovett became an instantly recognized symbol of something much greater than a single girl's experience. A week after the initial report, the *Sunday Tribune* gave two pages to Ann Lovett's and related stories, including personal experiences of the religious-run mother and baby homes that made headlines again and again over the following three decades.[21] In other media, 'a flood of stories told of similar experiences and episodes'.[22] But in Granard, the predominant feeling was of hostility towards the *Sunday Tribune* and other media for 'bringing shame on the town'.[23] In continuing coverage in the *Sunday Tribune*, Emily O'Reilly wrote of four other deaths of babies 'in unexplained circumstances'.[24]

The *Sunday Tribune's* openness to points of view beyond the spectrum generally covered in media was seen most clearly but also most controversially in relation to Northern Ireland and republicanism. In an exclusive report, Vincent Browne and Gerald Barry – very often the authors, individually or jointly, of page-one lead stories – detailed a signed commitment given in 1975, but not honoured, by the then Garda commissioner Edmund Garvey to maverick republicans Eddie Gallagher and Marion Coyle, kidnappers of businessman Tiede Herrema.[25] In another exclusive, Browne interviewed republican fugitive Dominic McGlinchey, leader of the Irish National Liberation Army, who admitted his involvement in many murders and bombings.[26] In an accompanying editorial, Browne denounced McGlinchey's actions but defended the interview on the basis that 'the public should know more about him'. Gardaí, who were actively hunting McGlinchey, visited the newspaper's offices in an unsuccessful attempt to secure information about his whereabouts. Tony Ryan was very upset about the interview and 'summoned' Browne and John Kelleher to his Dublin house, where the confrontation was physical as well as verbal.[27]

20 *ST,* 5 Feb. 1984. **21** *ST,* 12 Feb. 1984. **22** Colum Kenny, *Moments that changed us* (Dublin, 2005), p. 43. **23** O'Brien, *Fourth estate*, p. 163. **24** *ST,* 1 July 1984. **25** *ST,* 1 May, 1983. According to the report, Garvey had signed a document assuring Gallagher and Coyle that they would be released from prison after four and two years, respectively, in exchange for Herrema's immediate release. Gallagher was sentenced to twenty years' imprisonment and Coyle was sentenced to fifteen years imprisonment for their parts in the kidnapping. **26** *ST,* 27 Nov. 1983. **27** Richard Aldous, *Tony Ryan: Ireland's aviator* (Dublin, 2013), p. 88.

The already strained relationship between editor and sponsor was coming close to breaking point. The paper's sales for July–December 1983 were an average 93,266 per week, the response from readers was encouraging, and, according to a page-one notice, 'we have managed to cut costs drastically compared with the former *Sunday Tribune*'.[28] But there were frequent cash-flow crises, which occasioned 'phone calls to Kilboy [Ryan's Co. Tipperary home] on Friday evenings saying the paper couldn't come out unless money for the printer was immediately made available'.[29]

A 'PERMANENT STATE OF CRISIS'

Financial controller Martin Dobey, in one of a series of reminiscences on his blog, remembered 'three years in almost a permanent state of crisis' as the paper established itself.[30] Ryan and Browne were destined, Browne said later, to be uneasy business partners. Browne commented: 'We are much too alike, although he lacks my tact and I his patience.'[31] From an initial investment of £50,000 in shares and an agreed loan of £330,000, Ryan ended up pouring more and more money into the newspaper and came to view the newspaper's demands as constant and uncontrollable.[32]

In negotiations with the National Union of Journalists in early 1984, the company stated that 'special co-operation and commitments are required from the journalists involved in the newspaper to ensure its viability and success'.[33] The situation was such that the company made provisions in its agreement with the union for the possibility of the paper closing within a year. The company publicly committed to 'greater concentration of resources on the editorial side during the coming year'.[34] But despite the positive signs and an earlier denial that Ryan had put up his shares for sale, in June 1984, fifteen months after the *Sunday Tribune*'s relaunch, he withdrew his support.

When Ryan's departure was announced in the *Sunday Tribune*, Vincent Browne stated: 'I believe the future of the paper is assured'.[35] Browne had managed to find a small number of friends, including USIT managing director Gordon Colleary, to buy Ryan's shares.[36] He and associates had paid Ryan £50,000 for the title and made a long-term arrangement to repay loans. Despite the public assurance about the paper's future the company's agreement with the NUJ covered 'the emergency period from 30th July 1984 to 1st January 1985 or whenever

28 *ST*, 10 July 1983.   29 Aldous, *Tony Ryan*, p. 89.   30 Post at martindobey.blogspot.ie, 17 Apr. 2008.   31 Ivor Kenny, 'Vincent Browne – the *Sunday Tribune*' in Ivor Kenny, *Talking to ourselves: conversations with editors of Irish news media* (Galway, 1994), pp 101–30 at p. 123.   32 Interview with Martin Dobey, 9 Apr. 2017.   33 ST industrial relations documentation from personal papers of Deirdre McQuillan.   34 *ST*, 18 Apr. 1984.   35 *ST*, 8 July 1984.   36 *IT*, 5 July 1984.

an investor joins the company – whichever is the earlier'. *Tribune* staff members were asked to accept wage cuts in an effort to reduce weekly costs by 7 per cent.[37] The final deal with the unions was completed on 17 July 1984, Browne's fortieth birthday. But the crisis was far from over: finding the cash to pay the printers 'became a weekly obsession … We spent the next two years not really knowing from week to week if we could make it … it was really hand-to-mouth stuff.'[38]

The *Tribune* then set its sights on raising money through the newly established Business Expansion Scheme (BES), which allowed tax relief on investments of up to £25,000 per year for five years. The BES applied only to manufacturing companies and thus the *Tribune*'s company structure and printing arrangements were changed to meet this standard; effectively, the company 'manufactured' the newspaper each week. Investors were being lined up under the BES when a major libel case threatened to derail the campaign. Former industry minister Justin Keating took a defamation action against the *Tribune* for an article written by Browne in May 1984 about his role in the state's deal with Bula Mines. The court found in Keating's favour on 16 December 1985 and awarded him £65,000. Browne insisted this would not undermine the stability of the newspaper.[39] But there were other libel actions pending and the *Tribune* made a concerted effort to settle these in order to allay investors' fears that money put into the company would be going out again in libel awards. Deals were done and numerous apologies published. About the same time as the Keating award was made, John Birrane, a Britain-based Irish businessman, contacted the *Tribune* and agreed a £250,000 investment.[40] (Keating, in the end, accepted far less than the court award.) The BES investments brought in £500,000, as did the *Sunday Tribune*'s launch in 1987 on the Smaller Companies Market. Readers were invited to 'Buy the *Sunday Tribune*', with Browne and Dobey on-hand to take Sunday morning phone calls from interested parties.[41] Sales of the paper reached a weekly average of 96,666 in 1987, a credible performance at a time when competitors' sales were falling. The share offer was fully subscribed and the money from new investors was used to enlarge the paper and broaden its coverage.

REVOLVING DOORS

One key to securing the transition from the earlier version of the *Sunday Tribune* was Vincent Browne's offer of posts to *Tribune* journalists who had been laid off in October 1982. To these he added several writers who had cut their teeth on *In*

37 *IT*, 11 July 1984.   38 Dobey interview.   39 *IT*, 17 Dec. 1985.   40 *ST*, 26 June 1988.   41 *ST*, 27 Sept. 1987.

Dublin magazine, thus rejuvenating the arts team – the recruitment of popular music-industry personality B.P. Fallon as rock writer also helped in this department. The recruits from *In Dublin* included Michael Dwyer (cinema), Mary Raftery (radio), Fintan O'Toole (theatre and general news) and Aidan Dunne (visual arts), who joined in 1987. Paddy Agnew came from *Magill* to be sports editor; Gene Kerrigan later followed Agnew, while later again, John Waters, who had contributed a column to the *Sunday Tribune* from 1984, went in the other direction to edit *Magill*.

The *Sunday Tribune* became a scouting and informal training ground for new entrants to journalism, many of whom were later to go on to senior positions in other media. Orla Guerin, Lorna Donlon and Maggie O'Kane were among those who joined the *Tribune* in the mid-1980s soon after leaving college. All went on to build notable careers in British broadcast or print media. Rory Godson followed Donlon in winning an award as Young Journalist of the Year while with the *Sunday Tribune* and also pursuing a career later in Britain.

Others who worked with the *Sunday Tribune* relatively early in their journalism careers included Aileen O'Meara, Kevin Dawson, Fergal Keane and Anne-Marie Smyth, all of whom went on to long periods with RTÉ. Among those joining the *Sunday Tribune* with established track records in newspaper journalism were Ed Moloney returning from the *Irish Times* in 1986 to cover Northern Ireland, Ciaran Carty moving from the *Sunday Independent* as arts editor and Deirdre McQuillan, who had established herself in women's magazines and contributed strongly presented fashion coverage and other feature material to the *Sunday Tribune* as lifestyle editor. In sport, David Walsh joined the *Sunday Tribune* from the *Irish Press* and, through his special interest in the Tour de France, developed a relationship with cyclist Paul Kimmage, introducing him to journalism and working with him on investigations of drug use in cycling that became a decades-long theme for Walsh, later senior sports writer with the *Sunday Times*, and for Kimmage as contributor to the *Sunday Independent*.

Design and photography were key parts of the *Sunday Tribune*'s distinctiveness. Award-winning designer Andy Barclay had stayed with the paper from its first version, having previously worked with *Hibernia* and the *Belfast News Letter*. He designed notable and bold layouts, particularly for the colour magazine, while staff photographer John Carlos was supported by a changing crew that included Derek Speirs, Eamonn Farrell and Billy Stickland, all of whom became leaders in the field as independent operators or agency owners. Fergus Bourke, an art photographer with a long-standing specialism in theatre, was assigned the photography for the *Sunday Tribune*'s innovative 'Kindred' column, which presented the writers' views on and memories of their siblings or other family relations; Bourke's stark black-and-white pictures were a critical component of the regular feature.

Freelance contributors of many different kinds were an important element of the *Sunday Tribune*'s total package. These included satirist Dermot Morgan, who wrote a weekly column from 1984 before becoming much more famous as Father Ted in the cult television series of the same name, Mary Holland, who contributed her columns, mainly on Northern Ireland, up to 1985 when she moved to the *Irish Times*, and broadcaster David Hanly.

Whether staff members or freelancers, *Sunday Tribune* journalists came and went with great frequency. Fintan O'Toole estimated that the *Sunday Tribune* under Browne lost five books editors, three business editors, two arts editors, three sports editors, three chief sub-editors and three news editors.[42] To that could be added three managing directors, the last of them being Barbara Nugent, who was three years in that position before leaving due to 'irreconcilable differences' – only to return soon after for a further two years.[43] Northern editor Ed Moloney commented later that Browne 'could never make a friend without falling out with them', but also stated: 'If there was one man who made me the journalist I later became it was Vincent.'[44]

AHEAD OF ITS TIME

The *Tribune* had entered the newspaper market well ahead of its main competitors in terms of production and printing technology, with a look that was fresher, cleaner, more modern. In 1983, the editorial mix of news, sports, arts and business filled thirty-two broadsheet pages, with a separate sixteen-page lifestyles and features magazine, carrying full-colour advertisements. In 1989, after finances had improved, the paper was redesigned with a second broadsheet section that increased sport and business coverage.

Arts coverage was a consistently strong and substantial part of the *Tribune* package, reflecting its ambition as a quality broadsheet. When the *Irish Press* dropped the long-running 'New Irish Writing' page, the *Tribune* stepped in. Novelists Joseph O'Connor, Anne Enright and Hugo Hamilton were among those whose stories were published. As O'Connor later told arts editor Ciaran Carty, the call from the *Tribune* was pivotal. 'I don't think anything as exciting will ever happen to me [again] ... I wouldn't have been one of those very brave writers who kept on trying for years and years ... I would have stopped.'[45]

42 *IT*, 17 Nov. 1990.   **43** *IT*, 15 Feb. 1989.   **44** Post at Ed Moloney's blog, thebrokenelbow.com, 8 Feb. 2011.   **45** Ciaran Carty, *Hall of fame interviews, Hennessy literary awards* (Dublin, 2016), p. 13.

The decision in late 1984 to wrap the magazine around the broadsheet gave the paper a full-colour glossy front page and a stand-out presence on the news-stands. The wraparound was originally intended as a once-off photographic souvenir of the visit of President Ronald Reagan to Ireland but became the format for the *Sunday Tribune* until April 1992 when high-quality colour printing on newsprint became available. The colour cover played to Browne's strengths as a former magazine editor; a typical *Tribune* cover featured a strong news image and a provocative headline, like, for example, during the long-running Kerry Babies tribunal (see below), a cover with a colour close-up photograph of Joanne Hayes and the lines, 'What the Gardaí did to Joanne Hayes', 'By Deirdre Purcell, Woman Journalist of the Year'.[46]

The *Tribune* used the colour cover to push the paper's authority, offering readers 'the inside story' or an exclusive take on a running story, sometimes also with an irreverent and quirky perspective. When Charles Haughey dismissed from goverment Brian Lenihan, the man he had called his 'friend of thirty years', the *Tribune* cover featured a close-up shot of a pensive Haughey with the headline, 'Some Friend'.[47] The cover was also used as a vehicle to boost sales, featuring personalities who were reckoned to attract readers, notably broadcaster Gay Byrne, then in his heyday. When Deirdre Purcell wrote Byrne's autobiography in 1989, the newspaper sustained stories about him for six weeks, including two full covers, bringing *Tribune* sales over 120,000.[48]

But the colour wraparound was printed on a Friday and, while Sunday newspapers are generally less dependent on breaking news than dailies, big news events can happen on the weekend and, at such times, the Tribune was at a disadvantage. Both the Bradford and Hillsborough football stadium tragedies were Saturday events, given substantial space by the *Sunday Tribune* but not on its cover. The *Tribune* could not promote its own scoop by photographer John Carlos, who captured the dramatic moment (on a Saturday) when a Garda opened fire in central Dublin during incidents after the release of IRA suspect Evelyn Glenholmes.[49] The cover that Sunday featured actor Clint Eastwood, who was running for mayor in Carmel, California. (Carlos later won the Photographer of the Year award for his picture.)

The *Tribune* sought to mitigate this problem when a big event was scheduled for a Saturday. The cover for 1 July 1990, printed before Ireland's quarter-final defeat in the football World Cup in Italy, featured goalkeeper Packie Bonner's full-stretch penalty save in an earlier game against Romania, with an inset team photograph and the headline 'They've Done Us Proud', which worked whether Ireland won or lost. Boxer Barry McGuigan's Saturday-night

46 *ST*, 25 Jan. 1985.   47 *ST*, 4 Nov. 1990.   48 *ST*, 3 Sept.–8 Oct. 1989.   49 *ST*, 23 Mar. 1986.

world-championship fight against Eusebio Pedroza on 9 June 1985 presented greater deadline challenges and the solution was unorthodox but ingenious. Two covers were printed, one featuring a story about Mehmet Ali Agca, the Turkish man who shot Pope John Paul II in 1981, and the other a close-up action shot of McGuigan with the headline 'Champion of the World'. By placing a £5,000 bet against a McGuigan win but also selling two extra colour advertisements exclusive to that edition, the *Tribune* covered the cost of both covers. McGuigan won, the late edition carried the McGuigan cover and the ads covered the cost of the print run and the bet.[50]

On 26 April 1992, with the benefit of new printing technology and with award-winning designer Stephen Ryan at the helm, the *Tribune* was relaunched as a three-section, fifty-six-page colour broadsheet. A week earlier, the paper published a farewell to the wraparound cover, noting that Charles Haughey had been the person most often featured – forty-one times: 'Sometimes it drove us mad. Frequently it must have driven our readers mad. Almost always it drove Charlie Haughey mad.'[51]

PLURALISM AND WOMEN'S RIGHTS

Equality for women was one of the four key issues highlighted in Vincent Browne's first editorial, 'Where We Stand'.[52] Objectivity, he wrote, 'does not preclude editorial or personal opinions – opinions which are certain to inform the presentation of cases, and more particularly, the selection of issues'. It was a time of extraordinary events that put into sharp focus the position of women in Irish society. In April 1984, two months after the Ann Lovett case, mentioned earlier, the mutilated body of a baby boy was found on a beach in Cahirciveen, Co. Kerry, and the Garda murder squad devoted its full attention to a single mother eighty kilometres away in Abbeydorney. Joanne Hayes, like Ann Lovett, had concealed her pregnancy and had given birth at home, alone. Her baby died and the body was hidden on the family farm. Under Garda questioning, Joanne and her family confessed to involvement in the violent killing of the Cahirciveen baby – although they turned out not to have been involved.

The Kerry Babies Tribunal, set up to investigate how this happened, sat for eleven weeks in 1985 and Deirdre Purcell was there every day for the *Tribune*. For Joanne Hayes, it was a harrowing ordeal. No detail of her personal or, indeed, gynaecological life was left unexamined as the Garda sought to defend the investigation. Purcell wrote, 'Joanne Hayes is not on trial in Tralee. You repeat that to yourself now and then as you watch and listen.'[53] As the hearings went on,

50 Dobey interview. 51 *ST*, 19 Apr. 1992. 52 *ST*, 17 Apr. 1983. 53 *ST*, 20 Jan. 1985.

Tribune headlines and cover stories were dramatic and unambiguous: 'The Kerry Babies Barristers: the men behind the tears', and 'They Shoot Horses, Don't They?'[54] A *Tribune* editorial concluded that Gardaí had abused their power and 'Joanne and her family were denied rights which should be taken for granted in a normal civilized country'. The *Tribune* printed a photograph of the body of the Cahirciveen baby with multiple stab wounds to his back, and with the caption, 'It is a wrenching reminder of a far more horrible event than that which took place in the Hayes house in Abbeydorney.'[55]

As the Tribunal dissected the reproductive life of one woman, the Dáil was debating legislation liberalizing the sale of contraceptives. Fianna Fáil opposed the government bill, but Des O'Malley broke ranks and abstained, his now famous 'I stand by the Republic' speech leading to his expulsion from the party. O'Malley was on the cover of the *Tribune* that week with his speech printed in full.[56] But the larger fight between Garret FitzGerald's coalition government and the Catholic Church was over divorce. The *Tribune* supported the government's stance, believing 'the success of the referendum would represent a formidable symbol of the willingness of the Republic of Ireland to accommodate views and beliefs at variance with the tenets of the majority of the population'.[57] The newspaper believed 'the duty [of the electorate] is to vote yes', but columnist J.J. O'Molloy had brought a dose of realism with 'Divorce in our time? Don't hold your breath'.[58]

In February 1992 the attorney general sought and received an injunction preventing a 14-year-old rape victim leaving the country to obtain an abortion. The X case, as it became known, was covered over two successive weeks in the *Tribune*, which devoted the front covers and eight inside pages to the controversy. The paper's editorial stated, 'The constitutional amendment on abortion should be simply deleted,' leaving the issue to the legislature.[59] The *Tribune* sought to talk to the people most directly affected; journalist Nicola Byrne was dispatched to a London abortion clinic to report on the journey taken by many Irish women. The women's stories were published over two weeks and a full page was given over to readers' views.[60] Underpinning the *Tribune*'s commitment to covering women's issues was the talent of its many women journalists and the fact that, atypical of the industry at the time, women occupied many senior positions, both editorial and commercial. It is unlikely that there were many other companies on the Irish stock exchange that listed a commitment to equality for women in the company prospectus.[61]

54 *ST*, 27 Jan. 1985. 55 *ST*, 6 Oct. 1985. 56 *ST*, 24 Feb. 1985. 57 *ST*, 22 June 1986. 58 *ST*, 22 June 1986 & 29 Sept. 1985. O'Molloy was a pseudonym. 59 *ST*, 23 Feb. 1992. 60 *ST*, 23 Feb. & 1 Mar. 1992. 61 *ST*, 27 Sept. 1987.

Figure 9: The *Sunday Tribune* front page from 1 November 1987, featuring an interview with Dessie O'Hare, the so-called 'Border Fox', who was part of a gang that kidnapped dentist John O'Grady.

NORTHERN IRELAND

The *Sunday Tribune's* controversial interview with on-the-run INLA leader Dominic McGlinchey in 1983 was a clear indication the paper would talk to all 'sides' in the Northern conflict. Another INLA activist, Dessie O'Hare, whose criminal and murderous activities earned him the media moniker the Border Fox, later took to phoning the newspaper. One of these calls came while O'Hare and associates were holding dentist John O'Grady in a twenty-three-day kidnap ordeal. The *Tribune* ran the interview in the late edition on 1 November 1987, quoting O'Hare as saying that O'Grady was alive and well, and adding, 'I am the Border Fox and foxes are very clever.' Even as O'Hare made that phone call, Gardaí were in the *Tribune* office asking about earlier contacts.

Political developments in the North spanned the negotiation and aftermath of the 1985 Anglo-Irish Agreement, the rows and frustrations over extradition and the beginning of the Hume-Adams talks that eventually led to the Good Friday Agreement of 1998. Browne, Barry, J.J. O'Molloy and Northern editor Ed Moloney came at these from different angles. The paper was notable for the extent to which it engaged with events in the North, sending reporters from Dublin to talk to as broad a spread of people involved as possible. Emily O'Reilly spent a night with a Catholic family under siege from loyalists and she also spoke at length to sectarian killer and loyalist leader John Bingham; her interview could be published in full only after his murder.[62] It was a time of regular paramilitary 'executions' of people deemed to be informers or troublesome for other reasons. The *Tribune* printed a close-up colour photograph of the body of one such victim – Eamonn Maguire – on its cover, with the headline 'In Cold Blood'.[63] The editorial was unequivocal: 'Every one of those involved – and yes it does include Gerry Adams, Danny Morrison, Martin McGuinness and the rest who, if nothing else, are apologists for this kind of abomination – stand guilty of a despicable and mean act that defies all human values.'[64]

Sunday Tribune editorials on Northern Ireland continued to argue through the darkest days that the nationalist cause was justified but violence was not; there were political means available to address these problems. The paper sought to understand the republican mindset, however. Condemning the fatal ambush of eight members of the IRA by British security forces at Loughall, Co. Armagh in May 1987 under the headline 'Murder is Murder is Murder', the editorial stated: 'The eight IRA men, while killed in the act of attempted killing, are themselves victims in another sense of the Northern situation.'[65] The *Tribune*

62 *ST*, 24 Aug. 1986 & 21 Sept. 1986.   63 *ST*, 6 Sept. 1987.   64 *ST*, 6 Sept. 1987.   65 *ST*, 10 May 1987.

noted that the IRA drew recruits from a deeply and systematically alienated
community. An editorial on the inquiry into the killing of three IRA members in Gibraltar in March 1988, stated: 'It is difficult, certainly at this remove
and from an Irish nationalist perspective, to regard these killings as anything
other than premeditated murder.'[66] After the IRA's November 1987 bombing
of an Armistice Day commemoration in Enniskillen, which killed twelve people, *Tribune* editorials argued for allowing, albeit with safeguards, extradition to
Britain. It was a contentious issue, given the view that there was scant justice
for Irish nationalists in British courts. After the release of the Guildford Four,
an editorial noted there was not 'a single word of apology from the British'.[67]
The Birmingham Six were then still behind bars and the *Tribune* covered their
plight extensively up to their release in 1991, including reporter Kevin Dawson's
exclusive interviews with the men from prison.[68]

THE ECONOMY

The *Sunday Tribune* was committed to scrutinize in detail the management of the
economy, where 'the absence of accountability has been particularly glaring'.[69]
A decade's record of high levels of foreign borrowing was contrasted with the
continuously rising level of unemployment. The founding editorial argued that
'redistribution can mean only that those in jobs agree to hold back their wage
demands to allow resources to be freed for others to be employed'. The redistribution part of the agenda was reflected less in the paper's coverage of economic
issues and more in that of social issues such as poverty and drugs abuse arising
from or related to unemployment.

In a profile of Charles Haughey, then the leader of the opposition,
Browne identified as 'real crimes' the economic policies he pursued as taoiseach in 1980–1 when 'he allowed public expenditure to get out of hand'.[70]
This remained the emphasis of economic coverage; in that respect, the *Sunday
Tribune* in the 1980s was less disruptive in this area than in some other areas
of coverage, rather reflecting an emerging orthodoxy that has strongly influenced public policy in the following decades. The theme of wasted spending
recurred frequently, as, for example, in Paul Tansey's exclusive page-one
report on the £350 million over-run on the ESB's coal-fired power station in
Moneypoint, Co. Clare.[71] Waste was also a central theme of an exploration
by Tansey, Browne and economist Seán Barrett of the 'state of the nation'.[72]
In another extended examination of the theme, an editorial commented that

66 *ST*, 2 Oct. 1988. 67 *ST*, 29 Oct. 1989. 68 *ST*, 28 Jan. 1990. 69 *ST*, 17 Apr. 1983. 70 *ST*, 1
Jan. 1984. 71 *ST*, 5 June 1983. 72 *ST*, 20 Nov. 1983.

even with 'enormous' public expenditure and 'staggering' waste the incidence of poverty was high.[73] Ahead of the January 1986 budget, Tansey explained 'why we each owe £5,714' and, a week later, an editorial raged that the budget 'signalled the government's own confession of failure', as not cutting spending meant maintaining a high tax burden.[74] The editorial acknowledged the difficulty of making deep cuts but then went on to question the need for several named government departments, some major government agencies and for diplomatic representation in fifteen listed countries, starting with Argentina, Austria and Australia.

The concern about public spending easily turned into an argument about limiting public pay, which was claimed to be '£15 million over'.[75] Public-sector workers were often a target, which made life difficult for reporters working on these stories. In advance of a threatened teachers' strike over pay, the headline over Lorna Donlon's otherwise balanced report was 'Should Cooney Fire the Teachers?'[76] This triggered outraged letters from teachers, published over a full page, but with an editorial in the same issue again making the case against their demand for a pay increase.[77] Another year later Ireland was seen as 'A Nation in Peril' requiring 'a strategy for survival [that] has got to commence immediately'. In a full-page editorial, Browne wrote that 'another four years of the kind of government we have got used to could well see the country go beyond the possibility of survival'.[78]

Tansey's business coverage – and that of the *Sunday Tribune* in general, and Des Crowley in particular – often had a critical dimension. Tansey claimed that US companies were treating Ireland as a tax haven and, as excitement rose in political and financial circles about the potential of offshore oil discoveries, he warned of the lure of 'fool's gold' and estimated that a reported find could bring 'pennies from heaven', while Crowley observed that Ireland had 'oil millionaires before we had oil' and oil economist Peter Odell later warned against the lure of 'oil that glitters'.[79] However, there were contradictions here as in other areas. As Tansey was writing about 'fool's gold', Browne in the same edition congratulated exploration company Atlantic Resources and its chairman, Tony O'Reilly, on their success.[80] Browne then qualified the compliment, noting that the *Sunday Tribune* had 'little reason to praise O'Reilly – he went to considerable pains to obstruct the relaunch of the paper – but it [is] only fair to acknowledge the contribution he has made to the country'.

---

73 *ST*, 30 Dec. 1984. **74** *ST*, 26 Jan. 1986 & 2 Feb. 1986. **75** *ST*, 13 Oct. 1985. **76** *ST*, 9 Mar. 1986. **77** *ST*, 16 Mar. 1986. **78** *ST*, 18 Jan. 1987. **79** *ST*, 4 Nov. 1984, 14 Aug. 1983 & 16 Oct. 1983.

PERSONALITIES IN THE NEWS
AND IN ITS COVERAGE

Big personalities such as Tony O'Reilly, as much as big issues, shaped the *Sunday Tribune*'s character. The two dominant and contrasting political figures in the republic, Garret FitzGerald and Charles Haughey, fuelled much reporting, analysis, comment and imagery, as did Browne's contradictory views of these personalities, whom he criticized strongly and also admired. In FitzGerald's last months as taoiseach, the *Tribune* was relentlessly critical of the government: 'Garret, the Game is Up', 'As the Country Braves the Snow, Garret Stays in the Bunker'.[81] Yet when FitzGerald resigned, the *Tribune* cover declared, 'Garret: we will not see the likes of him again'.[82] As mentioned above, Browne charged Haughey with 'crimes' in his management of the economy but he was comfortable with Andy Barclay, a keen natural-history and wildlife enthusiast, and photographer John Carlos visiting Haughey's privately owned island, Inishvickillaune, to produce a flattering and rare feature about it.[83]

Personality-focused coverage also came in extended profiles and in Deirdre Purcell's interviews that became a staple of the paper. But Purcell's work for the *Sunday Tribune* in that time also included reporting on famine in Ethiopia before it became the stimulus for Band Aid in 1985 and an exclusive interview with US presidential candidate Gary Hart in 1987, when he sought refuge in the west of Ireland from US media pursuit of his alleged extra-marital affairs. Purcell and others were given space to stretch themselves – and to show their own personalities – in other formats. Purcell spent a long evening exploring the Dublin nightclub scene with photographer John Carlos.[84] As well as providing political and social features and being sent to South Africa to report on the dying apartheid regime in summer 1985, Emily O'Reilly went behind the scenes at a fashion show and at a snooker tournament during an appearance by the erratic Alex 'Hurricane' Higgins.[85]

Through 1988–9 Gene Kerrigan followed the William Dunne action against Holles Street maternity hospital, eventually writing a book on it, and Kevin Dawson followed the unfolding story of the damage to Kenneth Best from a rogue batch of the whooping-cough vaccine. In 1993 reporter Veronica Guerin tracked down Bishop Eamon Casey in Ecuador and the resulting interview, with exclusive photographs from John Carlos, ran over three weeks, totalling twelve pages.[86] Guerin was on her way to becoming a public personality, having developed a distinctive style of work largely detached from the editorial team of which she was a nominal part. The *Tribune* news editor of the time, Alan

---

80 *ST*, 14 Aug. 1983. 81 *ST*, 16 Oct. 1986 & 18 Jan. 1987. 82 *ST*, 15 Mar. 1987. 83 *ST*, 9 Sept. 1984. 84 *ST*, 29 May 1983. 85 *ST*, 28 Aug. 1983 & 1 Apr. 1984. 86 *ST*, 14, 21 & 28 Nov. 1993.

Byrne, recalled that 'the Casey story was one of the few stories where she was encouraged to do it by us. It was clearly the biggest story in Irish journalism at the time'. Despite this, Guerin left the *Tribune* for the *Sunday Independent* soon after, on bad terms with Vincent Browne.[87]

Columnists also provided personal insights and, in some cases, opinions contrary to the socially liberal thrust of current-affairs coverage. This was certainly the case for the pseudonymous J.J. O'Molloy, as mentioned earlier, but also for shorter-lived *Tribune* columnists, such as independent senator (and, later, minister) Shane Ross; adviser to the Catholic bishops and, later, president of Ireland, Mary McAleese; and Fine Gael TD John Kelly – all of whose opinions were to the right of the *Sunday Tribune*'s dominant editorial view.

Contrarianism was encouraged notably in the case of Helen Lucy Burke, who first contributed to the *Sunday Tribune* on gardening, then occasionally on restaurants, and then as the paper's established – and increasingly feared – restaurant critic. She took some time to find her strong voice, writing after some months as a restaurant reviewer that a lobster terrine 'tasted like brawn from a delicatessen', that 'rage set in at having to pay £1.95 each for vegetables. This petty meanness seemed on a par with the skimpy paper napkins', and that the crème brulée was 'mawkishly sweet, a disgraceful £1.95'.[88]

The promise of restaurant reviews like this became an essential part of the *Sunday Tribune*'s offering, as did contrarian coverage of football from Eamon Dunphy. As well as writing critically about the Irish international team he provided contemptuous coverage of the League of Ireland, which he repeatedly called the Famous Fried Chicken League in reference to its long-time lead sponsor. Writing on a short-lived manager of Dundalk FC, John Dempsey, he noted that Dempsey found 'the Famous Fried Chicken League was a joke. The Irish grounds were kips with rough, unprepared pitches. The League of Ireland was a cowboy outfit.'[89] Dunphy's second stint with the *Tribune* lasted less than two years; however, he went on to a longer spell with the *Sunday Independent*.

OVER-REACHING AMBITION

Fintan O'Toole reflected on Browne's achievement in 1990 that 'it is simply impossible to think of anyone else who could have kept the *Sunday Tribune* going through its early years never mind establishing it as the viable Sunday quality paper'. And therein, O'Toole added, lay the problem: 'The fundamental difficulty through Vincent Browne's remarkable career in journalism is that he has

87 Emily O'Reilly, *Veronica Guerin: the life and death of a crime reporter* (London, 1998), pp 40 & 48. 88 *ST*, 1 July 1984. 89 Ibid.

far too much energy and far too many ambitions for one man, yet he is virtually unable to delegate to others.'[90]

Earlier that year, the *Sunday Tribune* launched an ambitious new venture aimed at securing its financial future as an independent newspaper. It had the opposite effect and marked the beginning of the end of Vincent Browne's time as editor. *Dublin Tribune* was a twenty-eight-page, free, weekly broadsheet newspaper, with nine local editions, delivered directly to 165,000 homes. It was a lively mix of Dublin news and sports from a staff of eighteen reporters, with columns from established commentators such as Nell McCafferty and Shane Ross, all overseen by former *Sunday Independent* editor Michael Hand.

At the time, free-sheet newspapers were seen as potential money-makers, and there was a real fear that if the *Tribune* didn't grab this business opportunity, someone else would. As Browne recalled, 'if we waited … we believed that the Ingersoll organisation, which at the time had very successful free newspapers in the US, notably in St. Louis, would move in and rob us of the chance'.[91] Ralph Ingersoll had already invested in the ailing Irish Press Group and was for a short time feted as a man who could work newspaper magic: 'His newspaper pedigree is second to none,' noted the *Sunday Tribune*.[92] The son of a media magnate, he built his empire on local free sheets in the United States and in Britain and it was thought he would do the same in Dublin.

So the *Sunday Tribune* got in first, taking advantage of its technological lead over competitors. It was the first to introduce computerisation – 'direct input' by journalists of editorial copy – and on-screen page make-up soon followed, bringing down production costs.[93] Circulation had topped 100,000 and in the year to April 1990 a profit of £246,000 was reported. Arguably, it was a good time to expand. As Martin Dobey remembers it, 'the business was doing fine and *Dublin Tribune* killed the *Tribune.* But it was a fantastic idea, a good piece of work, very ambitious.'[94]

The *Dublin Tribune* had a profound impact: after five successive years of rising profits the company reported a loss of £1.4 million in the six months to the end of September 1990; this became a loss of £2.3 million for the 12 months to 31 March 1991.[95] The losses continued and in November 1990 disgruntled investors sold 29.85 per cent of *Tribune* shares to Ireland's largest media group, Independent Newspapers.[96] It was a blow to Browne, for whom the *Tribune's* independence was a large part of its *raison d'être*, but he and colleagues 'sought to make the most of it'.[97] He eventually proposed that Independent Newspapers

90 *IT*, 17 Nov. 1990. 91 Kenny, 'Vincent Browne', p. 125. 92 *ST*, 9 July 1989. 93 Post at martindobey.blogspot.ie, 17 Apr. 2008. 94 Dobey interview. 95 *IT*, 27 Mar. 1991 & 29 Feb. 1992. 96 *SBP*, 18 Nov. 1990. 97 Kenny, 'Vincent Browne', p. 128.

be allowed to take over the *Tribune*, to save jobs and bring stability and on the basis of 'undertakings on editorial independence which I believed would stick'.[98] When Independent Newspapers sought to acquire a majority shareholding, the matter was referred to the Competition Authority and Browne made a personal intervention with then minister for industry and commerce Des O'Malley seeking to persuade him that the takeover should be supported.[99] O'Malley ruled against the merger in March 1992, the *Dublin Tribune* continued publishing and losing money until May 1992 and Browne remained in the editor's chair until 20 January 1994, when he was sacked by the Tribune Newspapers board.

THE LONG TAIL

In the *Sunday Tribune*'s remaining seventeen years it had four editors, of whom the last three – Matt Cooper, Paddy Murray and Nóirín Hegarty – came from and went to positions in the wider Independent Newspapers group. Peter Murtagh was the exception to this pattern, working with the *Irish Times* both before and after his period as *Tribune* editor (1994–6). Each of these editors negotiated their own editorial autonomy within the overall control of the *Tribune* by Independent Newspapers. Many outstanding journalists worked with the title during this time and major stories in the *Sunday Tribune* often pointed the way for other media. Hegarty memorialized her tenure as editor with a collection of articles from the *Tribune* in those last five years of its existence.[100] Introducing the volume, she made no reference to the earlier history of the newspaper; the record of the *Sunday Tribune* as a pioneering, critical presence in the Irish newspaper market was not even a dim memory.

The paper's impact in the market was declining from the mid-1990s and, as sales fell, the subsidy from Independent Newspapers became an increasingly necessary lifeline. From Independent Newspapers' perspective, keeping the *Tribune* afloat was a deterrent to other media groups from entering or expanding in the Sunday newspaper market. It may have been effective in distracting the *Irish Times* from its plans for a Sunday edition, to which it dedicated significant resources. It did not, however, prevent the continuing development of the *Sunday Business Post* or the gradual growth of the *Sunday Times*' Irish edition.

The *Tribune* became subject to the same rationalizing pressures as other elements of the Independent group, eventually being accommodated in the same headquarters building as all other titles. Twenty years after Independent Newspapers first invested in the *Sunday Tribune*, it withdrew its life-support. Tony

98 Ibid., p. 127.   99 Ibid., p. 128.   100 Nóirín Hegarty (ed.), *The* Trib: *highlights from the* Sunday Tribune (Dublin, 2011).

O'Reilly, as long-time chair of Independent Newspapers, had been a relatively benign patron of the Tribune. According to one of his biographers and *Tribune* editors, O'Reilly was sidelined within the Independent group in 2011 when it came to the decision to close the Sunday paper.[101] Whatever his and his colleagues' precise motives for becoming involved with the *Sunday Tribune*, by 2000 the accumulated debt to the Independent group was 'of the order of £12 million'.[102] At the paper's closure in January 2011 the *Tribune*'s debts to Independent News and Media were estimated at about €40 million.[103] By any measure, it was an expensive adventure.

101 Matt Cooper, *The maximalist: the rise and fall of Tony O'Reilly* (Dublin, 2015). 102 John Horgan, *Irish media: a critical history since 1922* (London, 2001), p. 142. 103 *IT*, 2 Feb. 2011.

9 / 'A lightning rod for the anger and frustration that is out there': the *Sunday Independent*, 1984–2012

KEVIN RAFTER

Two editors define the history of the *Sunday Independent*. Between them, Hector Legge and Aengus Fanning ruled the title for over half a century. While they edited the newspaper in very different eras, these two men shared a remarkable consistency in twinning a drive for commercial and editorial success.

Always in search of an exclusive story, neither Legge nor Fanning was distant from the commercial realities of newspaper publication. Legge's diaries are filled with references to the pressures – and pleasures – derived from weekly sales figures. For example he wrote on 6 September 1952: 'RECORD street sales, over 11,000. General verdict paper very good'.[1] Fanning was equally interested in commercial success, bluntly observing that 'we live or die by the market'.[2] These two remarkable editors oversaw a commercially successful newspaper but also left indelible and controversial marks on the pages of the *Sunday Independent*.

But the interregnum between these two editors saw the Sunday newspaper market transformed by the launch of the *Sunday World* in 1973 and the *Sunday Tribune* in 1980. By 1976 the *Sunday World* was outselling the *Sunday Independent* – a lead it would hold in every circulation year until 1991. Already under pressure at the lower end of the market from the *World* – and a number of British tabloid titles – the *Independent* faced additional pressure in late 1980 with the launch of a new quality Sunday title. Sales of the new *Sunday Tribune* hit over 100,000 per week during 1981. Two years later, weekly sales of the *Sunday Independent* were down to just 249,021 copies – the *Sunday Press* was selling 319,105, the *Sunday World* 343,639 and the *Sunday Tribune* 103,000.[3] The Middle Abbey Street title continued to lose middle-class readers to the *Sunday Tribune* and working-class readers to the *Sunday World*. Circulation fell in 1987 to 222,361 copies per week. The newspaper had particular strengths in sports coverage and several high-profile columnists including Hugh Leonard and Ciaran Carty. However, there were concerns in Middle Abbey Street over an older readership profile

---

1 Hector Legge diary, 6 Sept. 1952.   2 Ivor Kenny, 'Aengus Fanning – the *Sunday Independent*' in *Talking to ourselves: conversations with editors of the Irish news media* (Galway, 1994), pp 208–24 at p. 214.   3 Kenny, *Talking to ourselves*, p. 9.

and circulation weakness among AB social class readers. The title was also seen as poorly designed, perceived as old-fashioned and considered to have more in common with the struggling *Sunday Press* than the new *Sunday Tribune*. In fairness though, the editors between Legge and Fanning (Conor O'Brien and Mick Hand) ran the newspaper with a very small editorial staff and an equally small budget. What followed was a radical reinvention of the title under Aengus Fanning.

'THE MOST PROFITABLE AND CONTROVERSIAL PAPER IN IRELAND'

Born in Tralee, Co. Kerry in 1942, Fanning was immersed in newspaper culture from a young age. His father, who had moved to Tralee to take up a teaching position, had at one stage been a part-owner of the *Midland Tribune*, and each summer Fanning would return to Birr, Co. Offaly, where his uncle still ran the paper. As a child and then as a teenager he hung around the newsroom, accompanied reporters to the courts, and read copy. Having completed a commerce degree at University College Cork he returned to the *Midland Tribune* as a reporter between 1964 and 1969 before joining Independent Newspapers as a reporter in 1969 – just as Hector Legge was ending his long association with the *Sunday Independent*. In 1973, at a time when Ireland had joined the EEC and when agriculture was important to political life, Fanning was appointed group agriculture correspondent. He spent a lot of time in Brussels and Strasburg detailing in the newspaper what joining the EEC meant.[4] In 1982 he became news-analysis editor at the *Irish Independent* before being appointed editor of the *Sunday Independent* in 1984. Fanning took over as editor at a time of political and economic instability. There had been three general elections between June 1981 and November 1982, along with a contentious constitutional referendum (adding the Eighth Amendment, restricting abortion) in 1983. All this took place against the 1981 hunger strikes in Northern Ireland and an inability on the part of several administrations in the republic to manage an economy in freefall. He would remain in this position until his death in 2012. It was during this twenty-eight-year tenure that the *Sunday Independent* became 'the most profitable and controversial paper in Ireland'.[5]

   It is worth noting that Fanning was not the first choice for the job. Tony O'Reilly initially offered the post to Conor Brady. He had just gone through a successful, if difficult, two years as editor of the *Sunday Tribune*. This culminated

4 Kenny, 'Aengus Fanning', pp 209 & 212.   5 Eddie Holt & David Quin, 'No more vanity fare?', *Magill*, Nov. 1997, pp 36–41 at p. 36.

in the closure of the newspaper after proprietor Hugh McLaughlin's attempt
to shore up the finances of the *Sunday Tribune* with the launch of the *Daily News*
went disastrously wrong. Brady, who had returned to the *Irish Times*, turned down
O'Reilly's offer which the future *Irish Times* editor later valued at €4 million
when stock options were taken into account.[6] It was Independent Newspapers
managing director Joe Hayes who moved his fellow Kerryman into the editor's
chair. Fanning's ideas about changing the paper to carve out a distinctive market
position appealed to Hayes, who had garnered a reputation for sharp marketing of the Independent Newspapers brand. After examining market research,
Fanning concluded that 'people were bored on Sundays and that if they were
going to read a Sunday newspaper, they would want something that was far
from boring'.[7]

He took over a newspaper he considered 'a bit staid and stale' and lacking
in female writers.[8] It was indeed a tired, poorly presented and clearly under-
resourced publication. The masthead was rendered in a limp italic font that
was small in proportion to the lead headline. Inside, the newspaper was equally
devoid of flair and excitement. Averaging thirty-two pages per issue, the title
was still news-driven – political reporting by Joseph O'Malley and Frank Byrne
and economic reporting by Martin Fitzpatrick – even if there were few reporters, as the paltry number of news stories showed. For instance, the edition of
15 January 1984, one of the last before Fanning took over as editor, had news,
or news features, on pages one to five; comment, tagged 'Leader Page', took up
pages six and seven; 'Your Letters' and a flabby feature, 'Redefining work for
all', dominated pages eight and nine, which were tagged 'News Focus'; pages
ten and eleven were tagged 'Business Page' and featured Martin Fitzpatrick's
admittedly sharp analysis on the week's events, along with a column by Colm
Rapple; fashion was on page twelve; a social diary by Trevor Danker was on
page thirteen; three arts pages, tagged 'Dialogue', edited by Ciaran Carty, occupied pages fourteen to sixteen, with reviews of art and movies (Carty), theatre
(Gus Smith) and music (John Honohan). Page fifteen was reserved for book
reviews, including contributions by regular critics Ulick O'Connor and John
Kearney. A travel page, 'Getaway' by John Coughlan, was on page seventeen,
while 'Motoring' shared page eighteen with bridge, a crossword, a 'Property
Brief' (i.e. a house for sale) and 'Cosmic Birth Chart', a horoscope column.
Pages nineteen to twenty-three featured recruitment ads, including one for
Fanning's old job, *Irish Independent* news-analysis editor. Page twenty-four con-
tained births, marriages and deaths, plus filler news items. Pages twenty-five to

6 Conor Brady, *Up with the* Times (Dublin, 2005), pp 52–5. 7 Matt Cooper, *The maximalist: the rise and fall of Tony O'Reilly* (Dublin, 2015), p. 154. 8 Kenny, 'Aengus Fanning', p. 214.

twenty-nine carried sport, dominated by GAA, rugby, racing and soccer, and the back pages featured Hugh Leonard's column, television previews, listings for radio and television and 'Backchat', a miscellany of political yarns and gossip.

Among the columnists, apart from Leonard, were *Irish Independent* Northern editor John Devine, and controversial Fr Michael Cleary, who wrote a religious column called 'Reflections'. This all-male line-up of journalists, columnists and contributors was supplemented by the lone female figure of fashion writer Ita Hayes. There was, one writer observed, 'little that was remarkable about the *Sunday Independent*. Its politics were slightly right of centre; it was hostile to republican sentiments, but it rarely produced anything that disturbed the political, social or economic status quo.'[9]

Within weeks of Fanning's appointment the paper has visibly changed. For the edition of 11 March 1984 the italic masthead is replaced with a cleaner, larger and more authoritative serif font. This sense of sharper, more reader-focused presentation is evident throughout the paper. While the architecture of the paper remains much the same, much of what is known as 'page furniture' (everything on the page except text, headlines and images) has been replaced. For instance, the fashion page is now termed 'Styles'; Motoring has become 'Autoworld' and the car-review text is now broken into sections – 'performance', 'economy', 'on the road', 'final verdict' – with stars awarded for how the car functioned. Almost all logos have also been redesigned, and the energy coursing through even old features is palpable. There is also now another female columnist, Brenda Costigan, providing recipes in 'Brenda's Kitchen'. A year on from Fanning's appointment and the newspaper had changed radically. The edition of 20 January 1985 looked different, sharper with more illustrations and caricatures, plus more punchy use of language and a greater sense of visual storytelling. Fanning was still working within the thirty-two page model; it was early days, but he and his team were creating something new, a broadsheet with tabloid tendencies, a newspaper 'that was far from boring'.

Fanning chose wisely in his appointment of Anne Harris, then editor of *Image* magazine, as features editor in 1985, noting that she had 'an instinctive sense of the market, she brought to the paper a remarkable flair for creative commissioning, for identifying, encouraging, inspiring and developing journalists of talent and unrealised potential'.[10] From almost the very beginning of Fanning's editorship, Harris began contributing to the *Sunday Independent* – her first column being a review of Germaine Greer's book *Sex and destiny*, in which Harris

9 Emily O'Reilly, *Veronica Guerin: the life and death of a crime reporter* (London, 1998), p. 49.   10 Kenny, 'Aengus Fanning', p. 214.

compared Greer's views to being 'almost akin to those of Mary Whitehouse and the Catholic Church'.[11] Fanning and Harris – who later married – formed a formidable journalistic double act. Fanning wanted to make the *Sunday Independent* a 'magazine wrapped inside a newspaper and Harris would be crucial in that regard, bringing what Fanning saw as a woman's intuition to an overwhelmingly male environment'.[12] Fanning later credited Harris with the development of what he referred to as the *Sunday Independent*'s 'people-based journalism'. 'Few enough people', he concluded, 'are interested in concepts or the logical thread of an argument. They are interested in people.'[13] Many commentators have, over the years, pointed to one article that has been interpreted as having strongly informed this move towards 'people-based journalism'. In June 1985 Harris declared that 'political observers long ago concluded that you can assess the political maturity of a society by the sophistication and openness of its gossip', and that British newspapers 'depend more and more on the quality of their gossip columns for sales'. Irish society, she concluded, was 'a hothouse of rumour and speculation … where rumour is never discounted – the more so if it's false. The fact that it existed changes reality and must be taken into account.'[14]

While the paper's news staff reported to news editor Willie Kealy, to inject more life into the newspaper new columnists and journalists were recruited. Among those hired over the years were Liz Allen, Sean Barrett, Jonathan Philbin Bowman, Anthony Clare, Liam Collins, Anthony Cronin, Stan Gebler Davies, Eamon Dunphy, Ruth Dudley Edwards, Barry Egan, Ronan Fanning, Eoghan Harris (Anne Harris' ex-husband), George Hook, Terry Keane, Gene Kerrigan, Fiona Looney, Declan Lynch, Colm McCarty, Michael McDowell, Brighid McLaughlin, John A. Murphy, Conor Cruise O'Brien, Brendan O'Connor, Eilis O'Hanlon, Patricia Redlich, Shane Ross, Sam Smyth and Colm Tóibín. Other key figures included future deputy editor Judy Corcoran and operations editor Campbell Spray. These writers were duly built up into larger-than-life personalities – although sometimes, as in case of individuals such as Eamon Dunphy and Terry Keane, they were in reality already larger than life. Fanning was utterly conscious that as a Sunday publication his newspaper was obligated to its readers on a 'leisure day' to provide a cocktail of 'entertainment, information, analysis, opinion, provocative pieces, gossip'.[15] While the newspaper's content may have been brash, gossipy and sometimes frivolous, the 'weekly mix' also included serious writers such as Tóibín and Kerrigan.

Fanning recognized that successful commerce underpinned his newspaper. As an editor Fanning sought to get Irish readers into 'the habit' of buying the

11 *SI*, 22 Jan. 1984. 12 Cooper, *The maximalist*, p. 154. 13 Kenny, 'Aengus Fanning', pp 220 & 214. 14 *SI*, 9 June 1985. 15 Kenny, 'Aengus Fanning', p. 220.

Sunday Independent by delivering 'a chemistry which makes a newspaper compulsive, that you can't ignore it, you've got to buy the bloody thing'.[16] By any measure the *Sunday Independent*, under Fanning, delivered huge commercial success. In 1983 – just before he was appointed editor – the *Sunday Independent* accounted for 24 per cent of the sales of the four main Irish Sunday newspapers (*Press, Tribune, World* and *Independent*). Six years later that circulation share had increased to 30 per cent. This sales growth is even more impressive when account is taken of the fact that the overall weekly sales of the four titles declined by approximately 196,000 copies per week (almost 20 per cent) between 1983 and 1992. The Middle Abbey Street Sunday title lagged behind the *Sunday Press* by nearly 70,000 copies every week in 1983. Fanning's title, however, overtook the *Sunday Press* in weekly sales in 1989, while also withstanding any serious threat from the *Sunday Tribune* and coping with the emergence of an increasingly localized edition of the *Sunday Times* in the mid-1990s. No competitor, including the mid-to-low-market Irish edition of the *Mail on Sunday*, had the ability to withstand the march of what was the best 'cash cow' of any newspaper group.

Influential and important journalism was produced – in particular, the newspaper's investigative reporting in the late 1990s on links between certain senior politicians and leading business people. In the same period, Veronica Guerin became a front-page staple for the newspaper, with exclusive investigative reports on Ireland's criminal underworld. Moreover, Guerin's story about a delay in processing an extradition request in a clerical sex-abuse case contributed, in part, to the collapse of the then Fianna Fáil-Labour Party coalition in 1994.[17] But there was a heavy price for this groundbreaking work. She had been threatened many times by the drugs gangs she was writing about and even had survived one assassination attempt. However, on 26 June 1996, she was shot dead by a gunman on a motorcycle as she sat in her car at traffic lights on the outskirts of Dublin. Following Guerin's murder, Fanning faced strong criticism for failing to protect his colleague from the criminals she was reporting on, and also for promoting her journalism as a means to drive circulation.[18] But her mother, Bernie Guerin, noted that after her death Fanning remained a friend of hers: 'I couldn't speak highly enough of him.'[19] Other high-profile news stories included Liam Collins' revelation of how Allied Irish Banks had facilitated the non-payment of deposit interest retention tax through the use of bogus non-resident accounts. Collins' story revealed that the bank's 53,000 bogus non-resident accounts contained £600 million and when Revenue started collecting tax on these, it netted €838 million in payments and penalties for the state.[20]

16 Ibid., p. 214. 17 *SI*, 23 Oct. 1994. 18 See O'Reilly, *Veronica Guerin*. 19 *IT*, 18 Jan. 2012. 20 Liam Collins, *The great Irish bank robbery* (Dublin, 2007); *SI*, 5 Apr. 1998.

Scandal and controversy were never too far away during Fanning's tenure. Notwithstanding the aforementioned editorial successes, the *Sunday Independent* ultimately came to be defined by what can best be described as 'macho-journalism' with a 'shock and awe' approach. Even Eamon Dunphy – who penned many of these contentious articles – later described the newspaper's strident and provocative journalism as 'evil … pernicious … and a cancer on society'.[21] The newspaper undoubtedly adopted an editorial line that sought out controversy to boost circulation and also to further its self-claimed role as champion of pro-business and 'anti-establishment' values. In pursuit of these editorial and commercial objectives, the tone of the newspaper was frequently unsavoury and even repugnant, while content was often biased and frenzied. Moreover, as one writer observed, on the pages of the *Sunday Independent* 'the nation's sacred cows were butchered with gleeful ferocity [as] targets were relentlessly singled out for vulgar abuse'.[22] The manner in which issues and individuals featured on the pages of the *Sunday Independent* frequently ranged well over generally accepted legal and taste lines.

Nowhere was this hostility more evident than in reportage in the early 1990s on leading figures associated with the Labour Party. In part due to conflicts with the newspaper's pro-free-market economic outlook, politicians including Mary Robinson, Dick Spring, Brendan Howlin and Michael D. Higgins were subjected to sustained criticism. When, in one of his columns, Eamon Dunphy referred to Labour Party leader Dick Spring as 'a bollocks of the highest order' after the party agreed to enter coalition with Fianna Fáil despite a pre-election pledge not to, Fanning felt the paper was 'breaking new ground. It was expressing something in the vernacular, in language in daily use.'[23] Others, however, viewed things very differently. Michael D. Higgins, who as minister for arts, culture and the Gaeltacht came under sustained attack for lifting the advertising cap on RTÉ and the Section 31 broadcasting ban, described the negative coverage as 'personally abusive' and without 'ethics or standards'.[24] This was a period when, as sometime contributor John Waters put it, the paper was 'engaged in the construction of a climate of fear in Irish public life as its journalists launched a succession of vicious, gratuitous and sustained personal attacks on certain politicians, writers and broadcasters'. This, Waters concluded, constituted 'an ideological war, whereby those who offer alternative views on issues like justice, the North, economics, history, culture and society are being targeted and undermined'.[25]

21 Holt & Quin, 'No more vanity fare?', p. 40.   22 Damian Corless, 'Profile of Anne Harris', *Magill*, July 1999, pp 19–22 at p. 20.   23 Kenny, 'Aengus Fanning', p. 223; *SI*, 28 Feb. 1993.   24 Holt & Quin, 'No more vanity fare?', p. 38.   25 *IT*, 18 Apr. 1995.

In spite of, or perhaps because of, such contentious content, sales increased throughout the 1990s. In 1992 weekly sales stood at 247,198; by 1998 sales had increased to 310,505, compared to 312,494 for the *Sunday World*, 85,056 for the *Sunday Tribune* and 47,232 for the *Sunday Business Post*.[26] Unlike the *Sunday Press*, which had disappeared with the collapse of the Press Group in 1995, the *Sunday Independent* reaped the benefits of the Celtic Tiger economy. When Fanning had taken over as editor in 1984 incomes in Ireland (measured by GDP per head of population) were just 63 per cent of those in Britain. By 1997 incomes in Ireland had surpassed those of Britain with the economy growing 10 per cent in 1995 and 7 per cent in 1996.[27] As consumer spending rose, so too did the demand for advertising space and lifestyle journalism.

The 'Living & Leisure' supplement was introduced in the mid-1990s to expand editorial reach and build on commercial opportunities. The thirty-two page configuration was simply too small to accommodate the ever-increasing volume of advertising and Fanning's and Harris' ambitious editorial plans. New technology had given journalists full control over editorial production and design. In effect, this meant that more pages could be produced more quickly and to a higher standard. The *Sunday Independent*, in common with other newspapers, took advantage of these innovations to create new products. For the edition of 22 January 1995, news, opinion, 'People' features (interviews and profiles), Trevor Danker's social diary, business and recruitment advertising filled the thirty-two page main section. The second, twenty-eight-page section was feature-led and included fashion, motoring and other staples, along with nine pages of sport. Ten years later, for the edition of 16 January 2005, this had expanded to a thirty-eight-page main edition, an eight-page property supplement, an eight-page 'Living' supplement, a six-page review section, a twenty-page business supplement with fourteen pages of recruitment advertising and a sixteen-page sports supplement. The main paper and all of these supplements were in colour and were supported by copious advertising. In addition, the package included a glossy heat-set colour magazine, *Life*, which was also heavily supported by advertising. This huge increase in pagination, editorial coverage and advertising had been made possible by the opening of the INM printing facility at Citywest, Co. Dublin, in 2000. Until this development INM newspapers had been produced on an old press in the Middle Abbey Street headquarters of the group.

But such success aside, the paper remained controversial. In 1999 one of its star columnists, Terry Keane, defected to the *Sunday Times*, bringing an end to

---

26 Kenny, *Talking to ourselves*, p. 9; *IT*, 3 Mar. 1999.   27 'Ireland's tiger economy', *Economist*, 17 May 1997, pp 25–8 at p. 25.

'The Keane Edge' column in which, over the years, various hints on Keane's relationship with Charles J. Haughey had been dropped. Keane's defection meant that her frank admissions appeared not in the *Sunday Independent* but in the *Sunday Times*, which, following Keane's tell-all *Late Late Show* appearance, published a three-page spread on the affair. That week's *Sunday Times* was its best-selling issue. The *Sunday Independent*'s attempt to seize the moral high ground by describing Keane's actions as an 'act of ultimate betrayal against the former Taoiseach Charles Haughey' rang somewhat hollow given that the paper had been hinting at the relationship for years in what Fintan O'Toole termed 'a very peculiar exercise, halfway between full-blooded British tabloid sensationalism and Irish cute-hoor reticence'.[28]

An article by May Ellen Synon in October 2000 represented one of the lowest points of Fanning's time as editor. The columnist took aim at participants in the Paralympic Games. Words such as 'perverse' and 'grotesque' were matched by descriptions of the athletes as 'cripples' who 'wobbled around the track in a wheelchair'.[29] Synon had form with over-the-top, controversy-seeking journalism. She had previously penned polemical attacks on the Travelling community and immigrants.[30] In the words of Fintan O'Toole, she 'had a penchant for targeting entire groups with hate-filled rhetoric'.[31] Fanning initially defended Synon's column in terms of the importance of a free press and not censoring writers. But a line had been crossed and public outrage continued to be heard, in particular on phone-in radio shows. Political criticism and calls for the withdrawal of commercially lucrative state advertising from Independent titles seems to have led to a change of stance. In a significant U-turn Fanning admitted that the article had 'caused great distress and offence to many people, particularly to the disabled and also to those athletes participating in the Paralympics. I wish to apologise sincerely to them.' The extent of unease at the exceptionally strong negative public reaction is evident in the fact that Fanning's front-page apology was followed by an apology from Synon and a statement from the board of Independent Newspapers – in the name of managing director Gavin O'Reilly – which also apologized for the 'distress and offence' caused by Synon's column.[32]

Alongside significant lapses in editorial taste, which caused considerable offense and generated huge public outcry – as in the Synon reportage – there were other errors of editorial judgment. The promotion of an 'exclusive' interview with Bishop Eamon Casey in 1993 led to a subsequent editorial apology under the heading, 'Error of Judgement'.[33] In radio advertisements the

28 *SI*, 16 May 1999; *IT*, 22 May 1999. 29 *SI*, 22 Oct. 2000. 30 See *SI*, 28 Jan. 1996 & 21 Nov. 1999. 31 *IT*, 28 Oct. 2000. 32 *SI*, 29 Oct. 2000. 33 *SI*, 25 Apr. 1993; the story appeared in *SI*, 11 Apr. 1993, the front page of which is visible in this volume's cover photograph.

newspaper had promoted an exclusive interview when, in fact, it was actually reporting the contents of what Casey believed to have been a private telephone conversation with a friend. In somewhat ambiguous language the editorial stated, 'we are not satisfied the bishop was interviewed in any normal sense of the word'. The apology is interesting, however, in throwing light on the approach to journalism at the newspaper at that time: 'this was a good story. A good human interest story with a significant public interest element.'[34] Defining what is in the public interest may frequently be contested but the 'human interest' angle was very much a determining factor in editorial choice at the *Sunday Independent*.

Several of these so-called 'exclusives' led to costly libel awards against the newspaper. A high court jury awarded £300,000 (€380,000) to politician Proinsias De Rossa over an article by Eamon Dunphy in the *Sunday Independent* on 13 December 1992. The 1997 decision was upheld on appeal by the supreme court.[35] There were many other high-profile libel settlements. Incorrect reporting around the death of politician Liam Lawlor in a car accident in Moscow in October 2005 resulted in a six-figure pay-out due to an article claiming that the other occupant in the car was 'likely to be a prostitute'.[36] Within hours of the newspaper being published the authorities in Russia confirmed the woman in question was in fact a legal translator. Fanning quickly apologized and accepted 'full responsibility' for the mistake.

'THE VOICE OF RADICAL OPPOSITION'

At the core of Fanning's approach was a desire to sell newspapers by challenging the consensus, although what was understood as 'consensus' often varied and certainly evolved over time. As Fanning himself put it, 'People may not like what the paper says but they like the fact we have the guts to publish opinions that sometimes go against the stream.'[37] As the Northern Ireland peace process moved out of the shadows and into the public arena in the late 1980s, contrarians such as former politician Conor Cruise O'Brien and broadcaster Eoghan Harris were given prominence to articulate views in keeping with the newspaper's own editorial positioning, in particular, a strong rejection of Sinn Féin. Fanning himself was no stranger to the North: his mother, as he put it himself, came 'from solid Presbyterian stock in Northern Ireland', though she converted to Catholicism and 'lived all her adult life in Tralee'.[38] In one interview he declared that 'the *Sunday Independent* is utterly implacable in its

34 *SI*, 25 Apr. 1993. 35 *II*, 31 July 1999. See A.J. Davidson, *Defamed! Famous Irish libel cases* (Dublin, 2008), pp 61–91. 36 *SI*, 23 Oct. 2005. 37 Kenny, 'Aengus Fanning', p. 217. 38 Ibid., p. 209.

Figure 10: The front page of the *Sunday Independent* on 30 June 1996, the first edition
following the murder of its journalist Veronica Guerin.

opposition to terrorism. The IRA and its loyalist counterparts have behaved like barbarians and put themselves outside the Pale of civilised society. I don't believe they should be entitled to the freedom or benefits of constitutional democracy.'[39]

This uncompromising stance sometimes infused columnists' reactions to the emerging peace process. In distasteful terms, SDLP leader John Hume was subjected to repeated criticism for his efforts to convince the republican movement to move away from its campaign of violence. Not without justification, Mark Durkan, of the SDLP, described criticism of his party leader as 'off the scale of legitimate hyperbole and journalistic metaphor'.[40] However, the attacks on Hume had an interesting culmination in 1994. Telephone calls from Hume to Fanning and appeals from the Irish and US administrations to Tony O'Reilly had had no effect and the attacks had continued. That is until O'Reilly attended a White House function and was seated – far from the centre of attention – at a table near the kitchen door. After that a meeting was held between Hume, Fanning and other company executives, and the *Sunday Independent* 'went quiet on the Northern question' for a couple of weeks. When coverage resumed, it was 'far more considered'.[41]

The newspaper was thanked publicly by Taoiseach Bertie Ahern in 1997 for not publishing details of Department of Foreign Affairs documents that referred to contacts between Irish and British government ministers in the run-up to the first IRA ceasefire in 1994. The documents were, according to the *Sunday Independent*, supplied to the paper by anonymous sources 'who said they were members of Fianna Fáil determined to bring down the Taoiseach'.[42] And, ultimately, when the Belfast Agreement was signed in April 1998 the newspaper declared that it represented 'the best chance of peace in a generation' and that John Hume 'deserves credit for his efforts to convert Sinn Féin from its dual support for the ballot box and the bomb to the constitutional path'.[43]

In Southern politics, the *Sunday Independent* was not uncomfortable with being politically partisan – in particular, in its favourable treatment of Bertie Ahern during his tenure as taoiseach from 1997 to 2008. Indeed, the former Fianna Fáil leader noted of media coverage of his difficult election in 2007 that, 'we hadn't had a fair shake during the campaign, except from the *Sunday Independent*'.[44] As speculation mounted over the exact date of the election, it was the *Sunday Independent* that exclusively reported the poll date – accompanied by a full-page interview of Ahern by Fanning.[45] Following the re-election of Fianna

39 Kenny, 'Aengus Fanning', pp 219–20. 40 Holt & Quin, 'No more vanity fare', p. 38. 41 Cooper, *The maximalist*, pp 232–3. 42 *IT*, 20 Oct. 1997. 43 *SI*, 12 Apr. 1998. 44 Bertie Ahern, *Bertie Ahern: the autobiography* (London, 2009), p. 323. 45 *SI*, 29 Apr. 2007.

Fáil, one of the paper's columnists, Eoghan Harris, was one of Taoiseach Ahern's nominees to the Seanad.

Ahead of the 2011 general election Fanning sought views from some of the key contributors to the *Sunday Independent* on how the title could maximise the additional sales that were likely during the imminent campaign. The context to Fanning's written memo was the dramatic collapse of the Irish economy, necessitating an international bailout agreement with the International Monetary Fund, the European Central Bank and the European Commission. The economic turmoil led to the unravelling of the incumbent Fianna Fáil-led coalition. Fanning wanted feedback on editorial direction as he signed off his message, 'I have no coherent idea of what we should credibly be proposing.' This significantly downplayed Fanning's considerable achievement – since his appointment in January 1984 – in driving the newspaper into the dominant position in the Sunday newspaper market, albeit assisted by the demise to the *Sunday Press* in 1995. If nothing else, the 330-word memo very much encapsulated the *Sunday Independent* under Fanning's frequently controversial stewardship:

> We must put Sinn Féin and its politics under relentless scrutiny every week. But more than that, I think that the image of the *Sunday Independent* requires it to be the voice of radical opposition. I believe that we have built up credibility in calling the shots since the early signs of the recession in mid-2006. When that element of the paper is at its best, we have been a lightning rod for the anger and frustration that is out there. Therefore, it should be our aspiration during the campaign to be seen to be not only the voice of the people, but the voice of radical change.[46]

Fanning's approach to economics – as outlined in the memo – was inherently free-market and pro-business: 'to maintain our position of radical opposition, we must put forward common sense suggestions that, if implemented, will get the economy growing again. Words like investment, profit, trade, commerce, enterprise, property must not be taboo in the party political lexicon, as they seem to be at the moment.'[47] This is very much in line with what he had always advocated the title's stance should be. In one interview he observed that:

> we really espouse the market in a way no other newspaper in this country does because they're afraid of alienating pretty powerful interest groups in

---

46 Aengus Fanning, 13 Jan. 2011. Memo in author's possession.   47 Ibid.

the public sector, the unions, and in some political quarters. I don't make
any moral case for the market, but I believe deeply that, while like democracy, it is a far from perfect mechanism, it's the better way of achieving
higher standards of living and employment.[48]

Similar to the 2007 general election, the *Sunday Independent*'s 2011 pre-election
edition carried an interview with the politician the paper viewed most likely
to become taoiseach, in this case 'taoiseach-in-waiting' Enda Kenny of Fine
Gael.[49]

'ONE OF A KIND'

When Aengus Fanning died in January 2012 he was described by Gavin O'Reilly
– then chief executive of Independent News and Media – as 'one a kind, possibly the greatest and most instinctively brilliant editor that Irish journalism
has ever produced'.[50] When Hector Legge retired he had been described as 'a
unique journalist ... a colossus of the Irish newspaper world if there ever was
one'.[51] Obituaries – be they in retirement or in death – of newspaper editors
tend to favour hyperbole and avoid any inclination to 'speak ill of the dead'.
Yet, with regard to Legge and Fanning, there is little doubt that they were
colossi of the *Sunday Independent*. They spent over a quarter of a century each
at the helm of the title, imbuing it with an individual ethos – albeit to serve
very different Irelands. While there may be the temptation to view each editor
and their version of the newspaper – one as conservative and one as provocative – in isolation, in reality they reflect Ireland at different stages of its social,
political and economic development. Sociologist Tom Inglis could have been
thinking of both men and the ethos of their editorships when he noted in
2006 that Ireland was going through 'a clash of cultures'. He observed that it
was 'a clash between the traditional culture of self-denial, humility and self-
deprecation and the culture of the Celtic Tiger that revolves around ambition,
success, getting and spending, going places and being proud of oneself and
one's achievements'.[52]

   The dramatic pace of technological change has caught up with print. In
line with all newspaper titles, circulation has declined in recent years. The
impact of online content availability on readership patterns and purchaser
behaviour has been augmented by the post-2008 economic crash. Weekly sales

48 Kenny, 'Aengus Fanning', p. 219. 49 *SI*, 20 Feb. 2011. 50 *II*, 17 Jan. 2012. 51 *SI*, 1 Nov.
1970. 52 Tom Inglis, 'From self-denial to self-indulgence: the class of cultures in contemporary
Ireland', *Irish Review*, 34 (Spring 2006), pp 34–43 at p. 38.

of the *Sunday Independent* in 2017 averaged some 182,000 copies — a long way short of the numbers achieved, albeit in very different times, by Legge and Fanning. Notwithstanding that fact, the *Sunday Independent* remains a major influence in Irish society though whether it still has, as Fanning had put it, the 'chemistry which makes a newspaper compulsive, that you can't ignore it', is open to debate.

10 / The business start-up: the *Sunday Business Post*, 1989–2001

ED MULHALL

When the presses rolled and the *Irish Times* printing machines produced the first edition of the *Sunday Business Post* in November 1989 it was the beginning of a journalistic and business venture the fortunes of which would often mirror the Ireland it reported on. It was a venture that would come close to collapse on several occasions, make millionaires of some of its founders, have several significant changes in its ownership structure, and yet still operate in 2018 under the banner of 'independent journalism on Sunday'. Its journalists and columnists would chart the story of an Ireland moving from high unemployment to Celtic Tiger to banking collapse, bailouts, austerity and recovery, a time of unprecedented political turbulence in Ireland, and significant economic and social change. It would break stories of major importance that would lead to tribunals of inquiry, cause political and business upheavals and spark controversy in its analysis and reporting with its distinctive approach to economic, social, political, and Northern issues. It would feature in its pages the work of some of the leading journalists and commentators of this era, giving many their first opportunities, and profile the leading players in business and politics as they adapted to the unfolding events. And, as the newspaper itself adapted to the changing economic environment, changing its structure and content to improve its viability, with its particular focus as an Irish business newspaper, it gave a unique perspective on the role of the media in a time of boom and crash.

The *Irish Times* was not the intended printer for that first edition. It was meant to be printed by the *Kilkenny People*, whose owner John Kerry Keane was to have been a key partner in the enterprise. But two days before publication it was realized that the *Kilkenny People*'s new presses would not be ready in time and an emergency solution was found with the *Irish Times*. The turbulence continued the following week, with the paper being printed at the *Meath Chronicle*, and the third edition was printed at the *Sunday World*. Only three months later did the paper settle into a regular print arrangement (with Drogheda Offset Printers). This turbulence on the printing side was a reflection of the efforts to get the paper established in the first place.

It was only five months previously, in June 1989, that four journalists had come together to found a national weekly business newspaper.¹ All were established business journalists or editors. Aileen O'Toole was editor of *Business and Finance* magazine, Damien Kiberd had been business editor of the *Irish Press* and *Sunday Tribune*, Frank Fitzgibbon was editor of *Irish Business* magazine and James Morrissey had been deputy business editor of the *Irish Independent*. Kiberd and Fitzgibbon, who had previously discussed launching a sports newspaper in the early 1980s, took the lead in formulating plans for the new venture. While Kiberd drew up an editorial strategy, Fitzgibbon developed a business plan. They conducted advertising research that pointed to a gap in the Sunday market for 'lost' *Irish Times* readers and an opportunity for a 'second buy' paper for the higher income groups in a quality market dominated by British titles. The proposed company structure was to have three major shareholdings: a printer, John Kerry Keane, of the *Kilkenny People*, who would earn his equity by printing the paper free of charge for the first year; the four founding journalists, who would earn 'sweat equity' by inputting their effort but not cash; and a promise of equity finance of £600,000 raised by Davy Stockbrokers under the government's Business Expansion Scheme, which enabled the founders to secure a bank overdraft of £500,000 and to rent premises and equipment.

O'Toole, who had resigned from her magazine editorship, began approaching journalists who might be interested in joining the venture, bringing two of her key staff from *Business and Finance*, Matt Cooper and Susan O'Keeffe. At the start of November 1989, fifteen staff members had been hired and the editorial side of the paper was taking shape when Kerry Keane decided he could not sign an agreement prepared by Davy Stockbrokers to launch the company. There was now no money and no printer and less than three weeks to the launch date. The founders had previously been in discussion with Groupe Expansion, a French media company led by Jean-Louis Servan-Schreiber, who published business magazines and newspapers and was forming a European network, Euroexpansion. The talks had initially been about syndicating some of Euroexpansion's content but, following a meeting in Dublin, Servan-Schreiber had offered to invest £400,000 in the company for a 20 per cent stake. This offer had, however, stalled on the issue of Kerry Keane and Servan-Schreiber having an equal shareholding. With Kerry Keane now totally withdrawing from the

1 Account of launch from Ivor Kenny, 'Damien Kiberd – the *Sunday Business Post*' in *Talking to ourselves: conversations with editors of Irish news media* (Galway, 1994), pp 53–79; Siobhan O'Connell, 'Why the boss had to go', 'Business Plus', Jan. 2000, and Aileen O'Toole, 'Enterprise – stories from the coalface', presentation at ISME annual conference, 19 Oct. 2007.

venture the founders turned again to Servan-Schreiber. Kiberd and Fitzgibbon
flew to Paris to meet Servan-Schreiber and he agreed to invest £600,000 for a
50 per cent stake in the company thus removing the need for BES investors; the
four founding members would share the other 50 per cent. The printing would
be done by contract without shareholding. As they left, Servan-Schreiber said
to Kiberd and Fitzgibbon, 'I know what it's like when you have a car and you
are all set to go and you have no petrol in the tank.'[2]

EARLY DAYS

While the initial printing moves involved different lay-outs and modes of
transmission of copy and added to the journalistic challenge of having a
compelling new product, the four founders – Kiberd as editor, Fitzgibbon as
managing director, O'Toole as news editor and Morrissey as senior reporter –
were determined to make the new paper stand out. Designed by Stephen Ryan
in a style later to win major awards, its use of character sketches and stylized
photography, often by Tony O'Shea, gave it a distinctive look that was unlike
the other papers in the market. The first issue of 26 November 1989 (which ran
to thirty-two pages) led with an exclusive by James Morrissey about Irish Steel,
which revealed that a secret subsidy worth £3 million had kept it in profit for
the past four years and that the new owner, German industrialist Willy Korf,
would remove the entire board. The front-page photograph was of Progressive
Democrats minister Bobby Molloy and was linked with a special feature on the
minister and his party conference. Inside there were three pages of home news
and two pages of world news.

The main news feature was an exclusive interview with Tony Ryan of
Guinness Peat Aviation, in which he spoke about the company he had founded,
Ryanair, his view of the Irish economy and his hopes for Ireland. On the 'News
Focus' page was an extensive piece by Susan O'Keeffe on Larry Goodman and
the collapse of the Goodman's group plans to invest £216 million in its Irish
factories, a plan that had been unveiled to great fanfare, with Taoiseach Charles
Haughey and two ministers in attendance. O'Keeffe revealed that the announcement had been made despite the fact that no deal with the IDA had been
finalized, and that now that Des O'Malley was back as minister for industry the
controversy over export credit relief and the Goodman companies was likely to
be pursued with more vigour.

The issue had two editorials, which was to become its usual format. The
first was 'Managing the Debt', which praised the efforts of Michael Somers,

2 Kenny, 'Damien Kiberd', p. 68.

the public servant in charge of the National Treasury Management Agency, and warned against importing fund managers into the system rather than rewarding those within. The second editorial, under the heading 'Fianna Fáil's Private Fears', urged the acceleration of the plans for the privatization of state companies and stated that Fianna Fáil worries of a clash with trade unions were misplaced. The theme of tax cuts was continued by Damien Kiberd in his economics column, which featured on the main editorial page, together with a politics column by former Fine Gael minister John Boland. Boland's theme was 'Bertie talk doesn't make real jobs', and it argued that the Fianna Fáil labour minister, and future taoiseach, had 'lost the run of himself'. Another opinion column, by James Morrissey, focussed on a rift between Taoiseach Charles Haughey and EU Commissioner Pádraig Flynn. Also in the main section of the paper were the specialist 'Markets' pages edited by Matt Cooper. Spread over three pages these included news stories, briefs, shares and gilts analysis, reports from London and New York and an international-markets commentary. Included was an analysis piece by George Lee, later economics editor of RTÉ, titled 'Sterling in decline as Thatcher's image fades', which argued that potential challenges to her leadership were a considerable negative influence on the currency. At the end of the main section of the paper was a page of more personality-based news items – 'The Last Post' – and a cartoon that lampooned civil servant 'mandarins' spending most of their day thinking of how much more they could be earning in the private sector.

The features pages of the paper opened with a major profile article, illustrated by a cartoon of the subject, Jim Stafford. Stafford, the investor in the national radio franchise Century Ireland, was a man, according to the article, prepared to take legal action against anyone who would take a photograph of him. Beside the profile was the first edition of a regular column – 'Counter March' – by Mary Ellen Synon. It focused on Thatcherism and noted that 'people are finally paying the price of a market that has not been based on liberty and good government'. Two pages centred on personal finance followed, with pieces by Kiberd on golden handshakes and tax and an investigation by Paul White into the hidden costs of mortgages. In the rest of the paper were columns on health (Orna Mulcahy), wine (John Bowman), architecture (James Dolan), motoring (Karl Tsigdinos) and the workplace (Mary Mulvihill), as well as marketing, media and communication pages with related stories and an advertising feature on mortgage plans. Finally came two commercial-property pages, one of which noted that developer Owen O'Callaghan was no longer involved in the £30 million sale of the Merchants Quay centre in Cork. There were no sports pages. The back page of the paper featured a question-and-answer segment

called 'The Finishing Post', between Aileen O'Toole and the chief executive of
Bord Gáis Éireann, John Lynch.

Despite the production challenges, it was a strong opening edition, as the
reporters had stocked up an impressive series of exclusive and in-depth stories for the launch. The booked advertising kept faith with the intended ratio
(60/40) of editorial to advertising and the initial optimism that Fitzgibbon
had found in presentations to advertising agencies. The *Post's* rates were lower
than other Sunday newspapers', and it was clearly aiming at the high end of the
market – which was reflected in the number of banking and insurance adverts
there were in the first issue. In his interviews to promote the paper, Fitzgibbon
had emphasized that there was a real difference in the fact that this new venture
was led by four journalists: 'In most newspapers, stories are dropped or slashed
in length for purely commercial considerations – to fit more ads in – but we
have set limits on the amount of advertising we'll take and we'll stick to that.'[3]
In the positive climate of the launch, however, there was one warning note when
RTÉ broadcaster Gay Byrne reacted to its prospects on his popular radio show:
'A newspaper dedicated to business? I can't see it lasting six months.'[4] Initial
interest in the paper was high, with a reported 38,000 circulation for early editions, which later settled to around 24,000 per edition.[5]

The first month of publication showed the approach the paper would
adopt. Among the lead stories during this time were revelations that SIPTU
was seeking state aid to axe 100 staff as the super union was created from the
ITGWU and FWUI, and an exclusive by Susan O'Keeffe on Larry Goodman.[6]
The continuing investigation into Goodman by O'Keeffe contrasted with the
editorial in the same edition. In a full column editorial, Kiberd wrote:

> Ireland is a land of great hatred and little room ... This week the perse-
> cution of Mr Laurence Goodman moved into top gear ... Mr Goodman
> is not a saint. He would not be the success he is if he were of a saintly
> disposition ... If Mr Goodman or any of his agents have broken the rules
> in relation to export credit insurance or any matter, then they should be
> given appropriate punishments by the relevant government departments
> and agents of the state. But this does not mean that Mr Goodman should
> be pilloried in the media and hounded by the organs of the state ... Some
> years ago the victim was Charles Haughey ... some years later the reality
> has begun to impinge on the collective consciousness of Dublin's moralis-
> ing journalists. Charles Haughey is no saint either. But he is doing a much

---

3 *IT*, 22 Nov. 1989.   4 RTÉ Radio One, Dec. 1989, quoted in O'Toole, 'Enterprise – stories from
the coalface'.   5 Kenny, 'Damien Kiberd', p. 70.   6 *SBP*, 3 & 24 Dec. 1989.

better job of running the economy than Dr FitzGerald did or could. And that is what counts.[7]

The *Post*'s distinctive editorial stance was also reflected in its first editorial on Northern Ireland: 'Hearts, Minds and Provos'. It was clear from the paper's use of the term 'six counties' when referring to Northern Ireland that the editorial perspective was to be a nationalist one. The efforts of the Ireland Funds to combat terrorism by investing in depressed areas would, the editorial argued, not work:

> Recently there have been claims that segments of Sinn Féin and the IRA favour reaching some form of short term accommodation with the British which would mean an end to violence … It would be wrong to be too confident, however, that such a process can be brought to fruition. The extreme violence deployed by the IRA this week indicates no softening of its attitude. It is difficult to see what future there would be for either the IRA or Sinn Féin were they to end their so-called armed struggle.[8]

The final paper of the year looked back at the previous decade and forward to the next, nominating business people and politicians it believed were of the past and those who would be of the future. Among the upcoming business people was Denis O'Brien, with his investments in Esat and his new radio station 98fm. O'Brien, it noted, 'has a keen interest in technological development of the communications business'. Among the politicians tipped to impact on the 1990s were Bertie Ahern, Charlie McCreevy, Emmet Stagg, Richard Bruton, Eamon Gilmore and Ivan Yates.[9]

In establishing the pattern of the paper in the first year it is notable that there was a strong business-and-politics focus in the news pages. There was little or no reporting from the North and no specific crime reporting. The media itself received a good deal of coverage, with the fortunes of Century Radio, minister Ray Burke's attempts to interfere with RTÉ's advertising and the travails of the *Press* group and *Sunday Tribune* all featuring regularly. One editorial was headed 'Burke should resign now', and Kiberd penned a feature on the *Irish Press* headed 'Press in whole new ball game' that used the example of a controversy over the *Sunday Press*' spot-the-ball competition as an analogy for the decline of the group and the exodus of quality journalists from it.[10] Susan O'Keeffe continued her persistent reporting on the Goodman story,

7 *SBP*, 24 Dec. 1989. 8 *SBP*, 17 Dec. 1989. 9 *SBP*, 24 Dec. 1989. 10 *SBP*, 10 Jan. 1990 & 27 July 1990.

but was away when it burst into crisis in August 1990. The paper covered it extensively with two-page spreads in subsequent weeks and revealed, in a James Morrissey exclusive, that Goodman owed £500 million, up to £100 million of which was to Irish banks and much of it unsecured.[11] An editorial headed 'The Goodman conundrum' described the scale of the crisis as 'breath-taking' and called for further investigation, including into the links between the government and Goodman. These links were the subject of a subsequent story by O'Keeffe which claimed that the government had pressurized the banks over Goodman.[12]

The central profile, accompanied by a sketch of the subject, became a lasting feature of the paper. In the first year the subjects were primarily from business (Denis Brosnan, Pascal Taggart, Paddy Wright, Craig McKinney, Oliver Barry, Philip Monaghan) or politics (Alan Dukes, Bertie Ahern, John Bruton, Dick Spring), with only two women profiled in that time (Mary O'Rourke and Mary Robinson). It also aimed to spot rising stars of business, with, for example, Seán Quinn being profiled in July 1990.[13]

By its first anniversary the *Post* was a much-expanded paper, and by mid-1990 its average circulation was 25,874.[14] In the second half of 1990 the news pages were increased, as was the 'Second Post' section, with more lifestyle coverage and a new 'Arts' page edited by Eileen Battersby. A new bi-weekly broadsheet section, 'Industrial Post', was introduced, with news stories and regional- and international-focus pages with associated advertising. The monthly 'Computer Supplement' had begun in May 1990 (soon featuring Brian Trench, who had joined the staff as sub-editor). Future editor Ted Harding was now on the staff and James Morrissey had become deputy editor, also taking responsibility for a Northern edition.

It was a stated aim of the founders of the paper that as well as a unique focus on business and politics, the paper would have a real investigative edge. Since the founders had between them many years of editorial experience, they would be better able to take on board the risks associated with backing a strong and important story. Reporters were encouraged to keep track of developing stories, often returning to them week after week with new developments and with the aim of generating some scoops. Susan O'Keeffe's work on the Goodman companies throughout 1990 is an example of this, with various angles covered and new stories broken. During her investigations O'Keeffe was alerted to irregularities in the labelling of exports in some Goodman plants and was assigned for a number of weeks to try to substantiate the allegations. However, the editors did not believe that the story reached the threshold to publish and it did

11 *SBP*, 18 & 26 Aug. 1990.   12 *SBP*, 23 Sept. 1990.   13 *SBP*, 22 July 1990.   14 *SBP*, 2 Sept. 1990.

not run. During her research O'Keeffe had met a producer from Granada TV in Manchester who was interested in the story. She joined Grenada and spent seven months working on the investigation that resulted in the *World in Action* programme of May 1991.[15] The programme caused a sensation and led to the establishment of a tribunal of inquiry into the allegations (under Justice Liam Hamilton).[16] O'Keeffe would later be charged with contempt of court when she refused to reveal her sources for the stories at the Hamilton Tribunal, but was subsequently found not guilty. Kiberd and reporter Brian Carey were also called before the tribunal to account for their reporting but were not charged with contempt.[17]

The *Post*, perhaps stung by being scooped by its former employee and the perception that its editorial defence of Goodman could have been perceived as a restraint on its investigative edge, followed up with extensive coverage of the fallout, with reporter Matt Cooper and deputy editor James Morrissey revealing significant new information about the business transactions of the Goodman group.[18] Morrissey was also investigating Greencore, the newly privatized Irish Sugar Company, and the involvement of some of its management in the ownership of subsidiary companies, with his reporting continuing over subsequent editions.[19] The controversy led to inspectors' reports, court actions and eventually out-of-court settlements.[20]

The Greencore controversy was followed by a number of others, many with links to Charles Haughey and the government: the sale of the Telecom site in Ballsbridge, involving Michael Smurfit and Dermot Desmond; the row over the sale of the Carysfort College site; land sales at Kinsealy; and investments in Haughey's son's company Celtic Helicopters. In a full-front-page editorial headed 'State of Emergency' Kiberd listed a number of revelations that week from the investigations into these various controversies, plus a recent vicious incident in the North and stark unemployment figures, and declared that:

> No country can continue to function in this manner. The people are heartily sick of it all. The time has come for a total change in Irish politics. Very few of those who currently hold high office in the Republic of Ireland should stay on. The country needs a total change of direction and this should begin, as we have stated before, with the declaration of an economic emergency.[21]

15 Mark O'Brien, *The fourth estate: journalism in twentieth-century Ireland* (Manchester, 2017), p. 214, and Damien Kiberd profile in the *Phoenix*, 3 Apr. 1993. 16 *SBP*, 1 May 1991. 17 *SBP*, 28 Nov. 2004; see also Elaine Byrne, *Political corruption in Ireland 1922–2010: a crooked harp?* (Manchester, 2012), pp 107–36. 18 *SBP*, 16 June 1991 & 19 May 1991. 19 *SBP* 6 Aug., 15 Sept. & 17 Nov. 1991. 20 *IT*, 13 Sept. 2013 has summary of the controversy's fallout. 21 *SBP*, 17 Nov. 1991.

Despite its steady weekly circulation the *Post* was not achieving its revenue targets and the French partner was becoming anxious. While Kiberd thought that adding sport coverage would increase sales Servan-Schreiber was not keen. Fitzgibbon felt that targeted direct advertising – selling directly to businesses – would improve cash flow and so the 'Industrial Post' was launched, an expert in trade magazines was brought in, and the advertising staff increased from five to thirty-eight.[22] When the paper expanded to sixty-two pages to deal with these special sections the increases in overheads led to clashes among the directors, with O'Toole and Morrissey on one side, Fitzgibbon on the other and Kiberd somewhere in between. In May 1991 the company ran out of money and Fitzgibbon asked that the second features section of the paper be dropped as it was not generating the revenue that the special sections were. This led to a major clash with the others and, as the dispute became public, the group held its first board meeting in eighteen months with the French shareholder.[23] By now Kiberd was in agreement with O'Toole and Morrissey and so Fitzgibbon was bought out and left the company in June 1991. Euroexpansion insisted on appointing its own chief executive, an English publisher, Jane Tolson. Relations with Tolson were not good (there were some reports of editorial meetings being held in Irish to exclude her), with clashes on advertising policy being the main bone of contention.[24] In January 1992 a business plan was adopted that reduced overheads, with up to one-third of the paper's staff being let go. Morrissey resigned as a director and left the paper in July 1992, later selling his shares to the other shareholders. Tolson also left that summer and the two remaining founders approached Barbara Nugent, who had been managing director of the *Sunday Tribune*, to join them as chief executive.

Nugent's arrival meant the paper now had the experience at the business end of the operation to align it with its editorial ambitions. The cost-cutting plan was implemented, a new advertising strategy was adopted and a new printing contract negotiated. However, just as these improvements were impacting on the company's finances another crisis hit, when Euroexpansion indicated that it could not continue to support the paper and wanted to bring in a new equity partner. At a crucial Christmas 1992 board meeting, Kiberd, Nugent and O'Toole secured agreement that they would source the new investor.[25] Among those interested in investing were the Pearson Group (then owners of the *Financial Times* and the *Economist*), which sought a controlling stake in the company, and a German publishing house, Verlag Norman Rentrop, which had, coincidentally, placed an advert in the paper in January 1993 seeking investment

22 Kenny, 'Damien Kiberd', pp 71–2. 23 See *IT*, 5 June 1991 & Kenny, 'Damien Kiberd', p. 72. 24 *Phoenix*, 1 Nov. 1991; also 9 Aug. 1991, 20 Mar. 1992 & 3 Apr. 1993.

Figure 11: The first edition of *The Sunday Business Post* on 26 November 1989.
The masthead was coloured green.

opportunities in Ireland. Rentrop ultimately took 40 per cent of the shareholding, with Euroexpansion diluting to 10 per cent and Kiberd, O'Toole
and now Nugent sharing 50 per cent. The balance sheet was cleaned out, with
Euroexpansion writing off debts. The new investments and cost reductions
allowed the company to move from a loss of £1 million in 1992 to a declared
pre-tax profit of £210,000 in 1993.[26]

ECONOMICS AND BUSINESS

As a business newspaper, editor Damien Kiberd was clear on its mandate: 'The
Post believes in wealth creation, in individual effort, in success, in improving the
stock of human capital in this country, in defending the rights of the business
people.'[27] So it was through its business and economic coverage more than anything else that the *Post* needed to establish itself as a distinctive voice offering
something not available from competing products. It did this through its in-depth
news coverage, its specialist pages, its focus on business and business personalities,
in its feature coverage and in its specialist commentary and editorial positioning.

   In pursuit of its pro-business stance, the *Post* continuously recommended tax
cuts as a way of stimulating activity. It was positive too about tax amnesties and
was not critical of revelations of off-shore accounts as long as they were legal.
On taxation, it supported the tax amnesty of 1993 and deemed it a success. It
promoted tax cuts ahead of the 1994, 1996 and 1997 budgets, and it praised
the tax cuts in Budget 1999,[28] though it recognized the problems with the tax
individualization proposals in that budget. But, by the end of 2000, it was recommending against further tax cuts.[29] Even during the period when the paper's
editorials were recommending tax cuts, the main economic columnist of this
period, Colm Rapple, offered a dissenting view, with columns headed 'Tax cuts
not the only option' in 1996, and 'Tax cuts won't help real losers in system' in
1997.[30] On currency matters the *Post* had, as early as 1993, argued for uniting the
currencies in the European Exchange Rate Mechanism (ERM) but was wary of
some of the policy downsides of the move to further economic integration.[31]
There were concerns about the single currency:

> the central problem is that not all of the pupils in this class of 11 can or
> will move at the same pace ... At worst, this could result in economic and

25 Account taken from same sources as footnote 1.   26 *IT*, 4 Feb. 1994.   27 *SBP*, 28 Nov.
2004.   28 *SBP*, 14 Dec. 1994, 6 Oct. 1996, 7 Dec. 1997, 18 May 1997, 6 Dec. 1998.   29 *SBP*, 3 Dec.
2000.   30 *SBP*, 6 Dec. 1996 & 18 May 1997.   31 *SBP*, 28 Feb. 1993 & 1 Aug. 1993. Columnist George
Lee dissented, arguing for the Irish currency to 'consider going it alone'. See *SBP*, 7 Feb. 1993.

political meltdown in one or more member states with governments facing
hostility from the poor and unemployed and getting little sympathy from
the bureaucrats of the European Central Bank.[32]

The birth of the euro in 1999 saw the publication of a special 'questions and
answers' section and an opinion poll full of optimism.[33] The business coverage
was supported by money and advice pages (pioneered by Gail Seacamp), some
specialist magazines such as 'Computers in Business' (2000) and guides to property tax, tax returns and even off-shore tax.

With dedicated property pages the *Post* was well attuned to the role property was already playing in driving the improving economy. In addition to
its investigations on planning corruption it charted the growth of prominent
builders and developers and chronicled the competition for major projects.[34]
In 1997 it published a major feature piece asking 'What's funding the property
boom?' and another on irresponsible lending.[35] It highlighted the reports by
economist Peter Bacon on measures to cool the market and closely followed
the rise in house prices into 2000.[36] It considered the second Bacon report
'too much stick and not enough carrot' and by September 2001, just after the
events of 9/11, it had an economist warning of a 20 per cent price fall in the
property sector.[37]

The high levels of borrowing associated with the Celtic Tiger economy of
the late 1990s was a theme of the now established column by economist David
McWilliams, who had first contributed feature articles to the paper, starting in
1996 with one highlighting the improved economy, headlined 'Celtic Tiger Irish
fundamentals the envy of Europe'.[38] He began his regular column with a stark
warning 'A tiger can become a lame duck very fast'. Using the example of South
Korea, he warned that pressures in the economy and the inability to adjust
exchange rates would give rise to falling productivity: 'Unfortunately, unlike the
Koreans whose undervalued exchange rate allowed them to rebound, our euro
may actually be rising in the years ahead potentially condemning us to years of
negative equity.'[39] This came just after the paper had begun a ten-page dedicated
property supplement in February 2000. The supplement was launched by then
Taoiseach Bertie Ahern at a reception attended by a 'number of leading figures
in the property sector', including developers Joe Cosgrave, Noel Smyth and
John Rohan.[40]

32 *SBP*, 10 May 1998. 33 *SBP*, 3 Jan. 1999. 34 *SBP*, 18 Jan. 1998. 35 *SBP*, 30 July 1997 & 7
Sept. 1997. 36 *SBP*, 19 Apr. 1999, 15 Aug. 1999 & 18 June 2000. 37 *SBP*, 18 June 2000 & 23 Sept.
2001. 38 *SBP*, 12 May 1996. 39 *SBP*, 2 Mar. 2000. 40 *SBP*, 13 Mar. 2000.

Ahead of the 2001 budget McWilliams was warning that 'this borrowing binge is blowing our bubble, this budget isn't that important; it's excess credit that is overheating the economy'. He concluded that:

> given the storm clouds building on the global stock markets, financial distress on a major scale here in Ireland can't be far away. Is it any wonder that this week Seán Fitzpatrick, one of the savviest operators in town, announced Anglo-Irish's purchase of a Swiss bank? The flight to quality begins.[41]

A year later – in a piece headed 'Borrowing bubble about to burst' – he challenged the predictions of other economists of a 'soft landing' for the boom economy. An editorial in the same edition, one of the last under Damien Kiberd as editor, took issue with a statement by the then governor of the Central Bank (Maurice O'Connell) that the Celtic Tiger was dead and growth was withering away. There was, it argued, no reason to panic: 'This is the first time in the history of the state that we have entered a recession with a strong cadre of experienced business people whose object is the creation of wealth.' Kiberd was even more direct in his 'The Rant' column: 'The Celtic Tiger is not dead. Mr O'Connell is a civil servant not an entrepreneur. Even as he communicates his dismal message, there are men and women out there rolling around and unable to sleep because of the dreams of wealth creation that obsess their brains. The Tiger lives. Floreat.'[42] If the seeds of the economic crash were well sown by this stage another portent was seen in a piece by newly installed markets editor Michael Murray. Focusing on the results of fast growing Anglo-Irish bank he noted that:

> many believe that this agile, fleet of foot, niche player will fall flat on its face once the economy turns down ... So far chief executive Seán Fitzpatrick has proved them wrong but the suggestion from the Anglo sceptics is that he is about to get a bloody nose. Anglo's sceptics argue that the bank's focus on property lending means that when the property market's fortunes turn Anglo's will turn with it.[43]

POLITICS, INVESTIGATIONS AND SOCIAL AFFAIRS

In reviewing his tenure as editor, Damien Kiberd took particular pride in the quality of the reporting staff.[44] In many cases the *Post* gave an early opportunity

41 *SBP*, 3 Dec. 2000.   42 *SBP*, 11 Nov. 2001   43 *SBP*, 3 Dec. 2001.   44 *SBP*, 28 Nov. 2004.

to young journalists, often taking the best of the crop from the journalism colleges. In some cases a journalist started off as a contributor and returned later as a staff member. Notable during this period were Mark Little, Richard Curran, Simon Carswell, Will Goodbody, Pat Leahy, Catherine O'Mahony, Gillian Nelis, Siobhán O'Connell and Ruth Marchand. Occasionally, the paper benefited from the problems in other newspapers, getting Des Crowley and Colm Rapple from the *Irish Press*, Kevin Dawson from the *Sunday Tribune* and Kieron Wood from RTÉ.

Part of the strength of the reporting came from the journalists building up expertise and contacts on specific stories and sectors through sustained coverage and, in some cases, through specialization, by editing topic pages or sections. Ted Harding, later an editor of the paper, took responsibility for property and planning stories in the early stages of the paper and this interest was sustained in his later reporting. He reported on planning corruption allegations and the role of Liam Lawlor in rezoning controversies and followed up with stories on Owen O'Callaghan in 1995 as well as providing many of the profiles of developers during that period.[45] He covered the mobile-phone licensing competition in 1995, when the *Post* profiled all the bidders, then as the main reporter dealing with the various controversies concerning Michael Lowry in 1996 and 1997 and on to the Moriarty Tribunal in 1999.[46] He followed Denis O'Brien, with the Esat mega-deal in 2000, through stories of a potential bid for Eircom to his embroilment in controversy in 2001.[47] Similarly, Kathleen Barrington, who later became one of the most astute commentators in advance of the crash in the subsequent decade, followed the early banking scandals at National Irish Bank and AIB during this period.[48]

The *Post*'s political coverage moved into another gear from May 1994 with the arrival of Emily O'Reilly, formerly of the *Irish Press*, as political editor. Her reporting on the major political controversies and personalities complemented that of Mark O'Connell, who regularly broke stories about forthcoming legislation and rows within the parliamentary parties. She also began a new political column titled 'Between the Lines'. At this time O'Reilly focussed in particular on the tensions within the Fianna Fáil-Labour coalition. Her style, often mixing reporting and commentary, culminated in an extended special report – '7 days in the death of a Government' – on the fall of Albert Reynolds.[49] Her sharply critical reporting of politics continued through the new John Bruton 'rainbow' administration, in particular in relation to economic and Northern

45 *SBP*, 15 Oct. 1995 & 29 Aug. 1997.   46 *SBP*, 22 Dec. 1996, 31 Aug. 1997 & 27 June 1999.   47 *SBP*, 14 Jan. 2000, 11 Feb. 2000, 17 Apr. 2001, 14 & 21 Oct. 2001.   48 *SBP*, 25 Jan., 29 Mar., 11 Oct. 1998 & 9 May 1999.   49 *SBP*, 23 May 1994, 2 Oct. 1994 & 27 Nov. 1994.

policy. Keeping with the *Post* practice of sustained coverage on significant running stories, O'Reilly followed in detail the controversy surrounding hepatitis
C and the blood bank and the women infected with the virus through con-
taminated blood transfusions.[50] She also revealed the Department of Foreign
Affairs memo at the centre of a 'green smear' against Mary MacAleese during
the 1997 presidential election (the memo alleged that she was 'too nationalist' to
be president).[51] O'Reilly kept contributing to the *Post* during two periods away
from the staff of the paper, while she served as editor of *Magill* (1999) and as a
breakfast presenter on *Radio Ireland* (1997). She became political correspondent
at the *Post* again in December 2000.

Maol Muire Tynan became parliamentary correspondent in early 1999.
One of her early notable stories was a survey of TD expenses, researched with
reporter Pat Leahy, later political editor of the paper. She also contributed to
the paper's coverage of the fallout of the mobile-phone licenses, with stories
on the clash between Esat and Denis O'Brien over a Fine Gael cheque, and an
exclusive interview with Michael Lowry.[52] Many of the *Post*'s exclusive political
stories concerned early warnings of new legislative proposals, such as the bills
on the financial regulator (Tynan), the scrapping of BES schemes (O'Connell),
the plans for Special Saving Incentive Accounts (Tynan), as well as drafts of
constitutional amendments (O'Connell).[53]

The reputation of the *Post* as an investigative paper, prepared to take risks
in its reporting, is exemplified by an examination of two of its most notable and controversial reporters: Veronica Guerin and Frank Connolly. Guerin,
the crime journalist who was murdered in 1996 while working for the *Sunday
Independent*, began her career as a serious journalist with the *Sunday Business Post*.
Kiberd recalled that she had sent a CV to the paper in 1990, looking to make
a start in journalism, and contributed as a freelance initially. She submitted a
story on aircraft leasing that he thought was very good and published, although
its literary style was 'very unsuited to newspapers'.[54] Her first major story was
an investigation into the Aer Lingus Holidays in January 1991, with a number
of follow up stories later that year.[55] Guerin also investigated aspects of the
Goodman story, particularly those concerning a bank in Cyprus where £2.5
million of company money was deposited. Guerin travelled to Cyprus on her
own initiative, showing her determination to follow a lead.[56]

50 *SBP*, 16 July, 23 Aug., 6 & 27 Oct. 1996 & 16, 23 Mar. & 1 June 1997.   51 *SBP*, 19 Oct. 1997.   52 *SBP*,
5 Sept. 1999, 18 Mar. 2001 & 14 Jan. 2000.   53 *SBP*, 10 Oct. 1999, 27 Apr. 1997, 11 Feb. 2001 & 3
Aug. 1997.   54 Emily O'Reilly, *Veronica Guerin: the life and death of a crime reporter* (London, 1998), pp
29–30.   55 *SBP*, 20 Jan., 10 Feb. & 31 Mar. 1991.   56 *SBP*, 12 Jan., 9 Feb. 1992; O'Reilly, *Veronica Guerin*,
p. 31.

However, some of her stories caused difficulties. An October 1992 scoop that revealed the contents of a taped telephone conversation involving John Bruton (ironically about phone tapping) resulted in Guerin and Kiberd being charged in the District Court for criminal breaches of the Postal and Telecommunications Act. Both pleaded guilty and they were fined £600 each.[57] Another political story, claiming to be the 'inside story of the Reynolds coup', led to one of the most comprehensive apologies published in the paper – to Albert Reynolds, Pádraig Flynn, Tom Savage and others – stating that there was no 'conspiracy' and that the reported meetings never took place.[58] A major investigation by Guerin into Aer Rianta and its attempts to secure new duty-free franchises, which involved leaked memos of Aer Rianta board meetings, ran into serious difficulty following a court injunction. The paper ran blank pages with a large INJUNCTED stamp across them.[59] However, in the courts, before the hearing of the case on the injunction, the paper's legal team was presented with an affidavit which alleged that Veronica Guerin was pursuing the story out of personal grievance with Aer Rianta and that a previous dispute with the company had involved the presentation of forged documents. The paper agreed not to publish and Aer Rianta agreed not to pursue their action.[60]

Guerin soon left the *Post* for the *Sunday Tribune* before moving to the *Sunday Independent*. But before she left she published her first major crime story, an investigation into the murder of a Dublin underworld figure named Travers and the killings that followed.[61] With this she began to establish the contacts that were the basis of her subsequent crime reporting. After her murder in June 1996 Kiberd praised her 'good old fashioned courage' and the paper's editorial noted that the events of that week had 'swept away the fog of complacency and excuses and blind eye turning that has allowed us, the people, to permit the political system to evade its responsibilities in the area of law and order'.[62]

By then, the *Post* had a dedicated crime reporter, John Mooney, and he (and later Barry O'Kelly) pursued the fallout of the Guerin murder, both in following the investigation and in reporting on other crime stories.[63] The crime coverage had included pieces critical of the use of 'supergrass' evidence in criminal trials and Frank Connolly would later investigate stories of Garda corruption

57 *SBP*, 28 Nov. 2004. 58 *SBP*, 13 Mar. 1994; original story 18 Oct. 1992. 59 *SBP*, 2 Dec. 1992. 60 O'Reilly, *Veronica Guerin*, pp 31–3. 61 *SBP*, 19 July 1992. 62 *SBP*, 30 June 1996. 63 See Mooney's interview with John Gilligan, 11 July 1996 and 'One year on', 29 July 1997; O'Kelly on Guerin investigation 6 Aug. 2000 and 'Probe into Gardaí' 3 Dec. 2000. 64 *SBP*, 9 Mar. 1997, 3 Nov. 1995 & 2 Mar. 2000.

in Cork and Donegal.[64] The most significant investigation in terms of impact was Connolly's into planning corruption, as it led to the establishment of the Planning Tribunal and the series of political crises that followed. It was through the solicitors firm Donnelly, Neary and Donnelly in Newry that Connolly was first put into contact with James Gogarty, a retired executive with the building firm Joseph Murphy Structural Engineering (JMSE).[65] Gogarty had gone to the legal firm with serious accusations concerning payments made to politicians and officials to secure planning permission, in response to a newspaper advertisement offering a reward for such information.[66]

The first story Connolly published on the allegations followed a meeting with the two men who had put up the reward for information about planning corruption, later identified as Michael Smith and Colm MacEochaidh, at their solicitors' premises. In August 1995, under the heading 'Politician link to property, rezoning pay-offs', the *Post* reported a current politician and three former Fianna Fáil office holders as having received pay-offs. Following a meeting with Gogarty at the solicitors' premises some months later, Connolly ran a story in March 1996 that gave more detail, under the heading 'FF politician paid off by developers'. It claimed that a 'senior Fianna Fáil politician was alleged to have received two substantial payments for planning assistance'.[67] Connolly then had a more comprehensive interview with Gogarty, which he taped, and this led to a story of how a 'former company executive' had stated he had been present when the two amounts of £40,000 were allegedly handed over to the politician.[68] When minister Ray Burke was named as the politician involved and Gogarty went on the record with his allegations in another series of stories in the summer of 1997, it became a major political controversy.[69] Burke was forced to resign and a Tribunal of inquiry under Justice Flood was established in November 1997. The second interim report of the tribunal found the payment alleged in the articles to have been corrupt and that those present (Burke, Gogarty, Joseph Murphy and Michael Baily) knew it to be such.[70] The third interim report contained adverse findings against those mentioned in the articles for obstructing the work of the tribunal.

However, following a number of appeals, many of these findings have been overturned. Most significant was a supreme court judgment in April 2010

65 For background see Frank Connolly, *Tom Gilmartin* (Dublin, 2014) & Paul Cullen, *With a little help from my friends: planning corruption in Ireland* (Dublin, 2002). 66 Michael Smith, 'The Mahon and Moriarty tribunal reports' at Magill Summer School, 2012. Smith was also the source for the exclusive stories on the Progressive Democrats donor files (rescued from a skip – story 14 Dec. 1997) and Liam Lawlor's tax returns. 67 *SBP*, 31 Mar. 1996. 68 *SBP*, 7 Apr. 1996. 69 *SBP*, 11 May, 27 July, 10 Aug. & 14 Sept. 1997. 70 Byrne, *Political corruption in Ireland*, pp 168–75; Tribunal of Inquiry into Certain Planning Matters, planning tribunal.ie.

involving an appeal by Joseph Murphy, Frank Reynolds and JSME against the tribunal's decision not to award them their costs as they had been found to have obstructed the tribunal. Central to the appeal was detail in the tapes of the interviews Frank Connolly conducted with Gogarty where accusations were made against other individuals. These had not been made available by the tribunal to the witnesses and as they could have been used to test the credibility of Gogarty's evidence, the process was undermined. The plaintiffs received their costs, and the findings that they had obstructed the tribunal were removed. Subsequently, Ray Burke too had the finding of 'corruption' deleted from the tribunal report.[71]

Just as the Planning Tribunal was beginning its work in 1998, the *Post* and the *Sunday Independent* had published stories in which it was claimed that an Irish businessman based in London, Tom Gilmartin, who had been involved in a plan to develop the Quarryvale site in west Dublin, had given Pádraig Flynn, the former environment minister and now EU commissioner, £50,000 for Fianna Fáil. The story by Frank Connolly ran under the heading 'Developer claims he gave Flynn £50,000 for FF funds' and in subsequent weeks further details of the claims were published, including the involvement of former government press officer Frank Dunlop and that Gilmartin would co-operate with the tribunal.[72] The tribunal widened its inquiries to include new allegations, but as these were reported in the press Gilmartin began to display a reluctance to give evidence and, as he was based in London, he could not be compelled to attend. This situation changed when Flynn addressed the issue in a *Late Late Show* interview in January 1999, claiming that Gilmartin 'was unwell, his wife's unwell, he's out of sorts', and denying that he had 'ever taken money from anyone to do a political favour for anyone as far as planning is concerned'. The interview incensed Gilmartin, who was now determined to give evidence and gave further details of his contacts with Flynn and other ministers, as reported in a number of further *Business Post* stories. These included Gilmartin's accusation that Taoiseach Bertie Ahern had been told of the payment and had also been present at a meeting in the Dáil after which Gilmartin said a man had approached him, seeking a £5 million offshore payment.[73] These events brought Ahern firmly into the ambit of the tribunal; its inquiries and the evidence given to it would eventually lead to his resignation in 2008.

At the time of the original Gilmartin claims, Ahern's resistance to the ongoing political fallout from the tribunal was assisted greatly by the publication

71 See Supreme Court 119/06, 21 Apr. 2010; *II*, 23 Apr. 2010; *Village*, 4 Mar. 2015 & 15 Dec. 2014; and *IT*, 28 Jan. 2015.   72 *SBP*, 27 Sept., 4 & 11 Oct. 1998. See also Connolly, *Tom Gilmartin* for full background.   73 *SBP*, 24 & 27 Jan. 1999; *Late Late Show* aired on 22 Jan. 1999.

in the *Post* of another accusation against him that was subsequently proven to be false. This was the claim by Cork businessman Denis 'Starry' O'Brien, who alleged that he had given Ahern a cheque for £50,000 from the developer Owen O'Callaghan in a car park of the Burlington Hotel on the night of the All-Ireland football final of September 1989. The *Post* had initially been wary of running the story and had passed on the information to the tribunal, but when it was alluded to at a discovery motion, the paper ran a Frank Connolly story outlining the basic allegation. It didn't name names, but it stated that if upheld, it could cause an election.[74] Ahern vehemently denied that he was involved in any such transaction and when the *Post* followed up with a more detailed account naming O'Brien, Ahern and O'Callaghan, the taoiseach sued O'Brien for libel. The accusation was soon seen as false and the *Post* subsequently published an apology to Ahern and O'Callaghan.[75]

Although the *Post* was responsible for some of the reporting that had led to the various tribunals of inquiry, its editorials were often sharply critical of the findings issued and stressed that enforcing the law was the best way to deal with business and political corruption – not expensive, drawn-out tribunals that had limited direct impact. 'Inquisition', it declared, 'is alive and well, tribunals are a failure to deal with business corruption through the normal channels'.[76]

From 1995 there was a major investment in the *Post*'s features pages under the 'Agenda' banner, with Aileen O'Toole establishing the in-depth interview as a major feature, and often conducting the interviews herself. These interviews went well beyond the business-and-politics focus of the main paper and have become one of *Post*'s lasting legacies. In November 2014, the paper's twenty-fifth anniversary, a special supplement, 'Ireland Interviewed', reprinted a selection of the most notable interviews. Some columnists who were to be central to the newspaper's success also joined in this mid-1990s period. Emmanuel Kehoe began a TV column in December 1995 (the playwright Frank McGuinness having written one for a short time). Also joining the *Post* at this time were Niall Stanage, Daire O'Brien (a regular profile interviewer) and Marian McKeown, who succeeded O'Toole as editor of the 'Agenda' pages for a time before Jennifer O'Connell revamped the section in 2001.

For diversity of opinion, the *Post* sought to have among its columnists some who would articulate a more 'conservative' approach to the social agenda, and who also presented pieces sharply critical of other media. Indeed, in one editorial it noted 'the virtual monopoly enjoyed by the so called liberal intelligentsia

74 *SBP*, 23 & 30 Apr. 2000. Also Connolly, *Tom Gilmartin*, p. 116 & Cullen, *With a little help*, p. 269.   75 *SBP*, 15 & 22 June 2001.   76 *SBP*, 9 Jan. 2000.

within the mass media [and] a society which is forever seeking to establish new "rights" while it abolishes old responsibilities'.[77] Initially it seemed Mary Ellen Synon would provide such a voice, but while some of her writings were critical of journalistic practice and she gave a distinctly conservative view-point on economic issues, her idiosyncratic columns never really looked in synch with public debate in Ireland. When she left the paper her position was taken by Tom McGurk, whose focus was more broadly political. McGurk was soon joined as a regular columnist by David Quinn (from early 1994 to April 1997), who also contributed a number of feature articles, including a major interview with Cardinal Ratzinger (later Pope Benedict) and with then Archbishop Desmond Connell.[78] When Quinn left he was succeeded by Breda O'Brien, who remained until 2001, and who was never reluctant to challenge the approach of media organizations to sensitive issues. Reacting to the airing of Mary Raftery's *States of Fear* series in 1999 O'Brien observed that 'to speak even a word in defence of the religious orders is now seen to somehow under-mine the truth of what the victims say. Yet it must be possible to accept totally the reality that desperate things were done without, in the process, demonising entire generations of priests and religious.'[79] Indeed, throughout Kiberd's edi-torship the *Post* took issue ethically with other elements of the media in their treatment of the private lives of public figures. On Bishop Casey it argued for 'less hype, less moralising'; on Emmet Stagg it debated 'the ethics of exposure, media and Stagg'; it saw the Terry Keane-Charlie Haughey story as 'Journalism of the lowest kind' and viewed the treatment of Celia Larkin as 'unwise and wrongheaded'.[80]

THE NORTH

One of the distinctive characteristics of the paper under Kiberd as editor was the apparent dichotomy between the stance it took on economic and busi-ness issues, and its political positioning, in particular in relation to Northern Ireland. It was summed up by the Northern Irish columnist Newton Emerson with this anecdote:

> I once asked a distinguished Dublin journalist to explain the editorial line of the *Sunday Business Post*, whose mix of Tory economics and republican politics struck me as intriguingly novel. "Oh that's easy", he replied. "It's our money and we want it back; it's our country and we want it back."[81]

---

77 *SBP*, 19 Nov. 1995.   78 *SBP*, 17 Dec. 1995 & 7 July 1994.   79 *SBP*, 16 May 1999.   80 *SBP*, 25 Mar. 1993, 13 Mar. 1993, 7 Sept. 1997 & 25 May 2001.   81 *IT*, 8 June 2017.

Kiberd, in his review of fifteen years of the paper, recalled justice minister Michael McDowell describing the paper as 'Greener than *An Phoblacht*' and countered this by saying that the reason the masthead was green was 'that green is the colour of money'.[82] Kiberd did not see a conflict in coming from a republican ideology but having a pro-business stance: he told one interviewer that 'despite the phobias about strong national feeling in Ireland, an awful lot of business people in Ireland are very proud of this country and they're very republican. You scratch a lot of business people and they're republican.'[83]

However, coverage of the North was not a major feature in the first two years. There was little direct reporting from the North and only occasional editorials, mainly on security or human rights issues. This changed significantly during 1993, partly because of the recruitment of Tom McGurk as a columnist and through the assignment of reporter Frank Connolly to cover Northern stories in tandem with his investigative work. But, more importantly, it was the changing dynamic of the Northern story itself that determined the increased coverage. The revelation of the Hume-Adams talks in the autumn of 1993 prompted an editorial, 'Time to grasp only chance left for lasting progress and peace', that claimed this to be a unique opportunity.[84] This editorial line was supported in a series of columns by McGurk writing almost exclusively on the North for a period. In addition to his column, McGurk was to contribute other significant feature articles, including an exclusive interview with Soldier A, one of the paratroopers involved in Bloody Sunday, and subsequently gave evidence with others from the paper to the Saville Inquiry.[85]

Frank Connolly began a series of question-and-answer interviews with Northern leaders, starting with John Hume.[86] Martin McGuinness, Jeffrey Donaldson, Peter Temple Morris, Gerry Adams and Albert Reynolds followed. James Molyneaux was interviewed by Emily O'Reilly, David Ervine by Mark O'Connell, Peter Robinson and Ian Paisley Jnr by Eddie Doyle. Editorials, as well as encouraging dialogue, also strongly condemned the acts of violence that were continuing during this period. The paper described the IRA's Shankill Road bombing as representing a 'severe loss of moral authority' and urged against 'the politics of the latest atrocity' in the context of renewed loyalist killings.[87] At the time of the Downing Street Declaration, it argued that 'Republicans have yet to be convinced', but saw the three-day IRA

82 *SBP*, 28 Nov. 2004. 83 Roger Greene, *Under the spotlight* (Dublin, 2005), pp 121–34 at p. 132. 84 *SBP*, 3 Oct. 1993. 85 *SBP*, 16 Mar. 1997 & 28 Nov. 2004. 86 John Hume (27 Nov. 1993), Martin McGuinness (2 Jan. 1994), Jeffrey Donaldson (23 Jan. 1994), Peter Temple Morris (6 Feb. 1994), Gerry Adams (20 Feb. 1994), Albert Reynolds (13 Mar. 1994), James Molyneaux (10 July 1994), David Ervine (4 Sept. 1994) and Peter Robinson and Ian Paisley Jnr (2 Oct. 1994). 87 *SBP*, 31 Oct. 1993 & 29 May 1994.

ceasefire in April of 1994 as a 'significant opportunity'.[88] It also urged republicans to test the clarifications coming from the two governments by halting activities for a significant period.[89] Extensive coverage in the North culminated in an editorial on the eve of the IRA ceasefire in August 1994 which claimed that 'what is on offer from Adams and McGuinness is a permanent end to armed struggle'. The edition following had a number of pages of reports and commentary under the banner 'Endgame for Peace', including interviews with Albert Reynolds and Gerry Adams, with the paper's editorial declaring that 'Everyone must seize the day.'[90]

The period that followed the ceasefire saw the paper take a strong line in resisting any change to Articles 2 and 3 of the Constitution and urging compromise on the issue of arms decommissioning in the talks then underway. When the ceasefire collapsed with the IRA bombing at Canary Wharf, its editorial lay the blame at the feet of 'British/Unionist leaders', but also declared that the republican leadership had a responsibility to explain what 'a resumption of violence' would achieve.[91] In the period between the IRA ceasefires the *Post* maintained a very critical stance on the two governments' handling of the situation and their giving in, as the paper saw it, to unionist intransigence. The practice of detailed interviews with key figures continued, but with more focus on republican leaders and their attitudes to the changing situation.

With a renewed ceasefire in place and the all-party talks under George Mitchell in session, the *Post* again made much of retaining Articles 2 and 3 of the Constitution, on which it held a stronger line than many of the nationalist representatives in the talks. This resulted in the *Post* alone of the principal Irish newspapers editorialising against the eventual Good Friday Agreement:

> This is no 'deal' for nationalist Ireland: … [it] is likely to copper-fasten partition on this island for many years to come, perhaps decades. It will permit the restoration of a fully functioning local administration in Belfast … and for the first time ever, the vast majority of republicans will be obliged to accept the legitimacy of the six county statelet.[92]

The emphatic vote in favour of the Belfast Agreement saw the editorial writer accept the outcome under the headline 'Ireland has a new beginning'. The paper believed that the republican movement had crossed the Rubicon, saw the prospect of Sinn Féin advancing North and South, and thought the DUP 'political dinosaurs … might wither away over time' and that, eventually, what was likely

---

88 *SBP*, 19 Dec. 1993 & 3 Apr. 1994.   89 *SBP*, 22 May & 26 June 1994.   90 *SBP*, 4 Sept. 1994.   91 *SBP*, 11 Feb. 1996.   92 *SBP*, 12 Apr. 1998.

to emerge was a 'coalition of forces whose aim is to make the Assembly work-able to a degree'.[93]

The Omagh bombing of 1998 saw the paper use black edging to enclose its coverage, with the editorial stating that the peace process was the best weapon against the bombers.[94] It also covered extensively the case of the Colombia Three, one of whom was the brother of reporter Frank Connolly.[95] When decommissioning of weapons began, it saw further unionist intransigence and the rise of the DUP as a vindication of the stance it had taken on the Belfast Agreement:

> We warned you that its network of ludicrous cross guarantees to both communities would render it unworkable. We were right. We also warned that regardless of how limp and ineffective the Agreement was in deliver-ing for republican aims and ambitions, the unionists would not be able to stomach it. Again, we were right … As has been the case since parti-tion, Ulster unionism wants to rule on its own terms and it wants to rule alone.[96]

INTO THE FUTURE

By 1997, with circulation having risen to near 42,000, the company in profit (£343,000 in 1996) and a strong editorial staff in place, the *Post* was in its prime. The fact that it had the highest proportion of social class AB readership of any national newspaper had 'important and enduring consequences for advertising as well as circulation'.[97] It received an unsolicited approach from the British regional paper group Trinity International Holdings to invest in the company. Trinity then published the *Belfast Telegraph*, which printed the *Post*, and it wished to expand its reach in Ireland. In August 1997 it announced the acquisition of the *Post* for £5.55 million. The three Irish shareholders, Kiberd, Nugent and O'Toole, who shared 60 per cent of the equity equally between them, each received £1.1 million. They committed to remain in their management roles in the company as part of the buyout.[98] The sale was controversial with staff, who did not gain from the transaction (apart from a double Christmas bonus)

---

93 *SBP*, 24 May 1998.   94 *SBP*, 23 Aug. 1998.   95 *SBP*, 19 & 26 Aug. 2001. Connolly later became embroiled in the controversy when justice minister Michael McDowell claimed that he had travelled to Colombia on a false passport. Connolly denied the allegation. See *Politico*, 14 Dec. 2005 & *SI*, 18 Dec. 2005.   96 *SBP*, 4 Nov. 2001.   97 John Horgan & Roddy Flynn, *Irish media: a critical history* (Dublin, 2017), p. 157. The *Post* had 49.5% of ABs, against the *Sunday Tribune*'s 25% and the *Sunday Independent*'s 16%.   98 'Business Plus', Jan. 2000.

except to see their bosses become millionaires and the company move from Irish control to becoming part of a British company, and a stablemate of the *Mirror* and *People*.[99] Kiberd would later assert that there was never any inter-ference with editorial policy from the new owners, and that having foreign ownership had also brought advantages: 'We have never had Irish shareholders who are telling us put pictures in of my friends or interfering with the editorial decisions of the paper.'[100]

As the *Post* began to migrate online in 2000, the last of the four found-ing journalists left the paper. Aileen O'Toole departed in May 2000 to pursue other interests, and in November 2001 it was announced that Damien Kiberd had stepped down as editor.[101] Kiberd remained as a columnist until he left to join the *Sunday Times* in 2002.[102] The new editor was Ted Harding, and Maol Muire Tynan, Kathleen Barrington and Seán McCarthaigh became assistant editors. Barbara Nugent remained as chief executive.[103] By then the *Sunday Business Post* was very much established and had found its niche. Looking back at fifteen years of the paper, Kiberd echoed advice given to him by *Irish Times* editor Douglas Gageby – 'never become poodles of the establishment'. The *Post*, Kiberd noted, had never fallen into that trap: 'You win some, you lose some but you never become part of the elite that is supposed to be held accountable.'[104]

99 *Phoenix*, 12 Sept. 1995. 100 *IT*, 20 Nov. 1999 & Greene, *Under the spotlight*, p. 132. 101 *SBP*, 25 Nov. 2001. 102 Frank Fitzgibbon was editor of the Irish edition of the *Times*; Barbara Nugent also joined in the same period. *Phoenix*, 25 Oct. 2002. 103 Thomas Crosbie Holdings bought out Trinity Mirror in Apr. 2002 for €10 million and Cliff Taylor replaced Ted Harding as editor in Nov. 2004. The *SBP* went into examinership in Mar. 2013 following a restructuring of Crosbie Holdings. Key Capital and Paul Cooke bought the company as it exited examinership in June 2013. Ian Kehoe became editor in October 2014 and having bought out Cooke, Key Capital put the paper up for sale in Sept. 2017. In mid-2018 Kehoe declared his intention to resign as editor. 104 *SBP*, 28 Nov. 2004.

11 / 'The English just don't get it': the *Sunday Times* in Ireland

MICHAEL FOLEY

'The English just don't get it', announced an advertisement for the *Sunday Times* in 1996, as the paper attempted to move from that place occupied by British newspapers in Ireland into the media mainstream. The move was made possible by a number of factors: the historic presence in Ireland of the British press, new technology that allowed a high degree of editorial change between Irish and UK editions and the health of the Irish economy as it entered what would be called the Celtic Tiger. This chapter examines the place of the *Sunday Times* within Irish society. It outlines how a British newspaper moved from the margins to the centre and considers the implications this has for the media in Ireland.

Following Irish independence in 1922 one might have thought interest in British papers would wane. That did not happen. There were reasons for this – including a continued post-colonial interest in the former colonial power, but also the attraction, however guilty, to a highly commercial and popular British press, compared with the more serious Irish newspapers. Britain's popular press developed largely in the early twentieth century, with the *Daily Mail* being established in 1896, the *Daily Express* in 1900, the *Daily Mirror* in 1903, the *Sunday Mirror* in 1915 and the *Sunday People* in 1888. Other than the *Irish Independent*'s cautious take on popular journalism, Irish newspapers tended towards Catholic conservatism, with the exception of the liberal *Irish Times*, a former unionist paper that served the Southern Protestant community. All were involved in the serious business of nation-building. With hindsight it is of little surprise that readers sought something lighter and possibly salacious. But if Irish readers enjoyed being scandalized, their betters did not necessarily approve, and their betters included the Catholic Church. Throughout the 1920s, '30s and '40s there was constant debate about the British press in Ireland. Censorship legislation in the 1920s – some of the earliest legislation passed by the Free State government – dealt with film, literature and advertising, especially relating to family planning, but the British press was still distributed, with its salacious reports on divorce trials, alongside British sports and racing, but without adverts for contraceptive products.

INDECENT LITERATURE

Enter Fr Richard Devane, SJ, a well-known campaigner against 'indecent literature' from the 1920s until his death in 1951. Today Devane might appear to be an
eccentric – he became increasingly authoritarian, admired the Portuguese dicta-
tor Salazar, and campaigned against Daylight Savings time and the imposition
of Greenwich Mean Time, but was highly influential in the early years of the
state. He worked with politicians and government ministers, but also outside
the law – organizing the burning of British newspapers when they arrived in
Limerick or at Dublin's docks. He was particularly against the *Sunday People*
and was at the forefront of the anti-'evil literature' campaign of the mid-1920s
that propelled the government to introduce the Censorship of Publications Act
1929. Of particular concern was the weekly influx of British Sunday newspapers, which, as one campaigner noted, contained nothing other than 'the vulgar
and the coarse, the suggestive, the unsavoury, the offensive, the smutty, the
ill-smelling; we have gilded filth, unvarnished filth, gross animalism, sex-knowledge series [and] sexual science'.[1] At this time, weekly sales of British Sunday
newspapers stood at over 350,000, and the *News of the World* was the best-selling
title, with sales of 132,444 per week.[2] It was this title, more than any other, that,
alleged another campaigner, 'depraved the minds of the younger section of our
community'.[3] And, it was this title that, along with five other British Sunday
titles, was banned – ostensibly for devoting 'an unduly large proportion of
space to the publication of matter relating to crime' – under the Censorship of
Publications Act.[4] While the ban prompted the development of a short-lived
Irish edition of the paper, the importation of British Sunday titles came to a
standstill during the Second World War. And, as British publishers rushed to
recapture lost Irish market share in the 1950s they prompted another moral
crusade.

For Fr Devane, indecent literature was a lifelong concern. In his late-career
pamphlet *The imported press: a national menace – some remedies*, Devane reiterated concerns that had been the focus of his public life: the need for censorship and the
building of a correct moral culture. The pamphlet, which makes for fascinating
reading, viewed Britain as a morally dangerous place and asserts that this fact
justified censorship of publications coming from there. He swipes at the 'cross

1 Michael Adams, *Censorship: the Irish experience* (Tuscaloosa, AL, 1968), p. 26.   2 Adams, *Censorship*,
p. 28.   3 Letter from Br J.C. Craven to minister for justice, 10 Dec. 1926, cited in Kevin Rafter,
'The Irish edition: from "filthy scandal sheet" to "old friend" of the taoiseach' in Laurel Brake et
al. (eds), *The* News of the World *and the British press, 1843–2011* (Basingstoke, 2016), pp 179–94 at p.
180.   4 DÉD, vol. 36, col. 719–20 (28 Nov. 1930). The other titles were *World's Pictorial News and
Competitor's Guide, Empire News,* the *People, Thomson's Weekly News* and the *Weekly Record.*

channel unclean press [and] cross-channel looseness, grossness and vulgarity that are nowadays being propagated with impunity throughout the country'. He writes of 'unclean and vulgar literature' and of the 'gutter press, which is dumped by the ton each week on the Dublin quays'. Meanwhile he writes of the 'clean tradition of the Irish press' and the innate purity of the Irish people.[5] His legacy was Cosg ar Fhoilseacháin Gallda (Ban on Foreign Publication), which in 1952 attempted to establish committees in every parish that would organize boycotts of foreign publications. When the organization approached the taoiseach, Éamon de Valera, for support, it was disappointed. His view was that only the most objectionable publications should be banned and that the importation of foreign publications was best dealt with by maintaining the import tax introduced in the 1930s.[6]

Despite his fame and influence, Fr Devane's impact on British newspaper sales and consumption was negligible. Ireland is one of the few countries in the world where the newspapers of another country are read so avidly. It is similar for television; British television was available in parts of Ireland before Irish television existed. The debates and discussions about setting up Irish television often mirrored debates about the British press and the fears of being culturally and politically swamped by foreign media. Why Irish people bought so many British newspapers is complex. The most popular tended to be livelier and offered something Irish newspapers did not, at least until the 1970s when the *Sunday World* was launched with its suggestive slogan 'Are You Getting it Every Sunday?'. Britain was also the main destination during this period for Irish emigrants and so many Irish people had, and have, friends and family living there. There was also no language barrier and a huge interest in British sport, and people often bought more than one newspaper, purchasing a *Sunday Independent* or a *Sunday Press* as well as the *Sunday People* or the *News of the World*.

The *Sunday Times* was selling far fewer copies in Ireland than many other London titles the year after Fr Devane published *The imported press*, but it managed to cause quite a stir with one story, and one that would have attracted Fr Devane's interest. 'A great day in the village', published in May 1950, recounted the tale of 79-year-old Canon Maurice O'Connell of Doneraile, Co. Cork, and his decision to build a new priest's house for himself at a cost of £9,000. The story was written by the English novelist and journalist Honor Tracy, who had worked with Sean O'Faolain on both the *Irish Digest* and the *Bell*, and was also O'Faolain's lover. She was also the *Sunday Times* correspondent in Ireland.

5 R.S. Devane, *The imported press: a national menace – some remedies* (Dublin, 1950), p. 8. 6 John Horgan & Roddy Flynn, *Irish media: a critical history* (Dublin, 2017), p. 78.

The article was a commentary on the relations between priests and people in Ireland. She revealed how funds for the new house were raised from among the parishioners. She reported the views of one parishioner thus:

> They do be saying we've built the finest parish priest's home in the country: and isn't it well for us? The Canon was saying on Sunday, not to bother with the Stock Exchange and that, but to lay up for ourselves the unspeakable joys of Heaven: and wasn't he right? Ah, he's a queer old fellow altogether mind, there's no harm in him, and mind, I didn't say anything, and mind, you didn't have it from me'.[7]

Canon O'Connell sued for defamation, and a year later the case was before the high court in Dublin, with the former taoiseach, John A. Costello, acting for the *Sunday Times*. The paper decided to settle, paid the Canon £750 in damages and published an apology. The judge, a former Fine Gael attorney general, Charles Casey, was satisfied with the settlement, having regard to 'the great wrong that had been done to the Canon'. The case had a twist though, because three years later Tracy sued the owners of the *Sunday Times* in London, on the basis that the terms of the apology libelled her reputation as a journalist. The judge in this case took a very different view to the court in Dublin: 'Her views were that there were too many priests, and that they lived on a scale which was quite disproportionately high, having regard to the comparative poverty of the majority of their parishioners.' Her article was true and fair comment, he ruled. Tracy was awarded £3,000 and costs.[8] What is interesting about the case, in the light of the criticism directed at British newspapers circulating in Ireland both from Fr Devane and from the Irish media industry right up until the 1990s, is that Honor Tracy, an outsider, 'had done nothing other than cast an impartial eye on how Irish society was structured – in this case the power of the church and the unwillingness of the people to question the power of the clergy; something no Irish journalist would have done at the time'.[9]

Such a case would not have gone unnoticed by other British Sunday titles, and the sensitivities involved in operating in the Irish market occupied the minds of editors and executives. The initial re-appearance, in 1961, of an Irish edition of the *News of the World* was characterized by caution, with 'the more racy pin-ups and court cases of the normal editions' being replaced with photographs and bland stories supplied by local stringers.[10] However, a 1961

7 John Horgan, *Great Irish reportage* (Dublin, 2013), p. 86. 8 *IT*, 25 Oct. 2014. 9 Mark O'Brien, *The fourth estate: journalism in twentieth-century Ireland* (Manchester, 2017) p. 151. 10 Cyril Bainbridge & Roy Stockdill, *The* News of the World: *150 years of the world's bestselling newspaper* (London, 1993), pp 212–14, cited in Rafter, 'The Irish edition', p. 184.

internal report for the paper noted that it had 'leant over far too backwards in trying not to offend', and that Irish readers were 'not merely disappointed, but cheated by the absence of pretty girls in bathing suits, and the occasional sensational story'. It was, the report's author concluded, 'better to be banned than just fade away'. Despite several complaints to the Catholic archbishop of Dublin and the department of justice no action was taken against the paper.[11] But as sales of British titles increased, Irish newspaper proprietors expressed concern. In 1971 a government committee heard that the volume of British newspaper imports had grown by 62 per cent between 1964 and 1969.[12] In 1969 the combined weekly sales of the *Sunday Independent* and the *Sunday Press* stood at 751,000 compared to weekly sales of 950,000 for all British Sunday titles, the most popular of which were the *News of the World* and the *Sunday People*, each of which had estimated weekly sales of 250,000 in the republic.[13] By the late twentieth century roughly one-third of Sunday papers purchased in Ireland were of British origin.[14]

A PIVOTAL DECADE, THE 1990s

The 1990s was a critical decade for the media in Ireland. Due to a buoyant economy there was increasing interest in investing in media. A number of British media companies bought into Irish regional newspapers and local radio, and when the Irish Press Group collapsed in May 1995 there was an assumption that the titles might be bought by a major overseas media company. One of the companies thought to be interested was News International, the owner of the *Sun, News of the World*, the *Times* and the *Sunday Times*.

The travails at the Irish Press Group have been well documented.[15] Its failure was some time coming. The decline was evident as the newspaper group passed to the third generation of the de Valera family. Various decisions, including tabloidization and a partnership with the US newspaper owner Ralph Ingersoll, did not work well. A lengthy court case followed the falling-out between the two companies. After a row with its trade unions the company closed in 1995. The closure of the three *Press* titles led to a major change in Irish media. The closure took place in the year economists date as the beginning of the Celtic Tiger economic boom. The boom led to increased corporate media interest in Ireland as a source of income either by attracting advertising to existing media products or by buying newspapers and radio stations. While all three

11 Rafter, 'The Irish edition', pp 184–7. 12 *IT*, 7 Jan. 1971. 13 *IT*, 13 Mar. 1971. 14 Ivor Kenny, *Talking to ourselves: conversations with editors of Irish news media* (Galway, 1994), p. 9. 15 See Mark O'Brien, *De Valera, Fianna Fáil and the* Irish Press (Dublin, 2001) and Ray Burke, *Press delete: the rise and fall of the* Irish Press (Dublin, 2005).

Press titles folded there was a view that if the *Sunday Press* had been a stand-alone title it might have been viable. There was also a belief, and possibly a fear, that News International wanted a bigger slice of the Irish market and that the company would bring with it different values, different labour relations and deeper pockets.

There was, however, an influential Irish media group, Independent News and Media (INM), chaired by Tony O'Reilly, a wealthy, successful businessman who had bought into the Independent Group in 1973, turning the titles into modern popular papers and expanding the group with the *Sunday World* and a half share in the *Irish Daily Star*, both tabloids and very different from traditional Irish publications. The *Sunday Independent*, with its mix of gossip, celebrity news and influential, if contentious, opinions, became the best-selling newspaper in the country. INM also underwrote the loss-making broadsheet the *Sunday Tribune*. O'Reilly had expanded INM outside Ireland and by the mid-1990s it owned newspapers, radio stations, cable and telecom interests in the UK, South Africa, Australia and New Zealand. In Ireland it also owned the *Irish Independent*, the *Evening Herald* and a number of national and regional newspapers.

O'Reilly had also bought a one-quarter share in the loss-making Irish Press Group, with the result that a sale of the titles was unlikely. O'Reilly and INM did everything it could to make investing in Ireland difficult for News International. It was unlikely that News International would buy the *Press* titles and share ownership with INM, and INM tried to have a title at nearly every level of the market to exclude News International. The *Sunday World* and the *Irish Daily Star* were to block any News International tabloid titles, such as the *Sun* and the *News of the World*, while the *Sunday Tribune* was to block the *Sunday Times* from expanding in the Irish market. News International, it turned out, was not interested in buying the *Press* titles, but did go after Irish readers by rebranding its titles as Irish editions. Such a move might be expected with its tabloid titles, but the decision to have an Irish edition of the *Sunday Times* was a surprise.

A GREAT BRITISH SUNDAY

The *Sunday Times* was one of the UK's great Sunday broadsheets. Founded in 1821, it was known for innovation. It published a wood engraving of the coronation of Queen Victoria in 1838. It was one of the first newspapers to serialize a novel, and in the 1960s it published the first newspaper magazine, or colour supplement. The colour supplement published the photographs from war zones and other disasters, including Northern Ireland, by the celebrated photographer

Don McCullin, and Antony Armstrong-Jones, later Lord Snowdon, was the art director. Circulation figures for Ireland are scarce for the *Sunday Times* until the 1990s. Prior to that, one assumes, there was a small, probably middle-class readership, who liked the book reviews and foreign coverage. Some *Sunday Times* coverage, though, did have a direct impact in Ireland. The Insight Team, an award-winning investigative unit founded in the 1960s, uncovered major stories that would have resonated in Ireland. The team covered events in Northern Ireland in a number of major investigations, including Bloody Sunday. Other investigations included the thalidomide scandal in 1972 and the exposure of Kim Philby as a Soviet spy in 1967. Those stories were reported in Ireland and were widely read. After a series of industrial-relations disputes the paper was sold, in 1981, to Rupert Murdoch's News International. The sale caused controversy when the Conservative government, led by Margaret Thatcher, decided not to refer the sale to the Monopolies and Mergers Commission, even though the company already owned the *Sun* and the *News of the World*. Andrew Neil, who succeeded Harold Evans as editor in 1983, closed the Insight Team. The word 'Insight' survived as a branding exercise rather than indicating a specific team of journalists giving time and effort to fully investigate a particular issue. Neil moved the newspaper to the right and gave support to Margaret Thatcher and, more generally, Thatcherism. During his tenure, the paper campaigned to prove that HIV was not a cause of AIDS and employed Holocaust denier David Irving to translate the diaries of Joseph Goebbels. Neil remained as editor until 1994.

Few had noticed that the *Sunday Times* had been developing its Irish coverage for some years, from roughly the time News International titles moved from the traditional home of British national newspapers, in and around Fleet Street in central London, to Wapping in London's docklands in January 1986, a move designed to destroy the print unions and their traditional practices. It succeeded in doing this, engendering much bitterness, and helped consolidate the place of the News International titles on the right of the political spectrum. The new technology in Wapping helped facilitate making changes to editions, so there could be more Irish stories in an Irish edition. Chris Ryder was the first Ireland correspondent who supplied Irish news to an Irish edition (from 1985). Liam Clarke succeeded Ryder. He concentrated on news from Northern Ireland; it was, after all, the height of the Troubles. Republic of Ireland news coverage was supplied by Dublin-based journalists, including Brian Trench. John Burns followed Trench and, except for a brief period as the *Sunday Times* correspondent for the north of England, has been with the paper in Dublin ever since. He is now associate editor. For most of this time the number three on the London news desk effectively acted as editor of the Irish edition.

In the early 1990s an Irish editor was appointed, the late Alan Ruddock, and an Irish office was opened in 1994. John Burns noted that having a city-centre office changed everything in that there was a place freelance journalists could call to with story ideas. The newspaper had a public presence.[16] The circulation was still small, at 20,000 to 30,000 copies per week. Costs, however, were low — rent for an office and salaries. There was still no Irish advertising, just the cover price. In 1995 Rory Godson became the second editor. Two years later the paper had a staff of four or five, a circulation of 70,000 to 80,000 and still no specifically Irish commercial operation. At least in terms of the *Sunday Times*, News International was not involved in an invasion — more an infiltration.

That infiltration went up a gear in 1996, the year after the closure of the Irish Press Group, when the Irish *Sunday Times* began a marketing push. Media-industry commentators in Ireland were constantly speculating on the lost *Press* readers, especially those who had read the *Sunday Press*. It was assumed much of the *Irish Press* readership was unlikely to turn to a British newspaper, but given the enmity between the *Press* and the *Independent*, between Fianna Fáil and Fine Gael, some readers might even prefer the *Sunday Times* to the *Sunday Independent*. There was also the vulnerability of the *Sunday Tribune*, just under 30 per cent of which was owned by INM, and which was relying on a stream of loans to keep it afloat. Part of the rationale for INM's propping up of the *Sunday Tribune* was, as explained, to try to block the *Sunday Times* from entering, or even worse, succeeding in the Irish market. But the drive to attract former *Sunday Press* readers did prompt a flurry of activity in the Sunday market. A new sports-only newspaper, the *Title*, was launched in July 1996 but later transformed itself into a more conventional Sunday paper. Retitled *Ireland on Sunday*, by late 1999 it had a weekly circulation of 65,000 copies and its editorial content was 'a mixture designed to appeal at least in part to the slightly more conservative, more nationalist readers who had been left high and dry by the collapse of the *Sunday Press*'.[17] Also in 1996 the *News of the World* launched a separate Irish edition. By the time it ceased publication in 2011 it was the third best-selling Sunday newspaper in Ireland with a weekly circulation of 115,000 copies and 12 per cent of the Irish Sunday market.[18]

The *Sunday Times* advertisement, telling us that the 'English just did not get it', was a new departure for British broadsheets in Ireland. British broadsheets had more or less dumped spare capacity in Ireland, with possibly a few editorial

---

16 Interview with John Burns, 5 Feb. 2018.   17 Horgan & Flynn, *Irish Media*, p. 177. In 2006 *Ireland on Sunday* was acquired by the publishers of the *Daily Mail* and relaunched as the *Irish Mail on Sunday*.   18 Rafter, 'The Irish edition', p. 169.   19 The *Sunday Times* lost a libel case over claims it had made concerning a witness whose testimony was included in the ITV documentary, *Death on the Rock*, about the shooting by the SAS in Gibraltar of three IRA volunteers in 1988. The *Sunday Times* was one of the newspapers that attempted to undermine the credibility of the programme.

changes, at little cost. There was always enough content to attract a small market of those interested in British news, cultural content and sport. But here was a British newspaper committed enough to actually advertise in the Irish market. The slogan attempted to distance the newspaper from its British mother ship – in effect declaring to Irish readers that the Sunday Times had enough Irish content to be an Irish paper – which was probably necessary given some of the newspaper's coverage of Irish and Northern Irish affairs since its move to the right.[19] The ploy and the slogan was described by journalist John Waters in the Irish Times as 'as cunning a piece of propaganda as can be imagined, suggesting as it does that this act of attempted recolonisation is actually the enablement of a self-distinguishing defiance'.[20] The media environment in which the Sunday Times, Ireland, was now operating was one that feared and distrusted the British media. It might not have been the moral fear of Fr Devane, more a fear of the deep pockets, resources and economy of scale of the British press, especially that owned by Rupert Murdoch's News International.[21]

COMMISSION ON THE NEWSPAPER INDUSTRY

The collapse of the Press Group meant media ownership was even more concentrated than it had been. There was a clamour for something to be done; for government to intervene; for some sort of protection for the indigenous press, at least a reduction in the rate of VAT. One result was the establishment of the Commission on the Newspaper Industry in September 1995. It was chaired by a former chief justice, Mr Justice Thomas Finlay, and had twenty other members, some of whom were prominent in the worlds of communications, academia, business, law, newspaper-management, advertising and trade unions. The late Dick Walsh, the political editor of the Irish Times, was also a member. It published its report in 1996.

The terms of reference included the need for plurality of ownership in order to maintain 'diversity of editorial viewpoints necessary for a vigorous democracy and to promote cultural diversity in the industry'. The commission was to look at the competitiveness of the Irish newspaper industry, 'which faces growing challenges from imports'. A huge concern of the commission and the minister who established it, Richard Bruton, was the British press and its presence in Ireland. One of the terms of reference referred to the 'importance of the industry in reflecting Irish identity'.[22]

20 IT, 1 Oct. 1996.   21 News International has changed its name and its Britain-based business, which includes Ireland, is now called News UK.   22 Finlay et al., Report of the commission on the newspaper industry (Dublin, 1996), p. 7.

The British press in Ireland runs right through the final report, but no representatives of the British press sat on the commission, and no one working for any Britain-based newspapers or their Irish editions, whether in Dublin or London, spoke to the commission or made a submission. There was mention of a growing range of electronic media, television channels mainly, but very little was devoted to digital technology.

According to the data published in the commission report, the *Sunday Times*, only two years after launching its Irish edition and opening its office in Dublin, was accounting for 31 per cent of the Sunday broadsheet market, up from 18 per cent in 1990, before the Irish edition was launched. As the report noted, 'As with the Sunday newspaper market, Irish titles within the daily newspaper market have steadily been losing market share to UK titles.'[23] Though a number of Britain-based newspapers benefitted with a price advantage, the *Sunday Times* did not, selling for £1, the same as the *Sunday Independent, Sunday World, Sunday Business Post* and *Sunday Tribune*.

The report defined indigenous newspapers as those that:

(i)   in their editorial and advertising content are directed to the Irish market either nationally or locally
(ii)   are published in Ireland and in the main controlled by Irish interests
(iii) are written by journalists and editors the great majority of whom are ordinarily resident in Ireland
(iv)   in most instances are printed and distributed by person working in Ireland.

The commission members clearly feared for Irish culture, with attacks coming from both electronic and print media producing a 'homogenising effect' that would be 'inimical to individual culture of smaller countries such as Ireland': 'The need for and value of the Irish newspaper industry must be viewed in the light of its vulnerability arising from the present activity and publicly stated future plans of UK publishers in the Irish market.'

The report observed a decline in newspaper readership, going back to the 1980s. In 1995 the slide was even more evident within the Sunday market. The research also showed a fall in double purchases, the result of which, the report stated, was that 'there is an identifiable segment of people who are primarily readers of English rather than Irish papers. Nearly one-quarter of Irish people now fall into this category. This pattern is particularly evident at the younger end of the market.'[24] Despite somewhat tentative warnings about the impact

23 Ibid., p. 18.   24 Ibid., p. 87

on Irish culture of British newspapers and the need to recognize the importance of newspapers, the report never went as far as the media scholar, Oliver
Boyd-Barrett, who in an academic article some years before wrote of media
imperialism as being:

> the process whereby the ownership, structure, distribution and content of
> the media are … subject to substantial external pressures from the media
> interests of any other country or countries, without proportionate recip-
> rocation of influence by the country so affected.[25]

It was difficult for the commission to go further for fear of being accused of
advocating censorship, and probably falling foul of the Constitution's protection of a free press. Given the make-up of the commission, with possibly two
exceptions, it was never likely it would recommend anything too radical, or
anything that would annoy Irish newspaper owners.[26]

Within that environment it is clear why the *Sunday Times* would try to rebrand
itself as Irish, and accuse its own masters of 'just not getting it'. The slogan was
a ploy, as the *Sunday Times* has always been, and remains, a British-managed and
-controlled newspaper. Today there is a London-based regional editor in charge
of the Irish and Scottish editions. That is who presents the Irish news list at the
two Friday editorial conferences, and the front pages of the Ireland edition and
the Northern Ireland edition are finally agreed, in London, at 6.00 p.m. every
Friday evening. The editor of the *Sunday Times* in Wapping is, ultimately, the
editor of the *Sunday Times*, Ireland. That is who has the final say on the content
of the newspaper.

The fact of the ultimate editor being in Wapping rather than Dublin
means that sometimes decisions are made without a nuanced understanding of
Ireland. The former editor, Andrew Neil, vetoed the publication of the story
concerning the former Labour Party TD and junior minister Emmet Stagg
– who had been instructed by gardaí on several occasions to leave a cruising
area of Dublin's Phoenix Park – on the basis that Mr Stagg had done nothing
wrong. That same Sunday the story ran in the *Sunday Press*, which assumed the
Sunday Times was running the story. It also ran in the *Sunday World*. Similarly, the
Sunday Times in Dublin had an exclusive story concerning the infamous priest,
Fr Michael Cleary, fathering a child with his housekeeper. According to one
journalist, London saw it as just a 'bonking vicar' story, beloved of some of

25 Oliver Boyd-Barrett, 'Media imperialism: towards an international framework for the analysis of
media systems' in James Curran et al. (eds), *Mass communications and society* (London, 1997), pp 116–35 at
p. 117.   26 It is reasonable to speculate that Dick Walsh and Professor John Horgan of DCU were
probably the two most radical voices on the commission.

Britain's mid-markets and tabloids, but not one for the *Sunday Times*. London never understood the place Michael Cleary had in Irish society.[27]

ULTIMATE CONTROL

If there was any doubt as to whether control of the *Sunday Times* lies in Dublin or London, it becomes clear when one examines the case of the sacking of columnist Kevin Myers. He was fired following the outcry over a column in July 2017 that was ostensibly about equal pay between men and women at the BBC, under the headline: 'Sorry, ladies – equal pay has to be earned'. Other than misogyny, he was also accused of anti-Semitism, when he alleged that two BBC presenters, Claudia Winkleman and Vanessa Feltz, earned more than other female presenters because they were Jewish. 'Jews', Myers wrote, 'are not generally noted for their insistence on selling their talent for the lowest possible price'.

Myers was 'suspended' and the Irish editor responsible for day-to-day decisions, Frank Fitzgibbon, and associate editor, John Burns, apologized and offered their resignations, which were not accepted. Of course, the column had gone through the production process, which included being seen by sub-editors and editors in London, as well as the staff in Dublin. The editor, Martin Ivens, also apologized and declared that Myers would never write for the *Sunday Times* again. What was interesting about this was that it clearly indicated that while the English don't get it, England is where the editor, power and decision making resides. Myers was effectively gone from the *Sunday Times* by 10.00 a.m. on the Sunday his column was published. The reason for such decisive action was probably due to British rather than Irish sensibilities and a fear of an accusation of anti-Semitism in the UK and a consequent intervention by Rupert Murdoch.

The background to Ivens' rapid decision was possibly an incident in January 2013. On Holocaust Memorial Day that year, the *Sunday Times* had published a cartoon by Gerald Scarfe, which showed Israel's prime minister, Benjamin Netanyahu, building a wall with the blood and bodies of Palestinians, with the caption 'Israeli elections – will cementing peace continue?' Scarfe, who is Jewish, had no idea when the cartoon would be published and maintained that the cartoon was aimed specifically at Netanyahu and his policies, and was a comment on his election. However, Scarfe and the *Sunday Times* were accused of being anti-Semitic by, among others, the Board of Deputies of British Jews and Britain's chief rabbi. Proprietor Rupert Murdoch took to Twitter to

27 The *Phoenix* broke the story in Dec. 1993 and the *Sunday World* later serialized Phyllis Hamilton's memoir.

apologize for this 'grotesque, offensive cartoon', and the acting editor of one week, Martin Ivens, promised to be more vigilant in future. The Scarfe incident raises a number of issues, including the danger of editors being undermined by Murdoch on social media. Murdoch is famous for telling the Leveson Inquiry – established in 2013 to investigate 'the culture, practice and ethics' of the British press following the News International phone hacking scandal – that he does not interfere in the editorial content of his papers.[28] By the time the Myers piece appeared, Ivens was editor and, given the history, one must assume, felt that, for his own survival, he had to act quickly. John Burns, one of those who read Myers' article, says five people viewed it before it was published, two in Dublin and three in London.[29]

In another area the relationship with London is subtle: the difference in the editorial lines between the UK and Irish editions. This becomes most pronounced in matters related to the European Union. In 2008, the defeat of the Lisbon Treaty referendum was blamed by some commentators on 'the nefarious role played by Irish editions of British newspapers noted for their Eurosceptic editorial slant'. On the weekend before polling day, the *Sunday Times* (Irish edition) had headlined its editorial 'Be positive, vote No'.[30] One former columnist, Sarah Carey, later recalled being told that, as the paper was privately owned, there was no legal obligation to offer opposing views. The headline on her *Irish Times* opinion piece was 'Don't let Rupert Murdoch decide Ireland's future'.[31] Before the Brexit referendum in the UK in June 2016, the *Sunday Times*, unsurprisingly, came out favouring the UK leaving the European Union. John Burns stated that he was editing the Irish edition that week and used the pro-Brexit editorial from the UK edition in the Irish edition, in order to make clear the position the paper was taking. The *Sunday Times* Ireland is not anti-EU or pro-Brexit, like the UK edition: 'Our editorial line', Burns asserted, 'is based on what is good for Ireland'. But whatever about differences in editorial lines, Burns adds: 'We do share basic values, of course.'[32]

TRIALS AND TEMPTRESSES

The *Sunday Times* has had a number of important stories that have had an impact in Ireland. Two led to major defamation cases: the case of Thomas 'Slab' Murphy, and that of former taoiseach, Albert Reynolds. The *Sunday Times* faced two trials (1987 and 1998) when sued by Murphy, who it accused of being a leading member of the IRA in South Armagh, and of importing arms from

28 London *Independent*, 29 Jan. 2013.   29 Burns interview.   30 See *IT*, 1 Oct. 2009 for an examination of coverage.   31 *IT*, 19 Nov. 2008.   32 Burns interview.

Figure 12: The front page of the *Sunday Times* on 16 May 1999. The edition, which featured details of journalist Terry Keane's affair with former Taoiseach Charles Haughey, recorded the biggest sales in the newspaper's Irish history.

Libya. In a high-profile trial, Murphy lost, but the judgment was later set aside and a retrial ordered because of omissions in the judge's summing up. Murphy lost the retrial also.[33] Subsequently, the *Sunday Times* published accounts of how weapons were smuggled from Libya via Greece. John Burns, associate editor of the *Sunday Times*, noted that the paper was brave to fight such a libel case, given the low success rate for newspapers in Irish courts. Going to trial rather than settling involved considerable financial and personal risk and Liam Clarke, then Northern editor of the *Sunday Times*, feared he and his family might be targeted.[34] Clarke, who died in 2015, covered events in Northern Ireland for thirty years. It was he who lined up the witnesses for the defamation case, who included members of the Garda Síochána and the customs service. He was described as a 'fearless journalist' when he died. 'Slab' Murphy was later convicted of tax evasion.

Albert Reynolds' case was over an account of the fall of the Fianna Fáil-Labour coalition in 1994 after it became embroiled in controversy over the handling of a sensitive extradition case. The story was not actually published in the Irish edition, but was written by the Irish editor, Alan Ruddock, and appeared in the English, Scottish and Welsh editions of the paper on 30 November 1994. Why it did not appear in the Irish edition was never explained fully, but much play was made of that during the court case by barristers for Reynolds. One can only speculate that the *Sunday Times* did not want a defamation action to be heard in an Irish court, where it was probably more difficult for newspaper defendants to win, and awards were high. The story that ran in the Irish edition on the same day, written by Vincent Browne, did not suggest that Reynolds had lied to his coalition colleagues. The case involved, among other issues, seeking to extend British press law and, with Reynolds being a former taoiseach, it attracted much interest. It was fought in the British courts right up to the House of Lords.[35]

Ruddock's story was provocatively headed 'Goodbye Gombeen Man' and continued with, 'a fib too far proved fatal for Ireland's peacemaker and Mr Fixit'. The *Sunday Times*' defence was that the story, accusing Reynolds of lying and corruption, was justified, and that the newspaper was protected by qualified privilege, a legal right that would give a newspaper protection from a lawsuit if the material was published in good faith and without malice. The term 'Reynolds Defence' has since become part of British media law, whereby a newspaper could now print untrue and defamatory information if the publication can prove the story was in the public interest and that it was the product

33 See A.J. Davidson, *Defamed! Famous Irish libel cases* (Dublin, 2008), pp 109–33 at p. 111.   34 Burns interview.   35 See Davidson, *Defamed!*, pp 29–60.

of responsible journalism. Unfortunately for the *Sunday Times*, it did not itself qualify for the Reynolds Defence, as the paper had not asked Reynolds for his side of the story.

In the first case, taken by Reynolds, the jury found for the plaintiff, but that there was no malice in the coverage, and Mr Reynolds was awarded one penny. When the case went to the House of Lords it ruled that the newspaper did not have qualified privilege. Reynolds appealed the one-penny award. In September 2000, six years after the article appeared, the case was finally settled, with Reynolds saying he was pleased with the outcome. Reynolds won another case against the paper's Irish edition when it published material from a draft memoir by Fergus Finlay, a former adviser to the Labour Party leader and former tanaiste in the Fianna Fáil-Labour Party coalition, Dick Spring. The *Sunday Times* stated that it accepted that Reynolds 'had not behaved in a corrupt manner'.[36]

While the strength of the *Sunday Times* has ebbed and flowed, the biggest circulation it achieved was in 1999 when it sold 145,000 papers on the day it carried the story about journalist and columnist Terry Keane and her long-term affair with former Taoiseach Charles Haughey, complete with photographs.[37] She had told her story on the hugely popular television programme the *Late Late Show* the night before publication, which made the *Sunday Times* almost compulsory reading the next morning. As recalled by John Burns:

> What put this newspaper irrevocably on the public radar in Ireland was the three-part serialisation of Terry Keane's kiss-and-tell memoir in May 1999, including photographs of the social diarist cavorting with her paramour, the former Taoiseach Charles Haughey … But it wasn't just about sales. Coming a year after the *Sunday Times* beat Thomas 'Slab' Murphy in a libel case in the High Court, it reaffirmed the newspaper's willingness to challenge the pusillanimous nod-and-wink mentality of Irish journalism, which often amounted to a conspiracy against readers.[38]

The characterization of Irish journalism as timid and of the establishment is an interesting trope. Where the *Sunday Times* is an establishment organ in the UK, it sees itself as a troublesome outsider in Ireland. In return for the story, Keane was given a weekly column in the newspaper. As Burns noted, 'that story put the *Sunday Times* on the map in Ireland, and it became a more serious player. We took the *Sunday Independent*'s biggest columnist and got a story everyone wanted to read.'[39]

36 *IT*, 11 Sept. 2000.   37 *Sunday Times*, 16 May 1999.   38 *Sunday Times*, 18 Mar. 2018.   39 Burns interview.

From the time the Dublin office opened in 1994 and the end of the decade, the *Sunday Times'* Irish circulation went from 59,000 to 89,000. Success was aided by such initiatives as putting Irish content into the popular 'Culture' section from 1997. By 2003 it was selling 120,000 copies per week in the republic and another 30,000 in Northern Ireland. The Northern Ireland edition is different to that sold south of the border, with a different news agenda. The success of the *Sunday Times* in Ireland was such that by the first decade of the twenty-first century, sales in Ireland, North and South, accounted for 10 per cent of total sales of the newspaper. Today, with the decline in sales, something experienced by all newspapers, weekly circulation is about 75,000 in the republic and 15,000 in Northern Ireland. The digital *Times Ireland*, which includes the *Sunday Times*, at the time of writing (2018), has around 8,000 subscribers.

For many years the newspaper industry body, National Newspapers of Ireland (NNI), now NewsBrands Ireland, campaigned on behalf of its members, the indigenous press, for a government response to the success of the British press in Ireland. The argument was that the British press was dumping newspapers on the Irish market and that they benefited from the scale of their operations, operating primarily in an environment – the UK– with a lower VAT rate. The threats from the British press were not totally cultural or moral, as Fr Devane believed. As far as Independent News and Media was concerned, an aggressive *Sunday Times* posed a threat to its own title, the *Sunday Independent*, and consequently it continued to keep the *Sunday Tribune* afloat, even though the Competition Authority had refused it permission to increase its holding in the *Tribune* to over 50 per cent. It continued to fund the newspaper in opposition to the *Sunday Times* until 2011, when the *Sunday Tribune* ceased publication and went into receivership. NNI's opposition could always be tempered by commercial gain, so while the industry was asking the government to act against the overspill of British print media into Ireland, the then *Cork Examiner*, an NNI member, took on a printing contract for sections of the *Sunday Times*, which was in direct competition with some of the *Examiner's* own NNI colleagues.

The *Sunday Times* and the other British newspapers with Irish editions formed a loose alliance and were involved in the lobbying for reform of the laws of defamation. It was probably with some reluctance that the *Sunday Times* and other Murdoch papers found themselves involved in supporting the establishment of a Press Ombudsman and Press Council, especially one that included the National Union of Journalists (News International famously refuses to recognize trade unions). It is believed that some members of the News International team were wary of the legal underpinning of the Irish Press Council, fully supported by the Irish newspapers, for fear it would be an example for the UK. The then *Sunday Times* Irish editor, Fiona McHugh, was a member of the committee that drafted the code of conduct for the new body. Other News International executives served on other committees formed to plan and establish the council. In 2004, the hatchet was buried and the *Sunday Times* joined NNI.

Since the early 1990s the *Sunday Times*, Ireland has given space to a strong line-up of columnists. They have included the historian and broadcaster John Bowman; European Ombudsman Emily O'Reilly; broadcaster and journalist Matt Cooper; Liam Fay; Damien Kiberd; Justine McCarthy; Brenda Power; former *Irish Times* editor Conor Brady; and many more. It provided a place for women journalists, alongside the female columnists. It had a woman editor, Fiona McHugh and a female political correspondent, Sarah McInerney. The well-known writer, broadcaster and controversialist Eoghan Harris was a columnist between 1993 and 2000 and used the fact of the *Sunday Times* being essentially a British newspaper to address a unionist readership. As he noted, his columns were designed, during the period from the IRA ceasefire through the Good Friday Agreement and beyond, to show that the republic was 'not a monolith of nationalist consensus' and did not have 'irredentist designs on Northern Ireland'.[40] The *Sunday Times* has a staff in Dublin of twenty-five journalists, looking after news, culture, property, finance and sport. Its attraction for Irish readers must also include its British coverage and content, and presumably columnists such as the late food writer A.A. Gill, along with Jeremy Clarkson, India Knight or Dominic Lawson, who never (or very rarely) comment on issues specifically of interest to Irish readers, or show particular sympathy for issues relating to Ireland. There is also its foreign coverage, some of it very fine, from well-known reporters such as Christina Lamb and the late Marie Colvin, who was killed covering the siege of Homs in 2012. Irish journalist David Walsh, famous for exposing cyclist Lance Armstrong as a user of performance-enhancing drugs, is the *Sunday Times'* chief sports writer.

DO THE ENGLISH NOW GET IT?

So after more than twenty years since the paper opened its first office in Dublin, where does the *Sunday Times* sit within the Irish media landscape? It is somewhat ironic that a paper owned by Rupert Murdoch has offered an alternative in the market to outlets controlled by Independent News and Media. News International (nowadays News UK) has been making slow and quiet inroads into the Irish market, beginning with the decision to set up Irish editions of it titles in the 1990s. News UK now owns, along with the *Irish Sun*,

40 In email correspondence with the author.

the London *Times* (now branded in Ireland as *The Times*, Ireland edition) and the *Sunday Times*, six radio stations and one in Northern Ireland as part of its Wireless Group.

We began by looking at the penetration of British media as one of the unique features of the Irish media market and the vainglorious attempts to turn back the tide. Changes in the media environment, especially in print, meant the Irish industry realised it had a lot in common with its British counterparts operating in Ireland. A common front in the face of a downward trend in circulations and a change in the newspaper business model was better than fighting for a 'level playing field', and so the British press joined the Irish newspapers' national body, NNI. Today digital technology means the end of attempts to maintain notions of cultural and commercial exclusivity, as articulated by the Commission on the Newspaper Industry. Every day, and especially every Sunday, newspapers still compete for hard-copy sales, but the competition has moved online and it remains to be seen if the glossy package of supplements, culture, style, travel, business, along with news and comment, works as well for Irish readers online as it has in print.

Appendix 1 / Circulations of Sunday newspapers[1]

	1955	1962	1977	1983	1994	1999	2010	2017
Sunday Business Post	——	——	——	——	29,710	49,621	49,637	30,202
Sunday Independent	380,995	317,355	280,000	257,000	253,291	315,600	265,455	185,080
Sunday Journal	——	——	——	60,000†	——	——	——	——
Sunday Press	383,716	355,192	384,000	303,000	158,924	——	——	——
Sunday Review	——	190,000*	——	——	——	——	——	——
Sunday Times	——	——	——	——	75,000††	80,000	111,640	79,751
Sunday Tribune	——	——	——	92,000	81,503	84,566	54,400	——
Sunday World	——	——	306,000	342,000	270,066	308,848	267,130	143,503

1 The 1955 figures are from DÉD, vol. 159, col. 659–60 (24 Mar. 1955).   * Figure from NAI, DFA/5/379/127.   † Figure from *IT*, 30 May 1981 and relates to 1980.   †† Figure from *IT*, 4 July 1994. Figures for 1962, 1977, 1983 and 1994 are from *Facts about Ireland*, 1963, 1978, 1985 & 1995 (Dept. of External Affairs/Foreign Affairs). The 1999 figures are from *IT*, 3 Mar. & 17 Aug. 1999. The 2010 & 2017 figures are from newsbrandsireland.ie/data-centre/circulation. The 1983 figures are July–Dec. measurement; figures for 1994, 1999, 2010 & 2017 are Jan.–June measurement.

Appendix 2 / Editors of Sunday newspapers

Sunday Business Post
Damien Kiberd (1989–2001)
Ted Harding (2001–4)
Cliff Taylor (2004–14)
Ian Kehoe (2014–)

Sunday Independent
P.J. Lynch (1905–21)
John Rice (1920s)
Thomas O'Donnell (1930s)
Hector Legge (1940–70)
Conor O'Brien (1970–6)
Michael Hand (1976–84)
Aengus Fanning (1984–2012)
Anne Harris (2012–14)
Cormac Burke (2014–)

Sunday Journal
Michael Miley (1980)
Willie Kealy (1980–2)

Sunday Press
Matthew Feehan (1949–62)
Francis Carty (1962–8)
Vincent Jennings (1968–86)
Michael Keane (1986–95)

Sunday Review
Austin Walsh (1957–9)
Donagh MacDonagh (1959–60)
Ken Gray (1960)
John Healy (1960–1)
Ted Nealon (1961)
John Healy (1961–3)

Sunday Times (Irish edition)
Alan Ruddock (1994–5)
Rory Godson (1995–2000)
Fiona McHugh (2000–5)
John Burns (assoc. editor) (2004–)
Frank Fitzgibbon (2005–)

Sunday Tribune
John Mulcahy (1980)
Conor Brady (1980–2)
Vincent Browne (1983–94)
Peter Murtagh (1994–6)
Matt Cooper (1996–2003)
Paddy Murray (2003–5)
Nóirín Hegarty (2005–11)

Sunday World
Joe Kennedy (1973–7)
Kevin Marron (1977–81)
Colin McClelland (1981–94)
Colm McGinty (1994–)

Index